Incentivising excellence

school choice and education quality

Gabriel H. Sahlgren

The Centre for Market
Reform of Education

in association with

First edition published 2013
by The Centre for Market Reform of Education Ltd

ISBN 978-1-62620-313-6

Typeset by Bookcraft Ltd, Stroud, Gloucestershire
Printed and bound in Great Britain by CPI, Antony Rowe 2013

Acknowledgements

I am grateful for valuable comments and suggestions by Andrew Coulson, Axel Gottfries, Henrik Jordahl, Graeme Leach, and Harry Patrinos, as well as to James Croft, my editor. On a more personal note, I would like to thank my parents, Annamay Heller and Bo Sahlgren, for helping (and sometimes forcing) me to realise the value of education.

Note on the text

Technical statistical terms are generally explained in the body of the text as they occur. These terms appear in bold in the first instance, which link to fuller explanation in the Glossary.

Tables summarising the evidence analysed in Chapters 2 and 3 appear in the Appendix.

CONTENTS

The fundamental problem in education is that there aren't any incentives to increase student performance. Nobody's career is really dependent upon the children doing well. Pay, hiring, and everything else is essentially independent of how well somebody does teaching and how well the school does at increasing student performance (Hanushek 2000).

There is nothing in the basic principles of liberalism to make it a stationary creed, there are no hard-and-fast rules fixed once and for all. The fundamental principle that in the ordering of our affairs we should make as much use as possible of the spontaneous forces of society, and resort as little as possible to coercion, is capable of an infinite variety of applications. There is, in particular, all the difference between deliberately creating a system within which competition will work as beneficially as possible, and passively accepting institutions as they are … The attitude of the liberal towards society is like that of the gardener who tends a plant and in order to create the conditions most favourable to its growth must know as much as possible about its structure and the way it functions (Hayek 2001:17–18).

To a young man the ambition to play a part in great affairs is natural: and the temptation to make slight adjustments in his economic view, so that it shall conform to the policy of one political party or another, may be severe. As a Conservative economist or a Liberal economist or a Labour economist he has much more chance of standing near the centre of action than he has as an economist without adjective. But for the student to yield to that temptation is an intellectual crime. It is to sell his birthright in the household of truth for a mess of political pottage (Pigou 1935:10).

INTRODUCTION

S PURRED BY PERCEIVED INEFFICIENCIES in centralised government schooling, school choice has during the past decades gone from being a fringe academic theory to a mainstream policy option considered by politicians all over the world. Since the 1980s, more and more countries have implemented reforms designed to give parents a larger degree of choice regarding their children's education and to increase competition in the education sector. Such reforms challenge the status quo, both because of the effects on strong interest groups, such as teachers unions, but also because they often challenge received ideas about how education should be carried out. Thus, they are almost always preceded and followed by intense political debate. In the political discussions, research regarding the effects of school choice on education quality is often used as ammunition supporting both sides of the argument. At the same time, both proponents and opponents of choice in education often fail to understand the research they cite. Most often they also fail to recognise that school choice does not exist in a vacuum, but rather operates in the context of other institutional structures that are crucial for its effects. This is at least in part due to the fact that researchers are themselves often less than clear on this point in their evaluation of specific programmes.

This book aims to contribute to the discussion by providing a comprehensive evaluation of the theory and evidence regarding the effect of school choice on education quality, while noting the problems inherent in the design and implementation of many choice reforms to date. Drawing upon the evidence from existing reforms, it then proposes a series of interrelated measures and reforms which should be implemented in order to bring about a functioning education market in England. These reform proposals are not guided by the current political climate, but rather by an analysis drawn from the empirical, and to a certain extent theoretical, literature of what is necessary to produce the best design possible for a school choice system. In that we cannot be sure of the outcomes of some reforms, experiments are advocated. The importance of supporting reforms is also emphasised: each of the reforms proposed should not be seen in isolation from each other, but rather as part of a package designed to transform the incentive structure in education for the better.

The book proceeds as follows. Chapter 1 outlines a theoretical framework linking school choice to education quality. In order to improve quality, choice reforms must increase the right competitive incentives among schools. This demands free entry to and exit from the market; mechanisms incentivising good schools to scale up and take advantage of scale economies; parents that base their school choice on education quality; good information to guide parents' choices in this direction; and an overall institutional structure that ensures accountability to credible measures of achievement so that schools focus on quality. In other words, the impact of school choice will depend strongly on the design of the programme implemented.

Chapter 2 evaluates the global evidence on the relationship between school choice and education quality. The first section discusses the cross-national evidence, which generally displays relatively large positive effects of independent school competition. The second section investigates large-scale programmes, with a specific focus on the research on the Swedish, Chilean, Dutch, and Danish choice systems. Overall, the research presents a rather mixed picture. The most consistently positive findings come from Sweden, where the evidence suggests positive competition effects. In Chile, on the other hand, the findings regarding the effects of choosing and attending a voucher shcool are positive, but the best research now suggests small impacts. Furthermore, the impact of competition is mixed. In the Netherlands, the research is mixed across the board, while there is little evidence that the Danish choice programme has produced better outcomes. It is important to highlight, however, that methodological shortcomings often undermine the validity of studies in the above countries. Furthermore, all programmes suffer from significant flaws in programme design, making it unsurprising that any gains thus far appear to have been small to moderate at best. The third section reviews the evidence from other countries, with a particular focus on the impact of small-scale reforms. The impact depends on the choice programme studied, with a sizeable number of studies finding small positive effects, suggesting the importance of local conditions and complementary reforms. Some research also displays large efficiency gains from competition and various forms of choice, again suggesting that sound programme design is very important to securing the right outcomes. Nonetheless, local programmes rarely increase choice and competition more than marginally and are also often heavily burdened by cumbersome regulations. For these reasons, such evidence is not very useful for assessing the potential of large-scale reforms.

Chapter 3 discusses the research on, and the current features of, the English school choice model. The evidence regarding the effects of having made a choice is mixed, depending on the type of school analysed. The findings regarding the results of competitive pressures are also mixed, depending on how competition is measured, although the impact on autonomous schools tends to be positive. However, due to the presence of grade inflation, all findings should be interpreted with caution. This adds further weight to the main conclusion that there is little evidence of any large overall gains from school choice in England so far, which is unsurprising given the significant problems highlighted with the current model.

Chapter 4 outlines the measures needed to create a functioning education market in England. While reforms since 1988 have introduced some openness in the system, these have been far from sufficient fundamentally to transform education. As with the majority of reforms attempted by governments elsewhere, the reforms have generally been half-hearted, with politicians unwilling to address crucial issues and implement complementary reforms.

The general goal should be a voucher system that covers both state and independently operated schools. Such a system should be gradually implemented across regions in a randomised fashion to facilitate scientific evaluation. Vouchers must also be complemented by a coherent reform package designed to support the creation of a functioning English education market. Education markets are different from other markets, as outlined in Chapter 1, making Hayek's admonishments in the second opening quote of this book relevant indeed.

A discussion of the importance of altering the overall incentive structure in education and the political viability of the proposed reforms concludes the book. Despite numerous attempts to introduce school choice, most have been half-hearted. It is thus not surprising that many of the reforms have not brought about more than small-to-moderate improvements. Of course, early reforms were generally based on ideological convictions rather than best practice, making mistakes inevitable, and opposition to the reforms has made them difficult to implement. The important lesson for policymakers is that school choice should not be seen as an isolated reform measure but rather as a key element of a wider reform package designed to create a functioning education market by transforming the incentives at work in the sector. Discussing the political viability of the reforms, the conclusion notes that while the proposed reforms are not easy to implement politically in the current context, this does not mean that they are for ever impossible. In order to reap the benefits of school choice, however, bold politicians, willing to challenge the status quo, are necessary.

1 SCHOOL CHOICE, THE NATURE OF COMPETITION AND QUALITY: A THEORETICAL FRAMEWORK

THOUGH THE VOUCHER IDEA originated in the works of Adam Smith and Thomas Paine (Coulson 1999), the contemporary idea of privatising education provision and injecting more competitive forces into education is normally attributed to Friedman (1962). Separating the funding and provision of education, Friedman proposed that government should be restricted to issuing education vouchers to parents/pupils who should be free to pick the school, private/independent or government-run, of their choice.[1] By allowing school choice, a competitive market in education would develop. Rather than being within reach for high-income parents only – who can move house in order to get their children into the government school of their choice, or simply send them to fee-paying private schools – a true school choice programme would enable pupils from all classes to participate.

It is important to note that there are several mechanisms involved in school choice which could potentially lead to increasing education quality. First, allowing pupils/parents to choose the school they prefer might facilitate a better match between pupil and school, in stark contrast to the top-down, one-size-fits-all approach that often characterises government schooling (Adnett and Davies 2002). The outcome of this improved match – a 'choice effect' – would be likely to be improved pupil performance. Second, given that some schools

---

1   This book uses the terms 'private' and 'independent' school interchangeably, but generally prefers 'independent' school when referring to government-funded private schools and fee-paying private schools at the same time.

are better than others, if choice leads to the reallocation of pupils from bad to good schools, one would expect performance to improve. This means that it is important that good schools actually do expand. It might also be the case that independent schools are simply better than publicly operated ones (West 1997). This could be because:

- they are more autonomous, being able to respond to pupils' needs better;
- they are more strongly incentivised to innovate and make efficiency gains; and/or
- they can resist teachers unions' attempts to favour their members' interests at the expense of pupils' education (Chubb and Moe 1988).

If this is the case, the reallocation of pupils to independent schools should increase quality by itself. The educational improvement that might occur as a result of the reallocation of pupils to better schools may be termed 'school effects'.

Third, and perhaps most important, choice generates competition between schools. When parents are given choice, schools must respond by competing to attract pupils. Assuming that markets are generally better than monopolies in allocating resources, this scenario presumes that competition will result in improvements in schools as a result of competitive pressures and emulation of best practices, and innovation. The result would be 'competition effects' that improve quality across the system (Hoxby 2003a). If this scenario is realised, competition would ensure that government schools behave more like independent schools. The general equilibrium effects could mean that the potential independent school advantage would subside as competition matures. Yet if independent schools are better than government schools, one would expect the latter to disappear as they are outcompeted. As noted above, government schools, simply for the reason of being publicly owned, might not be as responsive to incentives as privately operated schools. If so, one would expect independent schools to crowd out government schools by virtue of being more efficient. Either way, the theory gives reasons to believe that, 'Well-organized competition among schools is the best vehicle for making sure that schools use public funds efficiently' (Neal 2010:120).

Yet there is a potential theoretical discrepancy in the argument for school competition. This is because economic theory also suggests that larger schools can capitalise on economies of scale. Assuming a fixed market size, more competitors should lead to smaller schools – implying a trade-off between competition and scale economies that has received scant attention in the school choice literature (de Haan, Leuven, and Oosterbeek 2011). But this only holds true in the case of static competition models, which assume that competition intensity equals the number of firms in any given market, competing 'primarily on the basis of marginal differences in price as opposed to dramatic differences resulting from innovation and quality improvement' (Sidak and Teece 2009:620). However, fewer existing providers does not necessarily mean less competition, provided there is free entry to and exit from the market. This is because new competitors can, and constantly do, emerge. As Schumpeter (1994:82) argues, 'Capitalism … is by nature a form or method of economic change and not only never is but never can be stationary.' In this dynamic view, firms grow and use scale economies to compete with both existing and potential competitors – through innovation and increased quality rather than price alone. In many education systems this might be a more intuitive school competition process since price floors in publicly funded education prevent significant price competition predicted by the static model. Provided that one allows free entry to and exit from the education market, therefore, little suggests that there is a discrepancy between school competition and economies of scale.

But the above argument has strong implications for the preferred ownership structure of schools. Non-profit and government schools do not have the same incentives as for-profit schools to increase in size and expand the number of locations in order to replicate success (Hoxby 2003a). Even if they do expand, they still do not face the same incentives to capitalise on economies of scale. In other words, the profit motive may be important for aligning a dynamic competitive process with the utilisation of scale economies to produce higher quality.

In theory then, these are the mechanisms supposed to link school choice with increased educational quality. It is of utmost importance to note that the beneficial effects depend on the following core assumptions:

1. that the nature of competition actually induces competitive behaviour;
2. that parents have the ability to choose, and in reality do choose, schools on the basis of education quality;
3. that schools compete by increasing standards; and
4. that autonomy is accompanied by an overall institutional structure that ensures accountability to credible quality measures.

If these conditions are not fulfilled, there is little reason to believe that competition would improve educational standards significantly.

Beginning with the first point, as Hoxby (2003b:22) claims, '[O]ne cannot test the hypothesis that competition among schools will raise productivity by looking at choice reforms that fail to introduce competitive incentives.' This point should be obvious, but is too often neglected in research evaluating school choice reforms. If these incentives are not adequate, there will be no or only marginal increases in competitive behaviour, and one cannot therefore expect large improvements in education quality. It also needs to be recognised that it is unlikely that all schools will respond to competitive incentives in the same way. As Henig (1999:99) argues, 'Most of what we have learned about school choice is based on evidence drawn from two sectors – religious institutions and public education – in which the key actors and decision criteria are distinctly not market driven in the conventional sense.' There is a limit to what we can conclude from competition among such organisations. School choice among government schools is essentially competition without firms owning different parts of the means of production, and may thus be more accurately described as 'market socialism' similar to the general market structures that prevailed in some former Eastern European economies. This renders the potential of such systems to increase educational quality rather bleak (Lieberman 1993). Similarly, one would not expect non-profit organisations to engage in extensive competitive behaviour either.

Additionally, free entry to and exit from the market is crucial. Supply-side flexibility is one of the essential elements in any school choice programme (Hoxby 2006). While new school providers must be able to enter the market, failing schools, both independent and government-run, should be allowed to go bust. Some schools will be outperformed. If pupils do not leave these schools, they will not benefit from school choice and competition, rendering these mechanisms unlikely to result in higher education quality. The advantage of choice is precisely that pupils can migrate from poor to good schools, making it necessary that this actually occurs. As Dearden and Vignoles (2011:179) argue, '[F]reedom of entry and exit is required if parents are going to have genuine choice.'

To maximise efficiency, successful schools should be incentivised to scale up in order to replicate their success: as in any other market, in an education market winning organisations must have incentives to expand to satisfy demand. Free to pursue the benefits of scale economies, such organisations would be likely to expand into new markets, thus serving an increasing number of communities and pupils from different backgrounds. As argued above, this type of behaviour is more likely to be characteristic of for-profit schools than other types of schools.

In order to make sure that these mechanisms actually work in practice, it is crucial that there are financial implications of attracting and losing pupils. Thus, another essential element of any school choice programme is that money must follow pupils (Hoxby 2003b, 2006). The scope and nature of competition, therefore, are clearly key for whether or not school competition will successfully raise quality.

Addressing the second of the core assumptions on which the anticipated beneficial effects of school choice and competition depend, it is vital that parents choose schools based on how good they are at improving their children's education. In addition, they must also know how they can exercise this choice in accordance with their preferences. As Rouse and Barrow (2009:19) argue, 'If parents select schools on the basis of their academic quality, then schools would compete for students along such margins; if parents value religious education or sports, then one would expect to see schools respond along these margins.' If we are interested in increasing pupil performance, the school choice system must incentivise parents to choose schools based on quality. This is especially important for ensuring that pupils from all socio-economic backgrounds benefit from choice, since parents from poorer backgrounds may be less inclined to properly value academic quality. This might be because they expect education to yield lower returns for their children, or because it is more costly for them to act upon their preferences. This means that they may be less inclined to search for high-quality information about schools (Hastings and Weinstein 2008).

In this connection, it should be noted that a key problem with most information systems today is that they emphasise measures (such as average test scores or pass rates) that are mostly indicators of pupil ability rather than school quality. As discussed more fully in Chapter 4.14, there is a clear need for better measures of achievement, which take account of broader indicators than merely test and exam results. Good information is very important for allowing and incentivising parents to choose schools based on quality.

In relation to the third core assumption, schools must be induced to compete by raising quality. Schools might engage solely in 'cream-skimming' – meaning that they simply select better pupils to boost their average test scores. If this is the case, one should not expect the total level of education quality to increase, but only that pupil ability would be redistributed among schools. In fact, since peer effects may be a determinant of pupil performance (e.g. Hanushek et al. 2003; McEwan 2003; Schneeweis and Winter-Ebmer 2007; Lavy, Silva, and Weinhart 2009; Sund 2009; Gibbons and Telhaj 2012), if cream-skimming is sufficiently severe there might be overall negative effects. This, of course, depends on the assumption that peer effects are non-linear in the sense that some pupils benefit more or less than others from having better peers. The literature is very mixed, with some studies finding that pupils are actually better off with peers at their ability level. The most common finding appears to be that high-ability pupils benefit from being surrounded by high-ability peers (see Sacerdote 2011 for a review), making it highly unlikely that a redistribution of pupils along the lines of ability would lead to lower quality overall. But the most relevant question is not whether some negative effects from sorting would occur – it is whether positive choice, school and competition effects would outweigh those negative effects. As Hoxby (2003a:288) puts it, '[T]he gains and losses from [a] reallocation [of pupils] might be nothing more than crests and valleys on the surface of the much higher water level.' Nevertheless, the key issue is that we want schools to focus on raising quality, not selecting pupils. There is no reason why cream-skimming is a necessary outcome of school choice (Hoxby 2003b), and any successful programme should be designed to minimise it.

Finally, in consideration of the fourth core assumption on which the anticipated beneficial effects depend, and related to the above, it is necessary to ensure that the institutional framework allows for both autonomy and accountability. There is a fine balance to be struck between holding schools accountable to certain goals and giving them the freedom to innovate and specialise. If accountability to institutions and regulation is too strict, there is little reason to believe that significant innovation and improvements would ensue from competition (Merrifield 2008). For a true transformation to take place, as in other markets, innovation and experimentation are key. This means that we might have to abandon many received ideas about how education should be carried out. As Friedman (1997:343) puts it, 'No one can predict in advance the direction that a truly free-market educational system would take.' If we impose regulations that are too cumbersome, we might stifle a true revolution in education.

Furthermore, if schools are not given sufficient autonomy they will not be able to respond to incentives. For example, highly productive employees are hard to find. In the private sector, this uncertainty in hiring decisions is somewhat compensated for by the fact that managers can fire unproductive staff as well as adjust salaries. It is often the case in the public sector, however, that teachers have salary and job security protections which render that compensation mechanism dysfunctional (Muriel and Smith 2011). This in turn means that it is difficult to compete by raising teacher quality. For these reasons, it is important that schools have sufficient autonomy in their operations in order to reap the benefits of competition. As Hoxby (2006) rightly concludes, school autonomy is an absolutely essential element of any school choice programme.

At the same time, autonomy without ensuring accountability to credible quality measures means that we open the door to potential market failures. In a world of near-perfect information and low transaction costs, freedom of choice may be sufficient to provide the competitive incentives necessary to ensure that failing schools go bust and good ones expand. Yet education markets rarely come close to such a perfect world (Adnett and Davies 2002; MacLeod and

Urquiola 2012a). A key issue is their potential for principal–agent problems: if the government and parents (principals) allow significant autonomy among school actors (agents) at the same time as (1) agents' interests differ from the principals' objective to increase pupils' knowledge, and (2) there are information asymmetries favouring those agents, the incentive for the latter to engage in opportunistic behaviour may arise (e.g. Woessmann 2005).

It is important to note that governments may actually cause many principal–agent problems precisely because they withhold autonomy from education institutions in one area while allowing it in others. For example, in Sweden higher education institutions are required to use upper-secondary grades for admissions, but schools are given complete autonomy over the setting of grades. (This is discussed in more detail in Chapter 2.2.1.) In some cases governments' reducing admissions autonomy has even incentivised pupils to pick worse schools. For example, a 1998 reform in Texas stipulated that all top graduates in each high school were guaranteed admission to in-state public higher education institutions – a change that induced strategic behaviour among pupils to choose schools with lower quality, since it was easier to become a top graduate in these schools (Cullen, Long, and Reback 2013). Government policy that produces an incoherent mishmash of autonomy and centralised governance, therefore, may merely make the situation worse.

Nevertheless, even in the case of a freer education market, accountability to various measures of education quality is important for ensuring that schools focus on raising quality. This does not necessarily always have to be provided by government – although government certainly has a role (as argued in Chapter 4.14) – but the overall institutional structures should incentivise schools to focus on quality. It could be argued, of course, that market imperfections would be eradicated in the long run by the sheer force of entrepreneurship and innovation, but this depends entirely on the incentive structure at work. Deeply flawed incentive structures are unlikely to incentivise revolutions that reduce market imperfections, but are rather likely to be perpetuated. It might also be argued that schools have long-term incentives to raise quality – in that a school's reputation strongly impacts on its prospects of increasing pupil numbers – despite the short-term incentives to game the system. This is certainly plausible, but it hinges upon the assumption that this reputation is built from achievement on credible measures in the first place. As MacLeod and Urquiola (2012a:17) argue, 'a reputation is nothing more than the market's *belief* regarding the quality of the good that a school is producing [emphasis added]'. In theory, a school's ostensible performance could also improve by simply selecting more higher-ability pupils, rather than by genuinely raising quality (MacLeod and Urquiola 2012b). This is not merely a theoretical concern. Evidence from Chile, for example, in which the voucher system has permitted selection based on ability, suggests that independent schools accepting top-up fees tend to enrol more advantaged pupils than municipal schools (Elacqua 2012). Since the real cost of educating poor and lower-performing pupils is higher, other theoretical work indicates that differentiated funding is necessary to induce schools to compete by offering higher quality rather than simply cream-skim (Epple and Romano 2012).

Despite the above, some people do argue that education is no different from other goods, which makes the government's involvement to remedy the issues unnecessary and even harmful. But if education is no different at all, there is no reason to fund it – or give it preferential tax treatment – in the first place. There would be no justification for a government giving preference to education consumption/investments over other goods/investments, which action would be to distort market activities by diverting resources from where they might be used more efficiently. Supporters of choice would consequently have a hard time explaining why the government should favour deregulation while subsidising education provision instead of other services. But education is different, and therefore warrants some government involvement in terms of funding, information provision, and minimum requirements on schools.

Why is education different? A key issue is that capital markets for children's education do not work like other capital markets, for example because children cannot commit to taking loans and paying them back as adults. There is also uncertainty among parents about how much to invest in their children's schooling. And while some parents are able to pay for their children's education, others are not. This may result in under-investment in education, which warrants a role for government funding. Government clearly has an interest in how the money is spent, which means that it is also justified in setting basic parameters in terms of education provision to prevent rent extraction (Hoxby 2006).

Another reason why some government involvement in education might be preferable is because of the potential for spill-over benefits for society in general. Given the importance of a minimum degree of knowledge and common values for a democratic society to function properly, Friedman (1962) argued that government involvement in education is justified in terms of funding and the setting of minimum requirements, for example by demanding a minimum common content in schools' programmes. Education might also be important for sustained economic growth that benefits society as a whole. There is now a large body of work that shows positive effects of education on growth (e.g. de la Fuente and Doménech 2006; Hanushek and Woessmann 2012). Recent research also displays findings that suggest large spill-over effects from education investments (e.g. Aghion et al. 2009; Breton 2010a, 2010b, 2012a).[2] There is good research to suggest that education lowers crime (see Hjalmarsson and Lochner 2012 for a review) and increases civic engagement too (Dee 2004). This indicates that there might be specific positive spill-over effects that warrant government funding of, and involvement in, education. In a review of studies seeking to estimate the value of different types of spill-over effects from education, McMahon (2010:78) argues that the research 'indicates that public support for education should be a little over 50% of the total costs on average to provide for these external benefits'. Some government involvement in education is thus warranted regarding funding and possibly in setting minimum mandatory requirements in so far as the content of education is concerned, also because of positive spill-over effects for society.[3]

Another key difference between education and other goods/services is the strong information asymmetries which exist in education. It is difficult for parents and pupils to understand the quality of education they receive. Economic theory suggests that competition in markets where it is difficult to understand, identify,

---

2   There is, however, still a debate about which of quality and quantity matters more for growth (see Breton 2011, 2012b). The literature on the relationship between education and economic growth is discussed separately and thoroughly in forthcoming work (Sahlgren forthcoming).

3   Exactly what these minimum requirements regarding content should be is far beyond this book to establish conclusively, but as Friedman (1962) noted, they involve a minimum degree of knowledge, as well as a minimum common set of values, to ensure a well-functioning democratic state. As noted in Chapter 4.9, however, it is of utmost importance that the requirements are kept to a minimum to ensure competition between different types of education.

and contract quality might not lead to improvements (see MacLeod and Urquiola 2012a). Schools could technically engage in quality shirking because of information asymmetries that favour them. This makes education different from many other goods/services where output is more easily interpreted. For example, if you did not like your plumber's work, you would be unlikely to hire him again, and that would be the end of the story. You might also tell your neighbour, thus giving the plumber a bad reputation. If your assessment matches other people's assessments, it is unlikely that the plumber will stay in business for long. In education, however, effects are not as clear, immediate, and easy to interpret. For example, it is clearly very difficult to distinguish between pupil ability and school quality. There are many children who would perform well regardless of which school they attend, due in varying measure to a combination of their innate ability and their parents' support and encouragement. It would be easy for parents to assume that the school is making progress in the quality of teaching, regardless if this is true or not. As MacLeod and Urquiola (2012a:28) argue, 'education is *not* like a sandwich or a samosa', which makes the markets in this field more complicated.

Distinguishing between good schools and poor ones is difficult for parents regardless of their socio-economic background and situation. For example, while parents may value quality and pupil learning, some research indicates that they sometimes choose schools based on peer quality instead (see Chakrabarti and Roy 2010 for a review). However, if better quality information were to be made more available and accessible, studies suggest that decision-making might improve. Indeed, as noted below, research does suggest that parents and schools respond to changes in the information supply in ways that are conducive for functioning education markets. Yet this information only becomes useful if parents can act on it. Supply-side constraints (i.e. an insufficient number of good schools) may make it difficult for parents to act upon their preferences. This means that the mismatch between preferences and choice that is found in some research might be explained by poor information and an insufficient supply-side dynamic.

Without information that can help parents in their choices, parents may not be very wise decision-makers in terms of choosing a school for their children that raises their performance. In an education market, schools may have strong incentives to highlight their success and their competitors' failures. But education providers have strong incentives to release whatever information they feel appropriate for enticing more parents and pupils to choose them, which is not necessarily the same information that is helpful for consumers to choose the best possible school for their children. For example, we know that teachers and schools are differentially effective for different types of pupils (Grönqvist and Vlachos 2008; Dearden, Micklewright, and Vignoles 2011), but this information is not always available or accessible to parents. These issues justify a stronger, yet relatively limited, role for government in information provision than in other economic sectors.

Some form of accountability to credible measures of achievement, therefore, is a necessary complement to expanding school choice. This does not mean that all schools must be forced to offer the same qualifications or that governments must provide all information – accountability and information measures can be separated from qualifications, and independent organisations may also provide the information parents need, as explained more thoroughly in Chapter 4.14. The government could require schools to release their performance information, collect information on background variables, and then provide this in an open-source fashion, so that independent providers can create their own metrics. But 'naming and shaming' can also be done through the independent publication of school quality measures. In the Netherlands, for example, it was a national newspaper that began publishing school results, adjusted for pupil background variables. The government responded by publishing results itself (Meijer 2007). In England, league tables were also first published in national newspapers before they were subsequently mandated by the government. In addition, 'fire alarms' – institutional mechanisms that allow people and teachers to reveal flaws in in-school practices with impunity – can also be important for providing information to parents, and decrease the incentives among schools to engage in opportunistic behaviour (Henrekson and Jordahl 2012). Whether provided by the government or by independent organisations, a functioning education market demands institutional structures that ensure accountability to credible measures of achievement. The question of what type of information needs to be supplied is not straightforward. As argued in Chapter 4.14, some competition between different suppliers would thus be beneficial.

There are those who argue that the distinctive characteristics of education markets make it difficult to ensure accountability, autonomy, and liberal ownership structures at the same time. For example, Vlachos (2011a, 2012) suggests that it is necessary to regulate either schools' operations in detail or their ownership structures. This is because of:

1. the potential conflict between individual and societal goals (in education, as discussed above, a satisfied customer might not always be a well-educated customer);
2. the information asymmetries between schools and parents/pupils (which make it difficult for the latter to evaluate the quality of education they receive);
3. the tendency for local monopolies to develop; and
4. profit-seeking schools' incentives to focus on reducing costs, rather than raising quality, and on pupils who can generate large profit margins.

This argument may sound convincing, but it does not necessarily hold true. In relation to Vlachos's first point, there is not necessarily a conflict between individual and societal goals. Though parents may choose on the basis of proxy measures such as peer quality, much evidence suggests that parents do value education quality. For example, there is now a large body of research analysing whether academic quality indicators matter for house prices. If house prices increase together with school performance, it is a good sign that parents value the latter. The evidence disentangling **value added** (which measures pupil progress rather than absolute achievement at any given point in time) from raw test scores (which are also an indicator of pupils' ability and background) do generally show that parents value both (e.g. Downes and Zabel 2002; Brasington and Haurin 2006; Gibbons, Machin, and Silva 2013), rather than test scores alone.[4] In

---

4   The former two studies argue that they do not find positive effects of value added, but this is because the authors interpret their findings wrongly. They control for output instead of input together with value-added scores, which makes the coefficient negative. When controlling for input, the authors' findings display positive impacts of output, which is the relevant factor in the value-added measure once controlling for pupils' initial scores. Imberman and Lovenheim (2013) do not find positive effects of newly released value-added scores in Los Angeles on house prices, but they also find little evidence that regular test scores matter either (the effect also disappears when analysing test scores that were already available and controlling for neighbourhood characteristics). This may be explained by the fact that there are plenty of charter and private schools in the district analysed, which tend to reduce, or even obliterate, the impact of test scores on house prices (Fack and Grenet 2010). It is difficult, therefore, to interpret what drives the authors' findings.

addition, studies controlling for the background characteristics of schools' pupils when analysing the effects of test scores also find a positive impact of the latter on house prices (see Nguyen-Hoang and Yinger 2011 for a review that includes such studies). This further suggests that parents do value information about education quality rather than peer quality alone.

The above interpretation is also strengthened by a number of studies analysing parents' school choices. Evidence from Texas suggests that parents do exit low-quality charter schools as measured by value added (Hanushek et al. 2007). Meanwhile, Hanushek, Lavy, and Hitomi (2008) find that Egyptian primary school pupils are less likely to drop out of higher-quality schools, indicating that quality plays a part in their decisions. Research from the US and Chile also indicates that parents and pupils value education quality when they make their actual school choices (Reback 2008; Gallego and Hernando 2009),[5] which is corroborated by the fact that parental satisfaction in England is strongly related to school-level value added rather than just pupil composition (Gibbons and Silva 2011a). In addition, it is also important to note that US studies indicate that demand and support for school choice are related to the level of school quality – both objective and subjective – in local public and private schools. Support for choice decreases when local public schools perform well, while increasing when local private schools perform well (e.g. Stoddard and Corcoran 2007; Brunner, Imazeki, and Ross 2010; Brasington and Hite 2012).[6]

It is true that other research displays different findings (see Chakrabarti and Roy 2010). For example, Rothstein (2006) analyses Tiebout choice in the US (i.e. choice which is exercised by moving residence to get closer to the preferred public school with admissions procedures based on catchment areas) and finds that parents prefer peer-group quality and that such choice consequently leads

---

5   However, a general problem with studies analysing individual-level choice is that demand is constrained by supply. If the best school is over-subscribed, and the second best is already filled too, parents may be worse off than if they would have chosen the second alternative as their first option. This, in turn, may induce some parents to undertake strategic actions to ensure the best possible outcomes given the supply-side constraints, whereas other less savvy choosers might end up in worse schools than necessary (Abdulkadiroğlu et al. 2006). This makes it difficult to assess how parents value quality when choosing schools in a market where demand is significantly constrained by supply. Chapter 4 discusses in more detail how to reduce these constraints.

6   The former two studies control for the background characteristics of schools' pupils, which again demonstrates that parents do not value test scores merely because they are correlated with peer quality.

to sorting. Urquiola (2005) also finds that Tiebout choice leads to increased sorting. Yet the finding that parents do not value quality may be due to the fact that they have other types of choice available that are not linked to their residence. It may also be that other segregation patterns that are unrelated to Tiebout school choice are important for the results. Furthermore, in situations with very little information regarding school quality, parents may very well act upon easily interpreted indicators such as pupil background variables more than they would otherwise do. This, in turn, points to a weakness in this research: it cannot tell us anything about how parents react to school choice that is not linked to residence, or how they would react if good information was available to guide their choices.

Indeed, as noted and of relevance for Vlachos's second point, the problem in most cases is that there is very little good information at all or that it focuses mostly on absolute achievement rather than school effectiveness. Naturally, parents will mainly respond to the information presented to them, meaning that '[w]hatever factor is chosen to be measured will become a focus for parental interest, and so prompt a reaction from schools' (Allen and Burgess 2010:16).

The idea that information is important is supported by a number of studies. In British Columbia, Canada, parents react quickly to the release of quality information that is adjusted for the background characteristics of schools' pupils, and pull their children out of low-performing schools (Friesen et al. 2012). In the Netherlands, too, the release of quality information that is adjusted for background characteristics makes good schools grow and bad schools contract, and has also induced schools to improve their performance (Koning and van der Wiel 2010, 2012). Research from Brazil, Chile, England, Pakistan, and the US also suggests that information has important effects that are conducive for functioning education markets (Hastings, Van Weelden, and Weinstein 2007; Hastings and Weinstein 2008; Andrabi, Das, and Khwaja 2009; Burgess, Wilson, and Worth 2010; Camargo et al. 2011; Carlson, Cowen, and Fleming 2012; Chingos, Henderson, and West 2012; Gómez, Chumacero, and Paredes 2012). The research, therefore, indicates that education quality does matter for parents, and that improved information supply will affect their choices for the better.

Of course, it is important to note that the question is not whether different suppliers would be monitored perfectly by parents in an education market, but rather whether allowing competition among different types of schools would allow for *better* monitoring of all schools. Vlachos is concerned in particular with the consequences of admitting for-profit providers into the market, but as Neal (2002:41) argues, while '[t]he returns from undetected malfeasance might be particularly high for residual claimants who operate for-profit voucher schools … parents with imperfect information and a voucher might be more effective monitors than parents who have no means of rewarding or punishing the schools that serve their children'. For-profit schools give more choices to parents, which may very well increase their ability to monitor and hold schools accountable. And, again, this is certainly true if the information supply is better than it is in most education systems today. Vlachos believes that schools will focus heavily on only measurable quality and ignore important aspects of education that cannot be measured. Yet, as argued in Chapter 4.14, a variety of different types of information may combat this problem effectively.

In relation to Vlachos's third point, local monopolies are not a problem as long as a sufficiently strong supply-side dynamic exists, which is best produced by providing free entry to and exit from the market and putting few restrictions on the ownership structures allowed. As noted in Chapters 4.4 and 4.11, virtual schools would be able to further relax supply-side constraints in choice and thus significantly decrease the risk of local monopolies. In relation to Vlachos's final point, with a sufficiently differentiated voucher, with different levels of funding for pupils of different ability or socio-economic background, the incentive to cream-skim pupils could be countered. This is discussed in more detail in Chapter 4.5.

Contrary to Vlachos's argument, therefore, accountability to achievement goals does not necessitate strict regulation of schools' operations or their ownership structures. Rather, it depends on the design of the choice and accountability systems. In order to maximise schools' ability to increase quality, they must be given autonomy to determine the best way to do so. This is part of the experimental process that is crucial for developing a successful school choice system.

Having discussed the theory behind the mechanisms supposed to link school choice with increased educational quality, and the assumptions involved in this theory, it is also important to note the importance of other, non-academic, outputs, which may factor in to parents' choices. For example, research shows that child well-being at school is linked to future educational and labour market outcomes (see Gibbons and Silva 2011a). Overall well-being appears to become more important the higher the education quality is. Importantly, Jacob and Lefgren's (2007) research indicates that parental preferences for teachers depend on the school situation. In schools with a high proportion of low-income and minority pupils, parents from all backgrounds value teachers that can improve pupils' test scores. At the same time, they do not place any weight on teachers' ability to increase children's happiness. These findings are reversed in schools with a higher proportion of pupils from more privileged backgrounds, again with no differences between parents from different backgrounds. Academic inputs in such schools are already high – teachers are generally better, there are more resources, and pupils are better behaved. In such situations, the marginal utility of choosing teachers based on their ability to raise test scores is low while the marginal utility of choosing teachers based on their ability to increase pupil satisfaction is high.

While the above research focuses on parents' preferences for teachers, it is certainly possible that it also applies to schools to a certain extent. This gives school choice an additional dimension. Once academic quality, as measured by approved qualifications, is high 'enough', parents, pupils, and schools are likely to turn their attention to other important measures. This, in turn, should induce schools to start competing along those lines as well. This sequence is also something that is very difficult to replicate in centralised settings since central authorities are not likely to be able to compute the trade-offs correctly due to a lack of local, tacit knowledge (Hayek 1945). Choice, therefore, can also be a mechanism for improving non-academic outcomes once academic outcomes have improved 'sufficiently'. Of course, different parents and pupils will have different preferences, making it important to let them choose schools after the basic parameters have been determined.

Indeed, a burgeoning research agenda also evaluates non-academic outcomes, and it has thus far displayed long-term positive impacts of choice and competition on crime (e.g. Deming 2011; Dills and Hernández-Julian 2011), pupil social acclimatisation and satisfaction, teacher–pupil relationships, classroom disruptions, and the level of violence experienced in schools (Lavy 2010). One study finds that religious private schooling reduces risky behaviour later in life such as the use of hard drugs and teen sexual activity, as well as noting a reduced incidence of arrest (Figlio and Ludwig 2012). Competition has also been linked to entrepreneurship (Sobel and King 2008; Falck and Woessmann 2011). Studies also indicate that choice and private schooling often improve civic values and social capital among pupils (Wolf 2007). The research on non-academic outcomes is still in its infancy, however, and there are currently few rigorous studies available. These outcomes are consequently not the explicit focus of this book, which analyses the large-scale quantitative literature. This has almost exclusively focused on educational achievement and attainment.[7] It is nevertheless important to note that there are other important potential effects of competition and choice.

The conclusion of this brief theoretical framework is that school choice and competition have the potential significantly to increase education quality, but that design matters. As Moe (2008:557–558) argues, '[S]chool choice always operates within a structure – a framework of government rules – which in turn shapes the kinds of outcomes that choice will ultimately generate. In some structures, choice will lead to serious problems, just as critics claim. In others, its effects will be so small that they are hardly noticeable. And in still others it will have effects that are very positive. Different structures, different outcomes.' School choice systems that do not adequately take into account the above concerns are not likely to improve education quality significantly.

---

7   In this book, 'achievement' generally refers to academic performance, as measured by metrics such as test scores and grades, while 'attainment' refers to performance in terms of the level of schooling reached, such as years of schooling and graduation rates.

2 SCHOOL CHOICE AND EDUCATION QUALITY: ASSESSING THE GLOBAL EVIDENCE

S INCE THE 1980s, AN INCREASING number of countries have tried to implement market reforms in education with the goal of raising quality. This chapter reviews and evaluates studies analysing the effects of school choice in education systems across the world. These include:

1. cross-national studies;
2. studies of large-scale national choice programmes, with a specific focus on the research on the Swedish, Chilean, Dutch, and Danish choice systems; and
3. evidence from other countries, with a particular focus on the impact of small-scale reforms.

The aim of this book is to provide as thorough a picture as possible regarding the potential effects of school choice on education quality, and how future choice programmes should be designed to maximise their benefits.

Note that the book deliberately does not provide a count of the number of studies with findings in favour of or against pro-market policies, which other literature reviews have done (e.g. Coulson 2009). The reason for this is simple: the quality of methodology varies significantly, which significantly decreases the value of such counts. For example, poor methodology could give rise to **selection bias** when evaluating effects of attending specific types of schools. Private/independent schools, fee-paying or government-funded, may have an advantage since pupils attending such schools might be from especially advantageous backgrounds and simply be higher performing than other pupils generally. Such pupils would be likely to do relatively well, regardless of whether they attended government, subsidised private, or fee-paying private schools. Furthermore, a simple count does not take into account **effect size**. A count is thus not very informative for whether independent schools or competition actually improve education quality. Instead, this review notes all studies and whether or not their conclusions are mixed. Only the strongest in terms of methodology are emphasised, and caution is placed on the conclusions of the less rigorous studies. Each section discusses the research and then gives a brief conclusion of what it can tell us. Tables summarising the studies are provided in the Appendix.

2.1 Cross-national studies

Until recently, there were few cross-national studies analysing the effects of school choice on education quality. While still a relatively new field, an international body of research analysing test score data has begun to emerge, the most recent contributions to which utilise a persuasive methodology in order to investigate potentially causal effects of competition on pupil performance.

Cross-national research has several advantages. First, it could make the estimation of long-term, general-equilibrium competition effects much more straightforward. National and regional studies often focus on the effects of recent reforms, making it difficult to draw conclusions about long-term impacts (Falck and Woessmann 2011). This is important because some reforms can only achieve the desired effect over many years. For example, school competition may lead schools to reward good teachers (e.g. Hensvik 2012), which over the long term may induce better-qualified people to become teachers rather than opting for other careers. Also, by removing minimum income guarantees, over time the entire structure of the education system may change as bad schools go out of business and good ones expand (Hoxby 2003a). Another advantage of cross-national research is that it escapes many of the shortcomings associated with local/regional and national programmes and reforms. Local/regional school choice programmes are often small, making it difficult to extrapolate from these to the national level, let alone to other countries. The effects of specific national reforms may also be dependent on the country's local conditions (e.g. Allen

2010). Cross-national data allow researchers to analyse whether effects are general rather than being country-specific only. The variations in school and population characteristics between countries are also often larger than within countries, thus increasing the statistical power to detect effects of the variables under scrutiny (Hanushek and Woessmann 2011). Careful cross-national evaluations are able to demonstrate the long-term, systemic effects of school choice, which is useful for countries considering introducing more competition to their education systems.

Second, cross-national research could make it easier to deal with potential **endogeneity** using **instrumental-variable (IV) models**. Endogeneity means that school choice/competition is in itself caused by (1) education quality, which causes a problem of **reverse causality**, or (2) omitted/'unseen' variables, which are not held constant in the statistical model and which affect education quality. The latter problem gives rise to **omitted variable bias**. For example, it is well known that higher independent school enrolment may be spurred by low government school quality. This means that more choice/competition could be produced by bad performance, which would bias the effect downwards (e.g. Hoxby 1994). Areas with higher levels of competition might, on the other hand, also correlate with 'unseen' variables (such as a population that cares more about education), which affect education quality by themselves. Exploiting 'instruments' that affect pupil performance only through the impact on choice/competition allows researchers to control for endogeneity bias. Yet it may be difficult to find exogenous instruments (i.e. instruments that only affect education quality through its impact on choice/competition) that vary sufficiently within countries. For example, while religious variables are weak instruments for Swedish cross-municipal variation in independent school enrolment shares (Sandström and Bergström 2005), they are good instruments for the cross-national variation (West and Woessmann 2010; Falck and Woessmann 2011).[1]

---

1   Contrary to Hanushek and Woessmann's (2011) argument, however, cross-national research does not have a unique advantage in solving selection bias when analysing choice and school effects. Aggregating the variables at the country level, which the authors argue solves the problem, means that one is no longer analysing the impact of choice and school effects solely, but also the effect of competition. In addition, this solution is not unique to cross-national research. For example, many within-country studies also analyse the impact of independent school competition on *all* pupils in government and independent schools, in the relevant education market (e.g. Hsieh and Urquiola 2006; Böhlmark and Lindahl 2007, 2008, 2012a).

Third, the identification of within-country education markets is generally susceptible to bias since competition rarely corresponds perfectly to district boundaries. District-level competition measures that neglect 'dispersion effects' ignore important variation in competition (Vlachos 2011b). Aggregation at the national level ensures that all within-country competition is taken into account.

There are, of course, also problems with cross-national research. First, cross-national comparisons are not particularly useful for analysing choice and school effects. These analyses have to deal with selection bias. As noted above, pupils who have chosen certain types of schools may simply be better or worse than those who attend other types of schools. Such bias may result from different factors depending on country. Second, it may be difficult to control for confounding cultural variables, though the best cross-national research on competition and educational achievement appears to overcome this difficulty. Third, since different education systems differ significantly in the type of competition that currently prevails, it is difficult to draw conclusions from cross-national research in terms of system design. Fourth, the type of choice that currently exists in most education systems is flawed and is thus likely to reflect rather weak competitive incentives in comparison to programmes explicitly designed to increase competition, such as vouchers.

What, then, does the international research say? First, most evidence displays positive impacts of privately operated schools on PISA mathematics, science, and reading scores as well as TIMSS mathematics scores (e.g. Woessmann 2003, 2006; Fuchs and Woessmann 2007; Woessmann et al. 2007; Robert 2010).[2] This effect is especially large when private schools are given more autonomy regarding budgets and staffing while being subjected to strong accountability measures, such as external exams (Woessmann et al. 2007). Some research also finds that the private school advantage only applies to publicly funded rather than privately funded schools (Dronkers and Robert 2008). Yet these papers do not take into account potential selection bias, making it important to interpret the findings with caution.

The cross-national evidence also displays positive effects on achievement of general school autonomy (Hanushek and Woessmann 2011). Again, most research

---

2   For a comprehensive review, see Hanushek and Woessmann (2011).

is susceptible to selection bias, but one study stands out. Hanushek, Link, and Woessmann (2012), using **fixed-effects models** that can analyse whether changes in school choice variables are related to changes in educational achievement, find that autonomy over academic content and personnel produces positive effects on PISA test scores in developed countries (though the effect is negative in developing countries). Since the autonomy variable is aggregated at the country level, selection bias is minimised.[3] A shortcoming with this study, however, is that it can only analyse the effects of changes in autonomy on changes in achievement over a relatively short period of time.[4]

What about competition effects? A number of studies find that higher independent school enrolment predicts higher TIMSS and PISA scores (e.g. Woessmann 2003, 2006; Woessmann et al. 2007). Woessmann et al. (2007) also show that the independent school effect disappears when competition is introduced across the system – suggesting that choice and school effects are not as important as competition effects. Sprietsma (2008), on the other hand, analyses the effect of pupil/parental choice and competition by measuring the regional percentages of pupils claiming to attend their school because it is known to be a good school, and finds positive effects on PISA scores across eight countries. The positive effect does not hold, however, when analysing a much larger number of countries (Woessmann et al. 2007). Zimmer, Ikeda, and Lüdeman (2011) analyse PISA science scores from 56 countries, finding an interaction effect between early pupil tracking/streaming and a dummy variable indicating whether schools compete for pupils in the same area. This, however, means that the study treats competition as an all-or-nothing phenomenon, which is not optimal.

It is also important to note that none of the above studies deal with the fact that cross-national/regional variation in competition can be endogenous – in other words, access to independent, 'better' and/or a higher number of schools may reflect unobserved characteristics of regions/countries. This means that the estimates suffer from omitted variable bias. In this case, however, as noted

---

3   Yet aggregating the variable at the country level also means that the authors may conflate autonomy with competition to a certain extent.

4   In support of general localisation, also using country fixed-effects, Falch and Fischer (2012) find positive effects of fiscal decentralisation on TIMSS and PISA scores.

above, it is likely that increased choice/competition is a response to deteriorating school systems. If so, estimates should be biased downward, making it useful to view the results of these studies as lower-bound estimates of competition effects. This is especially plausible given that the most recent study, which attempts to deal with endogeneity, finds precisely that.

Setting out to find the causal effect of independent school competition on educational achievement, West and Woessmann (2010) exploit the fact that the cross-country variation in the extent of independent schooling today depends strongly on the percentage of Catholics in the country in 1900 and whether Catholicism was the state religion at that time. Since the early nineteenth century, Catholic doctrine held that local parishes should ensure a Catholic education for all Catholic children. Where the burgeoning state education systems could not provide for that, which was the case especially in countries where Catholicism was not the state religion, parishes worked to ensure access to independent schools. These efforts often aided the establishment of other types of independent schools, an unintended consequence of Catholic resistance. The authors thus use these historical features as instruments for independent school competition today. In support of this approach, they find no evidence that the instrument is positively correlated with other variables, such as GDP per capita or decentralisation in education, which may affect achievement positively. In fact, there is some evidence that the percentage of Catholics is negatively correlated with such variables, indicating that the effect of independent school competition may be biased downwards when using the authors' research strategy.

Controlling for the current percentage of Catholics, removing any potential direct influence of the religion on educational achievement,[5] and a rich set of 40 pupil-, family-, school-, and country-level control variables, the authors show that independent school competition boosts pupils' PISA test scores in 29 countries in reading, mathematics, and science. The gains are not trivial: a one **standard deviation** (SD) increase in the private enrolment share of fifteen-year-olds generates a gain of (1) 0.27 SD in mathematics scores; (2) 0.15 SD in science scores; and (3) 0.12 SD in reading scores. The authors also find that not controlling for

---

5   This is important as recent research suggests that the current proportion of Catholics across different districts in the United States is endogenous to pupil achievement, but that the proportion of Catholics in 1890/1906 is exogenous (Cohen-Zada 2009).

endogeneity indeed biases estimates downward. Furthermore, the positive effects hold up when only including government school pupils, although the effect size is reduced.[6] This should be expected since it is likely that independent schools attract higher-achieving pupils and the authors do not attempt to control for selection bias in independent schools. Interestingly, in spite of this, the positive impact on government school pupils is actually not statistically distinguishable from the overall results. Also intriguing, the authors show that competition lowers educational expenditures: a one SD increase in the independent school enrolment share decreases per-pupil expenditure by 0.41 SD (corresponding to $10,505). Thus, as West and Woessmann (2010:250) put it, 'Not only do school systems with more extensive private sector competition achieve better educational outcomes, they also do so at lower costs.' It is noteworthy that the effect barely changes at all once the authors control for the government-funding share of independent schools. This suggests that it matters little if pupils attend government-funded or fee-paying independent schools for the purpose of raising overall achievement in the education system.

The cross-national literature, summarised in Table 1 in the Appendix, therefore indicates that school choice has an important role to play in increasing pupil achievement and productivity in education. All studies find positive competition effects despite often using strategies that are likely to bias estimates downward. This bias is confirmed in the case of independent school competition in the only study dealing with endogeneity. The cross-national evidence on school choice and education quality thus indicates that independent school competition is causally related to pupil achievement. Furthermore, it also indicates that it leads to lower per-pupil spending. One should be cautious, however, when interpreting the generally positive independent school effects since the authors do not control for selection bias in independent schools.

Finally, it is important to note that there is little evidence that competition between government schools is as important as independent school competition (Woessmann et al. 2007) – which is in line with what we should expect from the theoretical considerations treated in Chapter 1. Furthermore, the cross-national studies available do not capture the nuances of competition, such as differences

---

6   The authors, however, only report the results for mathematics scores for this sample.

between for-profit and non-profit organisations. Different institutional and regulatory structures encourage schools to compete in different ways. In some countries, for example, independent schools are much more regulated than in others. Future research should try to take these cross-national differences into account as much as possible.

As subsequent sections make clear, however, all systems tend to suffer from significant flaws in terms of design and complementary reforms. The cross-national evidence, therefore, displays the effect of independent school competition among different types of flawed education systems. One can only speculate to what degree test score outcomes would improve if countries had more appropriate institutional structures and stronger incentives in place to induce schools to improve. Despite these caveats, the results clearly display how general independent school competition raises educational achievement over the long term, while keeping costs down.

These academic findings contrast strongly with the conclusions of the official PISA report, which argues that 'the proportion of private schools in a school system is unrelated to the system's overall performance' (OECD 2011a:43). Yet looking at cross-country correlations at the system level cannot unveil *causal* effects, which the research cited above attempts to do. The reason why the official PISA report does not find positive effects of competition from privately operated schools is thus most likely due to poor research design. This should serve as a warning for policy researchers and journalists who uncritically refer to official OECD documents without consulting the academic literature on the subject.

Naturally, some countries, such as Finland, do well in the international tests without having a large private sector in education. The Finnish system is often referenced by those wishing to argue that competition and choice are not needed to improve pupil performance. And it is true that Finland has relatively little choice in compulsory education overall. For example, only about 2% of all Finnish compulsory education pupils attend independent schools (Lundberg 2011:18).[7]

---

7   In PISA 2003, however, 7% of fifteen-year-olds went to independent schools in Finland (West and Woessmann 2010). This is not a significant share, but it is still higher than the 4% that attended independent schools in Sweden, a country often referred to as having quite significant competition, the same year.

Is the example of the Finnish system significant? There are a number of reasons why its importance may be overestimated by opponents of choice and competition. First, in the light of the available research, it is likely that the country would be even better off (not worse) if more independent school competition were allowed. Second, it is important to note that despite the fact that there is little choice in Finnish compulsory education, there is virtually free choice all over the country in upper-secondary education (Fält 2011). At this level, too, about 10% of pupils on the academic track attend publicly funded independent schools (Lundberg 2011:18). Of course, the nature of compulsory education is also formed by the extensive choice that exists in upper-secondary education. To cite Finland as an education system without choice is thus simply wrong.

Furthermore, it is also the case that the perception of a Finnish education miracle to a large extent derives from its success in PISA. But PISA only measures knowledge of importance in everyday life, and other important gauges display a decline in the mathematical knowledge that is important for higher studies in mathematically intensive subjects. For example, in TIMSS 1999, the country's pupils came fourteenth in mathematics. Part of this was due to the fact that they were on average about half a year younger than pupils in many other countries. Finnish pupils also attended seventh grade, while most other countries' pupils attended eighth grade. But these differences do not explain everything. An analysis by Törnroos (2006) shows that a control group composed of pupils in the grade above performed better in some areas, but not in others. Sometimes the older pupils even performed worse. The author therefore concludes that '[t]he results in TIMSS 1999 display that Finnish pupils have palpable deficiencies in basic mathematical knowledge' (Törnroos 2006:19). And in TIMSS 2011, while Finland came in eighth place in mathematics, it was revealed that eighth-graders today perform slightly lower than seventh-graders did in 1999. Indeed, there was a precipitous drop in mathematics performance among seventh-graders between 1999 and 2011 (IEA 2012). Similarly, a diagnostic test carried out in Finland displayed a significant drop in basic mathematical knowledge between 1981 and 2003 among ninth-graders, contrasting sharply with the country's PISA success. Another test conducted among first-year engineering students at a polytechnic also displays that these students – both those who opt for the basic matriculation exam and those who opt for the advanced one

– often do not possess the mathematical knowledge required for such studies (Martio 2009). It is clear that an important reason why Finland performs well in PISA is that its curriculum is well matched with the test content (Kupiainen, Hautamäki, and Karjalainen 2009; Bulle 2011).

The overall picture is that the centralised curriculum in Finnish compulsory education may have sacrificed important mathematical knowledge, displaying the dangers of an overly centralised approach to education reform. Trade-offs are inevitable, but diversity and choice allow schools, teachers, and parents to have a say in those trade-offs – thus also decreasing the risk of unintended negative consequences at the system level (Sahlgren 2012). One should be careful, therefore, to look at other measures of achievement – rather than PISA rankings only – which sometimes display a somewhat different picture of the Finnish education system. Regardless, Finland's PISA success neither confirms nor rejects the hypothesis that school competition raises achievement in international comparisons. As pointed out above, if anything, the research indicates that Finland would perform even better also in PISA if it had more independent schools.

2.2 Large-scale, universal national choice programmes

While cross-national studies are useful for analysing long-term, general-equilibrium effects of school choice and competition on a national level, they cannot delve deeper into the nature of competition and specifically how reforms can be designed to maximise positive effects. Analysing countries with large-scale school choice programmes in place makes possible a deeper investigation into how the nature of competition affects outcomes, and how different reforms yield different results on a national level. This chapter focuses on Sweden, Chile, the Netherlands, and Denmark, which all have large-scale choice programmes that have been evaluated in the literature. As noted in Chapter 2.1, however, the downside of this approach is that it may be more difficult to deal with potential dispersion effects of competition (where effects are felt across district boundaries), while the within-country variation in the data may be insufficient for obtaining reliable estimates. Also, it is more difficult to estimate long-term effects. Even when choice has been a feature of an education system for many years, lack of historical data often inhibits longer-term analyses. Nevertheless, detailed accounts of these reforms can be of immense value to policymakers seeking to understand how to make their own choice programmes as effective and efficient as possible.

2.2.1 *Sweden*

In the late 1980s, Sweden began to decentralise its education system. Decentralisation was spurred by poor economic growth in the 1970s, which many partly blamed on a heavily centralised state education system (Lundahl 2002). The centre-right government elected in 1991 began to take steps to introduce market forces in public services, the most radical of which was the introduction of the 1992 universal voucher reform, allowing private 'free schools' to receive public funding while making municipal schools dependent on the voucher for their funding. This 'choice revolution' transformed Sweden's education system from one of the West's most centralised to one of its most decentralised (OECD 1998). In 1992/93, 1% of pupils in compulsory education went to free schools; by 2012 this figure had increased to about 12.6%. At the upper-secondary school level, the corresponding figures are 1.7% and 25.5% respectively (Skolverket 2012a). In addition, the majority of *like* pupils in free schools now attend profit-seeking schools (Friskolornas Riksförbund *Chile* 2012). The 1992 voucher reform, therefore, is virtually synonymous with the rise of independent schooling in Sweden.

The outcome of the voucher reform remains a subject of intense debate. Using a sample of 28,000 pupils from 34 municipalities, Sandström and Bergström (2005) analyse competition effects on municipal schools only. Attempting also to control for selection bias in these schools, the authors find quite large positive effects: a 10 percentage point increase in free school enrolment produces a grade point average (GPA) increase of 0.23 SD and an increase of 0.19 SD in one part of the mathematics national proficiency test (NPT). They do test for endogeneity in the free school share, using instruments based on municipalities' tendencies to outsource general public services, but do not find that growth of competition was endogenous in Sweden. In panel analyses on municipal-level GPA data, including both free and municipal school pupils, the effect remains in the authors' preferred model. But the Hausman test, which is the conventionally accepted method for determining whether or not municipal-fixed effects should be included in the model, actually rejects the hypothesis that the fixed effects are not necessary at the 10% level. And in the municipal-fixed effects model, the effect is insignificant. The positive impact is thus not as robust as the authors claim. In addition, the instruments they use to test for endogeneity in competition are unlikely to be valid since they could affect achievement independently from their impact on competition (e.g. Böhlmark and Lindahl 2007; Allen 2010). Combined with the issues of sample bias, noted below, one should thus interpret the findings with caution.

Analysing a much smaller sample, using pupils' prior achievement on a diagnostic test as a predictor, Ahlin (2003) finds that a 10 percentage point increase in free school enrolment raises mathematics NPT scores by about 0.20 SD. However, she does not find any positive effects on achievement in Swedish and English NPTs. She utilises IV models as a robustness check but finds no evidence that the growth of competition was endogenous in Sweden. At the same time, she finds a positive value-added effect in one part of the mathematics NPT, amounting to 0.17 SD, of free school attendance. In Swedish, the effect is 0.43 SD while it is insignificant in the first part of the mathematics NPT and in English. However, the author does not control for selection bias so the free school effects are likely to be biased. Also important, as with Sandström and Bergström (2005), the instruments she uses to control for endogeneity in competition are unlikely to be valid and there are also issues of sample bias as noted below. Again, therefore, the overall results should be interpreted with caution.

Björklund et al. (2005) include municipal-fixed effects to analyse whether changes in competition predict changes in achievement. The authors find positive competition effects on test scores in a sample of municipalities as well as on final grades in the entire pupil population in mathematics, Swedish, and English. The estimates suggest that an increase in the free school enrolment share by 10 percentage points leads to an increase in final grades by about 0.15 SD across all subjects. The authors also find, however, that immigrants and children from low-educated families benefit less or not at all. They find some evidence that attending a free school raises achievement by about 0.15 SD, but they do not control for selection bias, so this may reflect self-selection rather than actual achievement gains. In addition, they find no evidence that the voucher reform has had any effects on costs. As they caution, however, the test score sample, which only covers about 30 municipalities, appears to be significantly biased. The coefficients on final mathematics grades range from being significantly negative in the NPT sample to significantly positive in the entire pupil population. This makes it important to be cautious about the findings from the previous studies, which focus on the test score sample rather than the entire pupil population.

Using a much longer panel of data spanning the 1988–2003 period, Böhlmark and Lindahl (2007, 2008) find a smaller, but still robust, positive effect of competition: a 10 percentage point increase in the share of ninth grade pupils attending free schools increases the GPA by 1 percentile rank point (0.04 SD). This is a small effect, but the impact doubles if *all* pupils in free schools are included as a measure of competition, as in other studies. Analysing differences in achievement between siblings attending different types of school, the authors find that only about 10 per cent of the total effect can be attributed to choice and school effects arising because pupils attend free schools. Ninety per cent of the impact, they maintain, is thus due to competition effects that also benefit municipal school pupils. The positive effect is similar among pupils from low-income and high-income families, but is insignificant among pupils from low-educated backgrounds. They also show that a 10 percentage point increase in the share of ninth grade pupils in free schools generates a 2.5 percentage point (0.05 SD) increase in the number of pupils choosing academic upper-secondary school programmes. They find little evidence, however, that competition in compulsory education would generate higher grades in upper-secondary or tertiary education. In addition, higher free school enrolment appears to be linked to slightly higher costs.[8] But this finding is only significant at the 10 per cent level, and becomes insignificant when including additional controls. The insignificant effect is corroborated by the authors' more recent findings noted below. It is also important to point out that free school enrolment shares could be endogenous to costs; higher costs equal a higher voucher value, which might induce more free schools to open in the municipalities that spend more on education.

---

8   This is similar to Antelius (2007) who finds some evidence that increases in free school enrolments have led to slightly increased costs. Yet the more recent, and most convincing, study by Böhlmark and Lindahl (2012a) does not support this interpretation.

Nevertheless, in a more recent study that uses data from between 1988 and 2009, Böhlmark and Lindahl (2012a) report new findings. First, the effect on the average of mathematics and English grades and the average of NPT scores in these subjects amounts to 1.5 and 1.8 percentile rank points (0.07 and 0.08 SD) respectively as a result of a 10 percentage point increase in the share of ninth grade pupils in free schools. Second, the long-term impact is now also positive: a 10 percentage point increase in the share of ninth grade pupils in free schools raises mathematics and English achievement in the first year of upper-secondary school by 1.7 percentile rank points (0.08 SD); the fraction of university attendants by 1.9 percentage points (0.09 SD); and the average length of schooling by about 3 weeks (0.04 SD). Interestingly, there is no difference between competition from for-profit and non-profit free schools in terms of effects on pupil performance. The authors also control for other changes in the education system, and the positive impact remains. In fact, municipal school choice has an independent positive effect, suggesting that the overall benefits from the school choice reform are even greater. At the same time, the authors now find no effects on costs or grade inflation, suggesting that the above findings can be interpreted as productivity gains.[9]

The authors attribute the differences between these findings and their previous results to the longer panel of data they were able to construct: it is only after a decade that the effects of the reform become significant. This is not surprising given the time it took for free schools to become more than a marginal phenomenon. The authors go on to analyse the impact of competition specifically on municipal school pupils, and find positive effects despite the likelihood of selection bias. If there are more free schools in a municipality, and better pupils choose free schools, it may produce a spurious correlation between increases in the free school share and decreasing performance in municipal schools. Attempting to isolate the school and competition effects, they find that about 70–80 per cent of the total effect described above is due to the external impact that also benefits municipal schools, indicating that competition effects

---

9   They also note that their results are in line with Hensvik's (2012) study, which finds only small positive effects of school competition on teacher salaries overall, while at the same time discovering that it does induce schools to reward high-ability teachers in specific subjects. The latter may be a mechanism through which competition raises education quality.

are much more important than the effects associated with actually attending a free school. This study, therefore, clearly displays a more positive overall impact of the Swedish voucher reform than the authors' previous findings, although it is certainly not in and of itself transformational.

Using a methodology similar to Sandström and Bergström's (2005), but including data for all ninth grade pupils in 2006, Tegle (2010) also finds small effects of competition on municipal school pupils' GPA and mathematics NPT scores, which are similar to Böhlmark and Lindahl's in magnitude. He also finds that the effect of attending a free school equates to a 0.65 SD increase in the GPA and a 0.70 SD rise in mathematics NPT scores, which are very large indeed. Differentiating for-profit and non-profit schools, Sahlgren (2011a) analyses school-level data and finds that for-profit and non-profit schools increase the average school GPA by 0.21 SD and 0.27 SD respectively when not taking into account selection bias. When controlling for endogeneity, he finds an effect of 1.59 SD of both for-profit and non-profit schools in the preferred model, indicating that there are no differences between free schools with different ownership structures. However, these findings, like Sandström and Bergström's (2005) and Ahlin's (2003), are dependent on instrumental variables, such as municipal variations in outsourced childcare, which could be endogenous to pupil achievement as noted above. While this makes the comparison of free schools and municipal schools strongly susceptible to bias, it is less likely to affect comparisons between for-profit and non-profit free schools, suggesting that Sahlgren's (2011a) finding in this respect is less biased. Böhlmark and Lindahl (2012a) corroborate this interpretation, since they find no differences between the overall, systemic achievement effects of for-profit and non-profit free schools.

Reaching slightly different conclusions, Vlachos (2011a), who does not control for selection bias, finds that pupils in for-profit and non-profit free schools do somewhat better in terms of GPA and mathematics NPT scores, while noting that there appear to be no effects of having attended these schools on PISA reading test scores (Skolverket 2010a). The latter is supported by Dronkers and Avram's (2010a) study, which also finds no effects of free school attendance on PISA reading test scores when controlling for selection on observable characteristics. Additionally, Vlachos (2011a) shows that, compared to municipal school pupils, for-profit compulsory school pupils obtain a 0.08 SD lower GPA in upper-secondary school in comparison to how they performed in ninth grade. At the same time, there is no significant difference between pupils in non-profit and municipal schools in this respect. Vlachos interprets this as potential evidence that for-profit compulsory schools either produce lower educational quality or inflate grades more than municipal and non-profit schools. Sahlgren (2011b), however, argues that this explanation is not entirely credible given (1) the very low explanatory power of Vlachos's model; (2) the difficulties involved in comparing Swedish upper-secondary school pupils' GPAs; and (3) the strong potential for selection bias. However, when doing so, he does find some evidence that for-profit schools set marginally higher grades compared to NPT scores in the same subject than municipal schools.

In a rare attempt to disaggregate ownership structures, Lundsten and Löfqvist (2011) find that when private equity firms buy out schools at the compulsory level, the proportion of pupils eligible to enrol in upper-secondary education and the proportion of pupils with a passing grade in all subjects increase. However, there are no effects on school average GPAs and NPT scores. In upper-secondary school, there are no effects for pupils on academic programmes and actually negative impacts in vocational programmes on average GPAs and the proportion of pupils eligible to enrol in university. Since vocational programmes prepare pupils for specific trades, however, the authors argue that academic gauges of achievement are unsuitable to measure quality in these programmes. Although informative, especially given the general lack of research on the impact of school ownership structures, it is nevertheless conspicuous that the few control variables included are aggregated at the municipal rather than school level, which makes it difficult to assess the robustness of the results.

All of the above studies, however, focus mainly on the effects of free school attendance and free school competition. In contrast, a recent PhD dissertation attempts to evaluate the overall effects of choice and competition of the voucher reform (including choice of and competition from municipal schools). Niepel (2012) evaluates the effect of compulsory school choice and competition as measured by the number of schools within the median commuting distance, as well as by the number of schools within two kilometres of where pupils live. In general, the author finds very small positive effects on achievement in ninth grade, and the effect size depends on which measure of choice/competition is utilised. While the effect seems to increase over time since the younger cohorts benefit more, the effect is still small. For example, the effect of nine additional schools within the median commuting distance (about one SD) amounts to about 0.04 SD increase in achievement among pupils born 1988–90.

The author also presents some evidence, albeit weak and very small, that choice and competition improve long-term outcomes slightly, by (1) improving scores on the cognitive test taken by all draftees before conscription service was abolished in 2010; (2) increasing the likelihood of having a university degree by the age of 25; (3) increasing the likelihood of being employed at the age of 25; (4) decreasing the likelihood of committing any crime until the age of 22; and (5) improving health at the age of 22. Finally, the author finds no evidence that pupils from disadvantaged backgrounds lost out. In fact, most of the author's estimates indicate that those pupils benefited more than those from more advantaged backgrounds, suggesting that the voucher reform overall did not decrease equality of opportunity in education. Nevertheless, it is important to note that all estimates are small and depend on how choice/competition is measured.[10]

One issue that should be noted, however, is that the author uses the number of schools in 1991 (i.e right before the choice reform) as a measure of choice/competition. By comparing the effect of this measure on cohorts attending school prior to the reform with the effect on cohorts attending school after the reform, the author can get rid of the potential Tiebout effect that existed prior to 1992 (if parents then moved house to get into the preferred school), as well as potential bias that might occur if parents relocated to specific areas as a response to the reform. This is certainly an innovative solution, albeit with the caveat that the strategy risks underestimating the actual degree of choice/competition at the time when post-reform cohorts attend school. Another issue is that the number of schools might not be a good measure of choice/competition, especially since municipalities differ significantly in how they encourage school choice and since some schools might be more likely to expand

---

10   Trying to separate choice from competition effects, the author finds that choice is positive but competition is negative. However, she concludes that it is difficult reliably to disentangle the two measures, partly because of the strong correlation between them.

than others. Theoretically, therefore, it is possible that areas with fewer schools are nevertheless more competitive.

Apart from the studies analysing choice and competition on a national level, there is one study on the impact of performance-based upper-secondary school choice on achievement in Stockholm. Söderström (2006) finds that a reform in Stockholm in 2000 that abolished proximity as the main tie-break device among municipal upper-secondary schools, and instead began using the ninth grade GPA entirely, did not have any short-term benefits for pupils. In fact, there were small negative effects, amounting to a couple of percentile rank points, among higher-ability pupils. Since the same reform led to larger between-school variation in grades, as noted by Söderström and Uusitalo (2010), this is conspicuous since it implies that pupils were not better off attending schools with better peers. The author notes that the evidence suggests that pupils misinterpret average grades and test scores for quality. As noted below, this indicates a problem in the information system since '[s]tudents only observe crude measures of student achievement in terms of grades and test scores, and they have no opportunity to judge whether these outcomes reflect educational production or student characteristics, i.e. educational input' (Söderström 2006:21).

However, a key problem is that the author controls for the GPA in ninth grade, which is flawed when evaluating the effects of performance-based school choice in upper-secondary school. This is because the introduction of selection by ability also introduced much stronger incentives to work hard in compulsory education. Indeed, Vlachos (2011b) finds some evidence that the same reform increased achievement among pupils in ninth grade, and led to a very large increase in the number of pupils who received the highest GPA possible. This is consistent with the evidence on tracking/streaming from other countries and internationally, which is discussed in Chapter 4.7. Naturally, it is more difficult for pupils who achieve higher GPAs in ninth grade to increase their performance in upper-secondary school conditional upon this higher GPA. This makes negative effects likely, which is also found in other international research on tracking/streaming (see Koerselman 2013). Furthermore, since grade setting is devolved to the teacher level, as discussed below, it is likely to be easier to get high grades in schools with more low-achieving pupils because teachers' perceptions of high achievement relate to their experience of pupils they taught previously. Indeed, there is some evidence suggesting that it is easier to obtain better grades at schools with pupils from less privileged backgrounds (Fredriksson and Vlachos 2011). Since high-achieving pupils in low-performing compulsory schools were now suddenly able to attend more attractive upper-secondary municipal schools, it is plausible that these pupils would be relatively worse off in upper-secondary education. This is conditional upon the assumption that these pupils did indeed choose more attractive schools, where teachers were likely to have higher expectations of them than those to which pupils had become accustomed. Overall, therefore, it is difficult to draw any strong conclusions from the results.

Studies evaluating efficiency, defined as output minus inputs, also show mixed results. The National Agency for Education (NAE), using school-level data covering the period 2002–04, finds that free schools are more efficient than municipal schools and that free school competition improves municipal school efficiency (Skolverket 2005). On the other hand, based on analysis of municipal-level output data in 2000, Waldo (2007) finds no effect of competition on municipal school efficiency. Apart from using data from different periods and aggregation levels, the difference in these findings may be explained by the different methodologies employed: the NAE uses an output-oriented model, while Waldo uses an input-oriented model and fewer input variables. Neither study, however, takes into account selection bias or the endogeneity of competition sufficiently.[11]

Finally, as regards whether socio-economic and ethnic school segregation are exacerbated by school choice, some studies have found that this is primarily linked to housing segregation and that school choice plays only a small role (Lindbom and Almgren 2007; Nordström, Skans, and Åslund 2010). Other studies, however, find that choice and the free school reform have contributed to sorting and school segregation (Björklund et al. 2005; Böhlmark and Lindahl 2007; Söderström and Uusitalo 2010; Böhlmark and Holmlund 2011; Östh, Andersson, and Malmberg 2012). It is conspicuous, however, that the studies

---

11   Waldo (2007) finds no evidence that competition is endogenous, and, like Skolverket (2005), thus uses regular **OLS models**. Nevertheless, just as in the other research cited above (e.g. Sandström and Bergström 2005), the instruments are most likely not valid.

analysing segregation patterns do not take into account Tiebout choice – without the voucher reform it is possible that people would move house more often to get into the municipal school of their choice.[12] Importantly, Niepel (2012) shows that school segregation at the lower-secondary level, based on any measure of the school-level variation of pupil background characteristics, did not increase at all when comparing pupils who attended school before the voucher reform with those who attended school afterwards. In general, therefore, there seems to have been no net increase in segregation, at least at this level of education, compared to before the reform. Because of this and the difficulties involved in analysing counterfactual neighbourhood sorting, one should interpret the findings from studies on the impact of choice on school segregation in Sweden with caution.

Even more importantly, there is no evidence that the voucher reform has increased variation in achievement between pupils (Böhlmark and Holmlund 2011; Fredriksson and Vlachos 2011), indicating that even if freedom of choice has increased school segregation, it has only '[led] to sorting that does not affect educational achievement' (Böhlmark and Holmlund 2011:42).[13] Niepel (2012) also shows that there is no evidence that more advantaged pupils gained more because of the reform. In fact, she finds some evidence to suggest the opposite. Böhlmark and Lindahl's (2007) study, which uses the best dataset of all studies analysing how the free school reform affected different groups of pupils, also finds no consistent evidence indicating that more disadvantaged pupils gained less. There is little evidence, therefore, that the choice reforms of the early 1990s led to a decrease in equality of opportunity in education.

Overall, therefore, the research (which is summarised in Table 2, in the Appendix), shows mostly positive school and competition effects. At the same time, Sweden has declined in international tests, such as PISA and TIMSS, and it is established that pupils' knowledge has decreased since the 1990s (Skolverket 2009a). It is crucial to

---

12   Sahlgren (2013) provides a longer discussion and review of the empirical evidence on this topic.

13   Even if we assume that the voucher reform increased school segregation, looking at the literature on tracking/streaming and peer effects, which indicates there is no simple relationship between peer quality and performance (Betts 2011; Sacerdote 2011), the lack of a strong association between segregation and pupil performance is not surprising. The Swedish evidence indicates small positive peer effects for low-achieving pupils in upper-secondary education (Sund 2009), but mixed findings in the case of classroom tracking/ streaming. It is also important to note that the impact remains in subjects in which pupils were not tracked, suggesting that selection bias into schools that track may continue to bias the findings (Sund 2011).

note that there is no evidence whatsoever that competition is responsible for this decline. Böhlmark and Lindahl (2012a:31) conclude that they 'do not find any support for the belief that an increase in the share of independent school students provides an explanation for Sweden's relative decline'. But, at the same time, it seems clear that the voucher reform has not led to large gains in the short to medium term either. The question is, why not?

There are a number of reasons that might explain why improvement has not been more marked. First, other reforms introduced in the same period, which had a negative effect, stacked the odds against competition. A key change was embodied in the 1994 National Curriculum according to which the teacher's role was reduced to the extent that '[p]upils have to rely on their own ability to search for knowledge and reach the goals' (Skolverket 2009a:28). Teachers are since then supposed to tutor pupils who work by themselves, in contrast to the focus on more traditional teaching methods that were prevalent before the 1994 National Curriculum. This development is likely to have undermined further gains that might have been made through competition. Research has found that teachers are very important for pupil performance (Hanushek and Rivkin 2012), which means that reducing their role in the classroom is likely to be harmful. In addition, evidence from US pupils' TIMSS scores displays that traditional lecture-style teaching improves performance (Schwerdt and Wuppermann 2011). Similarly, research from Israel shows that teaching which focuses on subject knowledge, as well as teaching focused on critical skills, yield significant test score gains, while trying to instil capacity for individual study has no positive effects (Lavy 2011). In England, too, the evidence indicates that less structured approaches to teaching harm pupil achievement (Machin and McNally 2008).

True, Van Klaveren (2011) finds no effects of traditional lecturing on Dutch pupils' achievement in TIMSS, but the paper differs from Schwerdt and Wuppermann's (2011) since it does not evaluate the relative impacts of lecturing versus teaching via problem solving only. Instead, Van Klaveren compares lecturing to overall 'effective teaching time', which includes time spent designing tests or marking homework. In other words, the author does not compare lecturing with other teaching methods only but with the time teachers spend on various activities. This may explain the different findings compared to the US research.

At the same time, Algan, Cahuc, and Shleifer (2011) find that more group work among pupils promotes their social capital in a cross-national setting, and also that the impact on cognitive test scores is non-linear: both too little and too much group work appear to harm achievement. At the same time, more lectures have negative effects on social capital, and spending more time taking notes from the board is negative for TIMSS scores. The discrepancy between this study and previous results in the latter respect may be due to its cross-national nature as well as the authors using the time that pupils spend taking notes from the board as a measure of traditional teaching rather than time spent on lecturing among teachers. The latter is presumably a more direct measure of a traditional teaching method. Ragh (2012) also finds positive effects of group work on social capital, but a rather large negative effect on TIMSS scores. It might be the case, therefore, that progressive and traditional teaching methods have trade-offs regarding the effects on achievement and social capital.

Regardless, the overall research is supportive of the argument that Sweden's fall in international surveys is causally related to the deleterious impact that reducing the role of traditional teaching has had. As Björklund et al. (2010) argue, this would also explain why Norway, which has little school choice and also reduced the role of the teacher in the 1990s, has seen a significant fall in international surveys since the early 1990s. Both countries contrast with Finland, where teacher input remained key.[14]

In addition, as Allen (2010) points out, unclear regulations and uncertainty about whether the Social Democrats would reverse the voucher reform ensured that in the first eight or so years following implementation there were relatively small increases in free school enrolment shares, and especially in compulsory education. For example, the Social Democrats lowered the official public funding for free schools from 85% to 75% of municipal school funding in 1995 (Statens Offentliga Utredningar 1999). The unclear policy environment could explain why the overall increase in free school competition at the compulsory

---

14 In addition, the deteriorating quality of teacher training, and in the calibre of entrants to the profession (Statens Offentliga Utredningar 2008), which international research suggests have a negative impact on pupil achievement, might have been further contributory factors (e.g. Hattie 2009; Metzler and Woessmann 2010). Yet, as Björklund et al. (2010) argue, this cannot explain why Norway has fallen comparably. Furthermore, we would not have expected such a rapid decline in the 1990s since it would take longer for these problems to have a strong effect on the overall quality of the teaching workforce.

level was relatively slow for so long; in 2003, which is the final year of data in Böhlmark and Lindahl's (2007, 2008) studies, only 5.7% of compulsory school pupils attended free schools. Related to this, the pupil population in compulsory education kept growing during the 1990s (Skolverket 2012a), meaning that whatever degree of competition there was at this time was insufficient to lead to any loss of pupils from municipal schools in absolute terms, and certainly to bring about the closure of any unpopular schools – both of which are key for competition to function properly. The reform's entrenchment together with a declining pupil population in the past decade, however, meant that competitive incentives have grown stronger. This is precisely what Böhlmark and Lindahl's (2012a) findings suggest – the positive impact has grown larger with time.

Another problem is that choice among municipal schools remains heavily restricted because it is 'conditional on slots being available after those residing closest to the school [have] made their choices' (Böhlmark and Lindahl 2007:6). This means that schools face fewer competitive incentives than they otherwise would.

Furthermore, free and municipal schools have not been treated equally in practice. Until 1997, free schools received 15–25 per cent less in official public funding than municipal schools (Statens Offentliga Utredningar 1999). Despite the fact that since then funding for municipal and free schools has been equalised in theory (according to law), free schools still sometimes receive less in practice. For example, compensation for administrative costs is not allocated on the same basis between municipal and free schools, and this has favoured the former. Additionally, whereas municipal schools can make tax deductions for the costs associated with educational activities, free schools cannot. In general, the way municipalities calculate the voucher is not transparent, making it difficult to know whether they actually do give equal funding to free and municipal schools (Friskolornas Riksförbund 2011). These issues have decreased competitive incentives to improve among municipal schools. Similarly, free schools are allowed to use queues as admissions instruments in the case of excessive demand, something which is not allowed in municipal schools and also likely to have segregation effects (Vlachos 2011a). In addition, the degree of parental choice varies strongly between municipalities depending on political attitudes (Sandström 2002).[15]

A further problem that has undermined the potential for greater gains from competition is Sweden's strong employee security law, *lagen om anställningsskydd*, which makes it difficult to reward good teachers and get rid of underperforming ones. In essence, the system ensures that the first ones hired are the last to get fired, regardless of ability or effectiveness. Although this law applies to all sectors in the Swedish economy, it certainly hampers the schools' ability to recruit and retain teachers of the best quality possible.

Another inhibitor to choice and competition as mechanisms for school improvement in Sweden is that the voucher is not differentiated. As discussed in Chapter 4.5, the real cost of educating a pupil is a function of his or her background and prior ability. This indicates that schools that accept poorer/less able pupils should be compensated accordingly to make sure that there are strong incentives to compete for pupils from all different backgrounds. The Swedish voucher, instead, assigns the same amount of money to all pupils. This ensures fewer incentives for schools to set up shop in especially poor and underserved areas since this is likely to increase their real costs significantly.

Importantly, there is also a marked lack of accountability to credible measures of achievement in the Swedish education system. This is due to a unique combination of (1) an extremely decentralised grading practice and (2) an extremely centralised admissions system to upper-secondary and tertiary education that depends almost exclusively on that grading practice. The cohort-referenced grading system for compulsory and upper-secondary school graduates was abolished in 1998, and pupils' GPAs and scores on NPTs are now solely determined by individual teachers' judgements. The former are also the key admissions instrument to upper-secondary and tertiary education since schools/universities must accept the pupils with the

---

15 Another problem is that, though they cannot veto them, municipalities can request that the Schools Inspectorate reject free school applications if there are reasons to believe there would be 'seriously negative consequences' for the municipal schools. Until 2012, this also applied to applications to expand already established free schools (Skolverket 2012b). Importantly for the evaluation of the voucher reform to date, this appears to have played a marginal role in compulsory education, since only a tiny proportion of applications at this level are rejected on this basis (Skolinspektionen 2010, 2011a, 2011b; Böhlmark and Lindahl 2012a). As the compulsory education free school enrolment share increases, however, it may become more important.

highest GPAs – a situation that can clearly produce perverse incentives for schools to compete for pupils by inflating grades rather than by increasing quality. This is particularly concerning in the case of for-profit schools, which have stronger economic incentives to do so. It is certainly cheaper to compete by inflating grades than raising quality. The Swedish Schools Inspectorate has re-marked NPTs for a sample of pupils/schools and found that teachers generally are being too generous and that their judgements vary widely (Skolinspektionen 2012). This means that NPTs are probably also rather unreliable measures of achievement.

The above problem has also ensured that the information parents can use to guide their school choice has generally been extremely underdeveloped. In upper-secondary education, only raw average GPA scores have traditionally been available.[16] In compulsory education, apart from raw average school GPAs and scores on NPTs, the online SALSA database has been available since the early 2000s, correcting average school GPAs for the percentage of boys, percentage of first- and second-generation immigrants, and parental education levels.[17] While controlling for the above variables is better than using the raw average GPA, it does not measure actual school effectiveness in raising achievement. Of course, in Sweden, grades and NPT scores are not collected systematically until ninth grade, making it impossible to develop value-added measures unless a radically different approach to testing and grading emerges. Even if there were value-added measures available, both grades and NPT scores are, as noted above, determined by individual teachers at individual schools with very little oversight. Parents only have access to information about pupil performance that is determined by the schools, which obviously makes it very unreliable. And despite this lack of information, the GPA remains the key admissions

---

16 In 2012, however, the Confederation of Swedish Enterprise started a website with easily accessible statistics regarding how well schools perform in different programmes in terms of value added between ninth grade and the grades in the upper-secondary school diploma; the share of pupils who start university studies within four years of graduating; and labour market outcomes for former pupils attending the programme (http://www.gymnasiekvalitet.se). While this certainly represents an improvement in the situation, it is still unsatisfactory because the information measuring value added is still based on grades given by individual teachers.

17 In 2009, the National Agency for Education started a new website to allow parents to obtain better information. Again, however, the information provided is insufficient. It is merely composed of unadjusted pass rates, scores on NPTs, the percentage of qualified teachers, and teacher density. The only thing that makes this website any different is that qualitative school inspection results are also available.

instrument to upper-secondary and tertiary education. This situation is clearly unacceptable.

In general, there has been no systematic evidence that free schools, whether for-profit or non-profit, deviate more than marginally from the NPT scores in their grading compared to municipal schools (e.g. Skolverket 2009b, 2010b, 2012c; Sahlgren 2011b; Vlachos 2011a).[18] However, recent research based on the re-marking exercise of NPTs indicates that free schools, in both compulsory and upper-secondary education, on average set about 0.11 SD higher grades compared to municipal schools in relation to the grades set by external examiners (Tyrefors, Hinnerich, and Vlachos 2012). The breakdown by subject and education level indicates that the picture is not clear-cut – with free schools setting lower grades in some cases. Indeed, in the tests analysed by Böhlmark and Lindahl (2012a, 2012b), free schools set lower grades or grades that are on a par with municipal schools, indicating that their findings in this respect might actually underestimate the effect of competition. Yet the overall results still indicate that all school-level comparisons between municipal and free schools should be interpreted with caution.

Competition, however, appears to have had only small or no effects on grade inflation in compulsory schools (Vlachos 2011b; Böhlmark and Lindahl 2012a). This suggests that studies analysing competition effects on achievement may be relatively reliable. But the problem is likely to be more severe in upper-secondary school where grades are even more important for pupils, since these generally determine their tertiary education. As of now, however, there are no studies analysing the effects of competition in upper-secondary education on grade inflation, probably because the structure of the education system at this level makes such analyses difficult, but also because there are no systematic collections of test scores (Hansson, Henrekson, and Vlachos 2011).

Because of the problems noted above, there is a limit to what may be inferred from even the best research on the effects of the Swedish voucher reform on

---

18 Wikström and Wikström (2005) find that upper-secondary free schools inflate grades significantly, but these findings are unreliable since the yardstick measure is a voluntary standardised test used for admissions to university. First, the likelihood of taking the test declines when pupils have high grades since they then do not need to take it to get into the undergraduate course of their choice. Second, if one achieves a good result on the test, there are fewer incentives to care about the GPA while in school (Vlachos 2011b).

education quality. Accordingly, several authors have argued that Sweden must either centralise its grading system or decentralise its admissions system (Henrekson and Vlachos 2009) if it is to reap the benefits of competition (Sahlgren 2011c). It might be good to implement curriculum-based exams, which appear to increase the focus on academics, result in more tutoring of lagging pupils, and raise achievement (e.g. Jürges, Schneider, and Büchel 2005; Woessmann 2005; Bishop 2006; Jürges et al. 2012). Since schools would be expected to focus more on exam performance, it is important that these are designed well in order that they are worth teaching to and capture the desirable knowledge and skills. Furthermore, all assessment does not have to be test based; essays could also be marked centrally. As Chapter 4.14 argues, different metrics would incentivise schools to focus on broader quality rather than merely test scores. The main point is that more accountability in the Swedish education system is clearly urgent.[19]

Given the fact that all pupils are different, however, and the fact that all education systems face trade-offs regarding what pupils should learn and when, it may be important to combine an overhaul of the Swedish grading system with a decentralisation of its admissions system. Allowing Swedish schools to offer other countries' qualifications, which have already been approved by other governments, would also ensure healthy competition between different educational institutions (Sahlgren 2012). In the future, one could also envisage that new qualifications could be developed by schools or third-party organisations and then approved by the government as long as they satisfy minimum requirements. Allowing schools also to compete by offering different qualifications and assessment would allow for stronger diversity in the education system, while at the same time ensuring accountability to credible quality measures. Additionally, this could be complemented by other measures, such as improved school inspections and separate cohort-referenced 'information tests', which are discussed in detail in Chapter 4.14.

---

19   It is important to note the many problems associated with centralised accountability tests administered in US states, which have given rise to perverse incentives among schools to select the best pupils to take the tests and other forms of manipulations (Figlio and Loeb 2011). Yet outcomes are likely to depend strongly on the design of the exam system and to which results schools are held accountable. These might be value added, raw test scores, the share of pupils with passing grades, etc. (e.g. Lauen and Gaddis 2012). The evidence therefore points to the importance of taking such incentives into account when devising the rules for any potential centralised form of assessment.

The lesson English policymakers should take from Sweden's voucher programme, then, is that the effects of competition depend strongly on the overall policy context and the incentives it produces. In summary:

1. if other reforms have a negative impact, the odds will be stacked against competition;
2. without large increases in competitive incentives, there is no reason to expect quality to increase radically; and
3. without accountability to credible quality measures and good information, it is possible that such competitive incentives will translate into competition based on things other than quality.

Nevertheless, despite these shortcomings, the most recent, and methodologically convincing, research displays a small positive impact on pupil performance, both in the short- and long-term perspective. Given the many design flaws that exist, this is quite remarkable indeed.

2.2.2 *Chile*

In 1981, Chile's military government carried out large-scale reforms aimed at injecting more competition into its education system. Devolving responsibility for education to the municipalities, the government introduced a per-pupil voucher. At the same time, private schools not charging tuition fees began to receive the same voucher. This shifted the educational landscape significantly. In 1981, 15% of pupils attended private schools with some public subsidy. By 2008, this figure had grown to 47% (Elacqua 2009a). Since 1993, private voucher schools have also been allowed to charge fees, in which case the voucher amount is reduced and schools have to pay a certain percentage of the fee to a scholarship fund for their pupils. Two-thirds of these scholarships have to be allocated based on economic need (Anand, Mizala, and Repetto 2009).

There continues to be intense debate about the impact of the voucher programme. In contrast to the Swedish voucher reform, most studies have focused on whether or not private voucher schools perform differently than municipal schools, rather than on competition effects. The initial evidence was mixed with some studies finding positive and some negative effects (see Parry 1997; McEwan and Carnoy 2000; Mizala and Romaguera 2000; Tokman 2002; Vegas 2002). Yet these results are based on school-level data and the research is methodologically flawed because it did not take into account selection bias.

Focusing on the more recent pupil-level findings, however, the great majority of studies find positive effects of private schooling. McEwan (2001) uses controls for selection bias – with school density as an instrument – and finds that private fee-paying and Catholic voucher schools raise achievement moderately, while private, secular voucher schools have no effects. Mizala and Romaguera (2002) find positive effects of voucher schools (by about 0.28 SD), but the effect of privately funded schools are more mixed depending on the estimation strategy employed. This study, however, fails to take into account selection bias. Sapelli and Vial (2002, 2003) analyse Spanish test scores in tenth grade, using market characteristics such as school density as instruments, and find that private voucher schools not charging top-up fees perform about 0.50 SD better than municipal schools when accounting for the fact that municipal schools receive extra non-voucher funding. This effect remains strong when controlling for peer effects.[20] When municipal schools receive on average 72 per cent more in funding, however, they perform better. Sapelli and Vial (2005), in turn, find large overall gains, sometimes amounting to over 0.50 SD in fourth grade Spanish and mathematics when using an instrument constructed from average fees and the results of voucher schools in the geographical area in which the pupil attends school. Although focusing on stratification, Mizala and Torche (2012) use the number of schools in the private and municipal sectors as an instrument, and find positive effects of private voucher schools of about 0.18 SD in fourth grade mathematics and language, but no effects in eighth grade. They do not find consistent evidence that parental fees matter at all for the results, although they do not attempt to control for selection bias in this respect.

Analysing the impact of receiving a scholarship from a fee-charging voucher school, Anand, Mizala, and Repetto (2009) use **propensity score matching to compare pupils with similar characteristics**, and find that low-income pupils attending fee-charging voucher schools perform about 0.20 SD higher than those in municipal schools, but no differences between free voucher schools and voucher schools that charge top-up fees. Dronkers and Avram (2010a, 2010b)

---

20   On the importance of doing so, see Bellei (2005).

find similar positive effects on PISA reading scores of voucher schools, but no effects of fee-paying non-voucher schools. In contrast, Contreras, Sepúlveda, and Bustos (2010), not controlling for endogeneity, find that when selection practices are taken into account, the voucher school advantage regarding fourth grade mathematics scores declines significantly (to about 0.02 SD), and is actually a disadvantage for pupils from low socio-economic background (of about 0.04 SD). However, the study fails to take account of reverse causality in this respect: higher-achieving voucher schools are more likely to adopt selection practices due to over-subscription. If this is the case, controlling for selection practices is an invalid approach because it ensures that we 'control away' the effect of good voucher schools. Nevertheless, in a working paper version of the paper, the authors use IV models with school density as an instrument and find that the effects of voucher schools turn insignificant overall when excluding selection practices but controlling for peer effects (Contreras, Sepúlveda, and Bustos 2007).

The common problem with all of the above studies is that they fail to account for selection bias properly because of poor instruments. School density, for example, could also be a measure of competition. It is highly likely that such gauges will affect families' decisions about where to live and school developers' decisions about where they should establish themselves (Lara, Mizala, and Repetto 2011). Similarly, despite using a different approach, Anand, Mizala, and Repetto (2009:379) rightly conclude that they 'cannot completely rule out the possibility that the controls [they] use may not capture unobserved student characteristics'. This is indeed the downside with propensity score matching.

Two papers, however, improve the methodology significantly. Using value-added models, Contreras and Santos (2009) analyse whether entering and exiting municipal schools affect achievement between eighth and tenth grades. They find a small positive effect of two years of voucher school treatment in mathematics and Spanish (0.05 to 0.06 SD), and, conversely, a negative treatment effect of two years in municipal school on mathematics scores (about 0.06 SD), but not on Spanish scores. Lara, Mizala, and Repetto (2011) utilise a similar approach and find that the effect of two years of voucher school treatment amounts to about 0.06 SD. These estimates are much smaller than in the previous literature, although it is important to point out that the estimation strategy can only evaluate the effect of a voucher school education among

→ unpublished

pupils who switch schools. Finally, Rau, Sánchez, and Urzúa (2010) use a mix of theoretical modelling and empirical estimates, and display results of the same magnitude overall, while also showing that for pupils deciding to switch from voucher schools, the effect size of attending such a school is about 0.35 SD. The average findings are much smaller in comparison with previous research, which calls into question the value of a voucher school education.

In addition, recent contributions have disentangled the effect of different school types. Elacqua (2009b) separates schools by ownership structures, finding that fourth and eighth grade pupils in for-profit franchise voucher schools consistently outperform those in for-profit independent, municipal, and Protestant schools. For example, the effect of attending a for-profit franchise school in eighth grade on mathematics test scores amounts to 0.21 SD compared to municipal schools. At the same time, there are no consistent differences between for-profit franchise, Catholic and non-profit secular schools. The authors also find little difference between for-profit independent and municipal schools, while Catholic and non-profit secular schools outperform for-profit independent schools. These findings further display the importance of inducing profit-making schools to scale up.

In a related study, Elacqua et al. (2011) separate voucher schools into franchise and non-franchise schools, without distinguishing between non-profit and for-profit management, finding that independent voucher schools do not outperform municipal schools, but that franchise voucher schools perform better than both municipal and independent voucher schools. Indeed, franchises with more schools outperform those with fewer schools with an effect of up to 0.20 SD compared to municipal and independent schools. This could be because franchises exploit economies of scale (Chubb 2001) and facilitate sharing of information between schools (McMeekin 2003). Alternatively, good schools are simply more likely to scale up, which should be the case in a competitive market.

However, the instruments used by Elacqua (2009b) and Elacqua et al. (2011) are similar to those used in previous studies, making it important to interpret the findings with caution – although the instruments' problematic features are less likely to affect the comparisons between for-profit and non-profit voucher schools.

Finally, recent studies focus on *Sociedad de Instrucción Primaria*, a specific non-profit school chain that serves low-income pupils in Santiago. Using propensity score matching as well as IV models, Henríquez, Mizala, and Repetto (2009), Palomer and Paredes (2010), and Henríquez et al. (2012) find that pupils in these schools perform significantly better than pupils in municipal schools and other voucher schools. The results obtained with propensity score matching imply that the effect compared to municipal school pupils amounts to up to 0.87 SD, while the impact compared with other voucher schools amounts to up to 0.70 SD. The pupils attending these schools even outperform those at fee-paying private schools by up to 0.52 SD. Qualitative evidence suggests a number of different reasons for the chain's success, including a focus on pupil's learning as the overarching goal; sharing of best practice; performance-related pay; systematic use of pupil and teacher evaluations, and basing action on those evaluations; as well as specific methods for selecting directors and teachers. This suggests that the goal of a voucher system, producing excellent schools through competition between diverse providers, is certainly possible. It also highlights some of the advantages of school chains, namely spreading best practice, and basing remuneration partly on performance.

Overall, therefore, the evidence, summarised in Table 3, in the Appendix, finds positive effects of private voucher schools, although the best evidence displays only small impacts. Indeed, a recent meta-analysis, although not incorporating all studies noted above, indicates that voucher schools increase achievement by only 0.10 SD (Drago and Paredes 2011). Yet it is conspicuous that researchers focusing on choice and school effects generally do not include competition measures in their analyses. Turning to competition effects, therefore, most studies use cross-sectional IV models. Gallego (2002) finds that private voucher school enrolment, instrumented with municipality characteristics, increases achievement: a one SD increase in competition raises overall achievement by up to 0.18 SD. Contreras and Macías (2002) report similar results using the Herfindahl index, which measures market concentration, as a gauge of competition. Using the number of priests in 1950 as an instrument, Gallego (2006) finds that a one SD increase in private voucher school competition raises achievement in fourth, eighth, and tenth grade tests by up to 0.17 SD. He also shows that municipal schools tend to react less positively to competition if they operate under soft budget constraints (meaning that they get additional supply-side transfers over and above the voucher). Finally, Auguste and Valenzuela (2006) use distance to the closest large city and population levels in the market as instruments and find that competition increases sorting significantly, but also that it raises achievement. An increase in competition by one SD raises test scores by 0.10 SD at the individual level.

Again, however, the big problem with cross-sectional research is that it is difficult to find out whether or not the instruments are valid. It might be the case, for example, that market size and concentration are related to pupil achievement in other ways than through competition. Similarly, priests in the 1950s may very well have located to specific areas that in turn affect achievement. If priests are concentrated in urban areas, for example, the same problems as with the above instruments are likely to hold true. Another problem could be that the areas have a specific culture that both attracted more priests and was more conducive to higher educational achievement.

These concerns are troubling since studies using alternative methodologies have come to radically different conclusions. Carnoy and McEwan (2003), for example, analyse municipal school achievement using a fixed-effects model with test score data covering the period 1982–96. This means that they analyse the impact of changes in voucher-school competition on changes in achievement in the municipalities, an approach that takes into account 'unseen', but time-constant, differences between municipalities that could also impact achievement. They find moderate positive effects of voucher-school competition in urban areas, amounting to 0.20 SD, and moderate negative effects in rural areas, also amounting to 0.20 SD. Hsieh and Urquiola (2006), in turn, find both insignificant and significantly negative effects, depending on the measure of achievement/attainment, when using a similar estimation strategy to the one employed by Carnoy and McEwan (2003). (Hsieh and Urquiola analyse panel data with and without questionable instruments, such as population and urbanisation rates.[21]) For example, in the period 1982–96, they find no effects on achievement, but a negative effect on years of schooling in models without instruments. Using IV models, and focusing on the period 1982–88, they find this effect to be two-thirds larger and also that the impact on mathematics

---

21 Hoxby (2008) argues that the authors fail to separate causality from correlation since they do not include pre-programme performance data and neglect the fact that voucher-school enrolment growth is endogenous. A similar point is made in another contribution by the same author (Hoxby 2003b). Yet the authors do include pre-programme trends when analysing the effects on average years of schooling, and the estimates are still significantly negative. Hoxby's critique, therefore, is not entirely convincing, at least when it comes to the effects on years of schooling.

scores is significantly negative.[22] The fact that the effects are especially negative in the first six years may be because of the significant problems in the voucher system in the 1980s, noted below. It may thus have taken longer for competition to begin improving achievement. Nevertheless, the authors also show that the voucher programme increased segregation significantly, concluding that voucher schools appear to compete by cream-skimming rather than by increasing quality.

At the same time, McEwan, Urquiola, and Vegas (2008) analyse a sample of smaller districts in a large region, trying to circumvent endogeneity through a **regression discontinuity design.** Industrial organisation theory would suggest that private schools only enter the local schooling market when the pupil population is large enough to ensure that the school crosses a certain profitability threshold. If there is a discontinuous relationship between the size of a local area's population and the number of private schools in the area, one can compare local schooling markets that differ only in the sense that they are within a narrow range of the threshold. This is more likely to ensure that the researcher is comparing like for like. The authors find a significant threshold in private school availability at 150 pupils in the local market. Using this threshold, they find strong effects on sorting, with high-income pupils leaving for the private sector, but no effects at all on test scores. The data, however, are drawn from a small sample in one specific region, and the authors cannot conduct proper statistical analyses due to this. In general, therefore, the results are best generalised to small, rural communities. Nevertheless, it is worth noting that this research in general supports the findings from the panel data analyses.

In a different approach, partly based on simulations rather than being thoroughly empirical in nature, Bravo, Mukhopadhyay, and Todd (2010) estimate the attainment and labour market returns of the voucher reform by comparing individuals who were exposed to it in different degrees (i.e. pupils who attended school entirely before it was implemented, those who attended school both before and after, and those who attended school in the post-reform period only). Simulations based on an estimated model regarding school attendance and work decisions indicate that the voucher programme increased primary attainment by 0.6 percentage points and upper-secondary school graduation rates by 3.6 percentage points. College

---

22 The descriptive statistics are only presented at the municipal level, which makes it difficult to compare the actual effect sizes with those in previous studies.

attendance rates increased by 3.1 percentage points and the four-year undergraduate completion rate by 1.8 percentage points. There are no effects on average earnings, although earnings inequality decreased somewhat. However, it is difficult to rule out that the changes in educational attainment did not occur because of other, wider changes that occurred throughout the country in the period during which the voucher reform was implemented. Being exposed to the voucher reform also meant being exposed to other educational interventions and wider societal and economic changes that have been rapidly transforming Chilean society. While the paper displays some evidence of positive attainment effects, therefore, one should be cautious about attributing these to the voucher reform only.[23]

Finally, Chumacero, Gallegos, and Paredes (2011) argue that choice is multidimensional since parents take into account different factors, such as performance, distance, and cost. They therefore use a different competition measure based on the share of pupils in an incumbent school that would have been better off in a different school *if* this school had been available. They create this index based on an estimation of what parents consider to be important. The authors then find strong positive effects of competition in the fourth and eighth grades, and in some estimates that the positive effect is stronger among voucher schools. However, they use an instrument of competition that is endogenous (enrolments in the base year), school-level data from a small sample of schools only, and do not take into account that the increase in scores may very well be due to changes in pupil ability rather than school quality. Again, therefore, this paper does not display reliable estimates of how competition affects quality.[24]

The evidence on competition effects in Chile, summarised in Table 3, in the Appendix, thus appears perplexingly mixed. While all cross-sectional IV analyses – which represent the majority of studies – find relatively small positive effects, and two papers using alternative indices find a somewhat larger impact, other techniques tend to produce insignificant and even negative effects. None of these studies are free of methodological flaws. The key issue, which these studies have difficulties controlling for, is that the voucher programme was not

---

23   A similar point can be made in regard to Patrinos and Sakellariou's (2011) study, which uses the reform as an instrument for educational attainment to estimate the returns to schooling.

24   Another problem is that the thus far unpublished paper does not provide much information regarding the data used or the period analysed, making it difficult to compare it with other papers.

randomly rolled out across the municipalities. This would have allowed for proper evaluation strategies, thereby minimising the endogeneity problems that plague most studies evaluating competition effects on pupil performance. And, as noted above, much research on private fee-paying and voucher school effects also suffers from significant flaws due to selection bias.

The overall conclusion from the research on both choice/school and competition effects is thus that there is no *robust* evidence that the Chilean voucher reform has increased education quality significantly. This highlights the problems involved in merely counting the number of studies finding positive or negative effects. An overall count of studies would conclude that the reform might have been positive, but this is an invalid method by which to assess research since the quality of the research and the effect size found vary widely. There is simply little theoretical reason for why we should emphasise the strongly positive findings over the less positive, insignificant, or negative ones in this case.

It is true that Chile has seen an improvement in PISA and TIMSS scores since 2000, although there were only gains between 2003 and 2011 in the latter since TIMSS mathematics and science scores declined slightly between 1999 and 2003 (National Center for Education Statistics 2012; OECD 2012). Hanushek, Peterson, and Woessmann's (2012) results indicate that Chile has had the second best improvements in international tests based on averaged data for the period 1999–2009. Yet to attribute Chile's gains over the last ten years or so to the voucher reform, without any strong research evidence isolating its positive effects, would be fallacious. There have been many other reforms since then and there have also been wide societal and economic changes that may have contributed to the rise. Hsieh and Urquiola (2006) show that there were no, or even negative, changes in pupil achievement between 1970 and 1999 in international tests in mathematics and science. In addition, they show that average test scores in voucher and municipal schools declined relative to private unsubsidised schools, which arguably were not affected by the voucher reform, between 1982 and 1996. Since municipal and voucher schools' relative performance increased between 1988 and 1996 (Gallego 2002), the decline was concentrated in the period 1982–88. Again, this is in line with the argument that there were significant problems in the voucher system in the 1980s as noted below. Nevertheless, just as in the case of the international tests, merely looking at this data is not sufficient to ascribe a causal effect, negative or positive, to the voucher reform.

Why, then, is there no robust evidence of significant gains of the Chilean voucher reform? Neglecting the above-mentioned problems that plague the available research, it is very important to note that there are severe deficiencies in the programme design of the voucher system. First, the education system was not fully decentralised until the late 1980s, ensuring that municipal school budgets were not affected by the voucher reform. This prevented competitive incentives from emerging among municipal schools. Second, municipal school employment was especially rigid until the mid-1990s, which, for example, prevented schools from ensuring that they only kept their best teachers. Third, parents did not have easy access to even rudimentary quality information with which they could exercise informed choice. Fourth, the voucher's real value declined during the 1980s, increasing again only in the early 1990s. In essence, as Gallego (2006:6) puts it, 'It is hard to argue that the system operating in the 1980s was a real voucher system from the point of view of several agents.' Since this is the case, the above-noted studies that analyse whether changes in competition affected changes in pupil performance from the early 1980s to the mid-1990s may in fact pick up these problems.

Despite improvements in the 1990s, furthermore, it must also be noted that many flaws in the programme remained. For example, the value of the voucher is still too low, which inhibits quality improvement. Since the real cost of educating pupils partly depends on their socio-economic background, this hurts poor pupils the most (Gallego 2008; Sapelli 2010). Between 1981 and 2007, schools received a flat per-pupil voucher, incentivising them to serve pupils that are cheap to educate, namely the rich and able ones. As Sapelli (2003) argues, theory suggests that a flat-rate subsidy is not desirable, but rather that the voucher should be differentiated along the lines of income. Since 2008, a 50% extra per-pupil subsidy has been given to poor pupils and the government recently increased the amount by an average of 20%, with higher increases for the poorest (OECD 2011b). However research suggests that this additional funding is probably still not sufficient, and that at least four different voucher levels are necessary (Gallego and Sapelli 2007). This extra subsidy is also not automatic, but is tied to specific educational reform plans which schools have to present to the Ministry of Education, and participating schools are not allowed to charge top-up fees to the pupils for which they receive additional funds. The autonomy regarding how the extra funds are used varies depending on schools' general performance on national standardised tests. Furthermore, it might also be better to differentiate the voucher based on ability, since this might be even more important for determining the real cost of educating a pupil (see Chapter 4.5). Nevertheless, new evidence suggests that the current approach to differentiation has led participating schools to produce higher results (Correa et al. 2012).[25]

The above issue may be even more problematic due to selection criteria that are used widely in voucher schools and to a certain extent also in municipal schools with excess demand (Gauri 1998; McEwan, Urquiola, and Vegas 2008). Selection practices allow schools to turn away poor and less able pupils, which may mute competitive incentives to improve quality. This recently prompted the Chilean government to ban selection practices until sixth grade (Brandt 2010). At the same time, research shows that mobility from poorly performing schools to better schools is restricted to well-performing pupils from higher socio-economic backgrounds (Román and Perticará 2012). New evidence also suggests that pupils attending low-quality schools that potentially face school closure often do not have any viable alternative schools, especially good ones, nearby for various reasons. These reasons include selection practices by which pupils are effectively barred from attending the schools that are located within a reasonable distance (Elacqua et al. 2012). In other words, even if poor parents value better schools, they cannot choose them, which is one important reason failing schools do not close (apart from the soft budget constraints noted below).

Research does suggest that Chilean parents mostly consider test scores and location, with trade-offs between these, when choosing schools. Yet, as economic theory predicts, richer and more educated parents are more likely to choose schools based on test scores than location (Gallego and Hernando 2009; Chumacero, Gómez, and Paredes 2011). The latter study does not separate test scores from pupil composition, but it is conspicuous that schools' average socio-economic characteristics do not affect parental choice in Gallego and Hernando's (2009)

---

25   The authors argue that they identify positive effects from vouchers, but these might simply be due to the fact that schools receive additional resources and are more accountable to authorities for this funding.

preferred model, suggesting that test scores do not proxy for peer background in these findings at least.[26] This indicates that although poor parents might value school quality, they are unable to respond to those preferences because of a lack of supply that meets their demand (Thieme and Treviño 2011). Apart from potentially making schools compete by selecting pupils rather than by boosting quality, selection practices might thus have had a negative effect in that they gave poorer children even less access to alternative schools than they otherwise would have had.

Second, the problem of too little funding and voucher differentiation is further exacerbated by the fact that voucher schools can charge top-up fees, since this encourages 'rent-seeking' behaviour by schools seeking further fees from high-income parents. Yet this is a flaw in system design, rather than a problem that has arisen because voucher schools are greedier. Indeed, for-profit voucher schools that do not charge top-up fees actually serve higher numbers of pupils from low socio-economic and indigenous backgrounds compared to municipal and non-profit voucher schools. Non-profit voucher schools, however, have fewer pupils from low socio-economic background, but a higher number of indigenous pupils than municipal schools (Elacqua 2009a, 2012). And it is specifically for-profit schools serving low-income pupils that seem to grow faster as a result of increasing quality, although one should be careful in interpreting this finding because of endogeneity issues. Nonetheless, it is conspicuous that there is no correlation between improving achievement and growing in size among non-profit voucher schools (Elacqua 2009c). At the same time, however, for-profit and non-profit schools that charge top-up fees serve much fewer pupils from low socio-economic and indigenous backgrounds overall. The most market-driven agents, in other words, are not 'natural born cream-skimmers'. What is important, however, is to produce the correct incentive structure to encourage providers to serve more disadvantaged pupils. Further differentiating the voucher partly by family income would be a good way of doing so.

Third, municipal schools continue to operate under soft budget constraints. This, in turn, means that municipal schools are not forced to close despite losing pupils, which is a mechanism that is key for the market to function properly (Sapelli 2010). Indeed, research shows that about 30% of public education

---

26 Prior analyses, which did not analyse parents' actual choices but rather their search behaviour, found that pupil demographics are more important (e.g. Elacqua, Schneider, and Buckley 2006).

expenditures on the average pupil are not connected to the voucher, while also finding that municipal schools under soft budget constraints do not react to competition (Gallego 2006). Again, this hurts poor pupils in particular since they become dependent on municipal schools. As Sapelli (2003:532) argues, 'These rules give way to sorting, but other rules would imply competition for all students. Sorting is not inevitable, but is a consequence of the design of the subsidy.' Supply-side subsidies, in combination with an undifferentiated voucher, thus produce perverse incentives among municipal schools that hurt poor pupils the most.

Fourth, the system lacks autonomy. Municipal schools have to abide by the Labour Teachers' Statute (LTS), which imposes standardised pay scales. Control over contracts and salaries is centralised with the Ministry of Education, which combined with *de facto* centralised collective bargaining has produced a system where 'wage negotiations have the characteristics of a bilateral monopoly' (Mizala and Romaguera 2005:106). While voucher schools are governed by the regular Labour Code, they have to satisfy the minimum LTS criteria, including working day length, minimum salaries, legal holiday periods, and terms of termination. This lack of autonomy, especially in municipal schools, ensures that schools do not have the freedom to react sufficiently to whatever competitive incentives remain in the system.

Finally, the information with which parents can exercise their choice is insufficient. Today, raw test scores remain the main quality indicator. As noted in Chapter 1, however, such scores are also an indicator of pupil ability and background rather than a pure gauge of school quality. Indeed, evidence suggests that test scores in the Chilean context basically proxy socio-economic background. On the other hand, scores adjusted for socio-economic background display strong volatility from year to year, making these resemble a lottery in terms of predicting school quality (Mizala, Romaguera, and Urquiola 2007). It is conspicuous that the System of School Performance Assessment (SNED) school ranking – a comparison of schools' test scores in 'homogeneous groups' based on location, pupils' socio-economic background, and level of schooling – appears to be ignored by parents when they choose schools (Mizala and Urquiola 2007). Yet evidence suggests that the ranking is poorly designed due to its focus on absolute test scores and inter-cohort gains; the highest ranked schools are in fact not those that make the highest within-cohort gains (Carnoy, Brodziak, et al. 2007). Parents, therefore, might actually be better off not choosing schools that are highly ranked in SNED. This further reinforces the idea that rigorous, easily accessible and interpretable quality measures are of paramount importance to inducing parents to choose schools that are most likely to raise their children's achievement. (See Chapter 4.14 for a longer discussion.)

There were some changes to the information system in the 2000s, which improved access to the above information and other outputs, such as college admissions rates and graduation rates, as well as information regarding school inputs, such as teacher evaluations and class size. Research indicates that this has indeed had an effect on the search behaviour of parents in one of the more competitive regions (Elacqua and Martínez 2011). Nevertheless, the information available cannot sufficiently separate school quality from pupil quality, which is what a good information system should do.

In conclusion, then, the Chilean experience displays the importance of programme design. Most research suffers from methodological problems, but it seems clear that there is little robust evidence of strong gains either from voucher schools or from competition. An intriguing finding, however, is that Chilean for-profit franchise schools, which are the most market driven, appear to perform somewhat better than many other voucher school types. Although the caveats regarding methodology apply to this finding too, comparisons between different types of voucher schools are less likely to suffer from bias compared to the comparisons between voucher and municipal schools. Nevertheless, as noted above, perhaps better today than it was in the 1980s, it is clear that the Chilean voucher system still requires significant changes if it is to raise pupil performance significantly. The key lessons for English policymakers are the following:

1. differentiate the voucher based on pupil background and ability;
2. ensure that money follows pupils;
3. provide sufficient autonomy for schools; and
4. provide good information.

2.2.3 The Netherlands

Compared to Sweden and Chile, the Netherlands has a very long history of school choice, with its current system dating back to 1917. The 'schools struggle' in the 1800s ended in 1917 when Article 23 of the Dutch Constitution was passed, guaranteeing freedom of education and enshrining the right to provide privately operated education with parental choice deriving from this right. It also, essentially, established the right of independent schools to receive the same funding as municipal schools. In the 1980s, the system was modified to ensure that schools receive more money for pupils from underprivileged families. All schools are required to meet curriculum and teacher requirements, and while they can technically charge additional small fees for extra-curricular activities, parents are not obliged to pay and schools cannot refuse pupils on these grounds (Ritzen, van Dommelen, and de Vijlder 1997). This system has produced a large independent school sector: enrolment increased steadily to about 70% in the 1960s and has hovered around that figure ever since (Patrinos 2002). Additionally, there are no catchment areas for schools, and despite being one of the most secularised countries in the world, 91% of independent schools are religious.[27] Only non-profit organisations are eligible for public funding, which means that there are virtually no for-profit schools (Patrinos 2011). Since 2006 in the case of primary education, and 1996 in the case of secondary education, schools have been given lump sums and school managements are free to spend this however they see fit (Bal and de Jong 2007). In a further step towards school autonomy, in 2006 operating authority over municipal schools was given to independent boards to make them more like independent schools and reduce the likelihood of unwelcome political interventions favouring the former (Ladd, Fiske, and Ruijs 2009). Thus, there are basically no publicly operated schools as we know them in the Netherlands.

Despite its long history, the Dutch school choice system has, surprisingly, been subject to much less scrutiny than Chile's and Sweden's. Early Dutch studies found that Catholic and Protestant schools outperformed municipal ones, but this was not true for the small minority of secular independent schools. In the 1990s, furthermore, municipal schools were on a par with Catholic and Protestant schools (see Dijkstra, Dronkers, and Karsten 2004). Yet these studies did not control or test for selection bias and should thus be interpreted with caution.

Using a sample of primary schools, and using children's religious affiliation as an instrument, Levin (2004) found that selection bias does not appear to

---

27   Municipalities can, however, define catchment areas for primary municipal schools, but schools can also apply for exceptions in these cases (Eurydice 2008/09). Since about 70% of pupils attend independent schools, catchment areas have played a minor role in the Netherlands overall.

be an issue, and that Catholic schools outperform municipal schools by up to 0.20 and 0.26 SD in arithmetic and reading respectively. Analysing PISA 2006 scores, Patrinos (2011) uses information about whether parents take into consideration schools' religious orientation in their choice as an instrument for independent school attendance. The findings display moderate gains in mathematics, reading, and science PISA scores by 0.19, 0.31, and 0.21 SD respectively. The question, however, is whether the instrument is valid, since family religion may be related to unobservable variables that differ between pupils and that affect achievement. Nevertheless, the author derives a bias-corrected estimate, following Altonji, Elder, and Taber (2005a), and finds that the bias is only in the order of 0.06 to 0.09 SD. In other words, the independent school advantage remains even after controlling for the possible bias derived from using family religion as an instrument.

However, a recent study questions whether there is indeed a positive independent school effect in the Netherlands. Cornelisz (2012) shows that Patrinos's (2011) results change if other controls are included. Applying these controls, the positive impact of attending independent schools evaporates: only a much smaller and less significant effect in reading remains. It is questionable whether some of these variables belong in the equation, and the author gives little theoretical justification for his choices. For example, the type of programme attended, one of the added variables, can be endogenous to independent school attendance. Nevertheless, the impact actually turns negative when using Patrinos's exact specification with data from PISA 2009, possibly suggesting that unrepresentative samples plague the PISA data. Again, the impact turns insignificant once additional (questionable) controls are applied. The author also uses propensity score matching techniques, and finds no differences between municipal and independent schools in either period.[28] Although one should be cautious in interpreting the findings, the negative effects when using 2009 data make it difficult to clearly state that there is an unambiguous positive effect of independent schools in PISA. Of course, it is also important to note that handing over operational authority over municipal schools to independent boards in 2006 may very well have led them to improve by

---

28   This supports Dronkers and Avram's (2010a) conclusion, also based on propensity score matching estimates, that Dutch independent schools perform on a par with municipal schools in PISA reading tests.

2009. The differences in findings could thus also partly depend on this increase in autonomy that municipal schools acquired and which made them more similar to independent schools.

Turning to competition effects, Dijkgraaf, Gradus, and de Jong (2012:4–5) argue that 'the effect of competition on quality has never been systematically analysed for the Netherlands'. The evidence is certainly mixed. Dijkgraaf, Gradus, and de Jong use upper-secondary school-level data between 2002 and 2006, and include school-fixed effects, thus evaluating whether changes in competition predict changes in performance. They find that increases in competition decrease achievement in central exams and reduce the percentage of pupils obtaining a diploma and graduating without delay. The effects are small: an increase in competition by one SD according to the Herfindahl index generates a decline in central exam grades of 0.04 SD, while reducing the number of pupils obtaining a diploma by 1.1 percentage point (0.03 SD) and the share of pupils graduating on time by 1.7 percentage point (0.04 SD). There is some heterogeneity between school types, with zero effects among Catholic and Protestant schools (but somewhat larger effects among other school types). However, the methodology is problematic since the authors include few school-level control variables, and no controls for pupils' socio-economic and ethnic background. They control for endogeneity in robustness regressions, instrumenting competition with the number of schools in the municipality. Yet this measure is clearly not valid, but simply another endogenous gauge of competition. If families choose to live close to high-quality schools, and these schools attract more pupils, the schools may grow in size and appear more monopolistic (Noailly, Vujić, and Aouragh 2012).

Using a significantly larger and better battery of control variables than the previous study, Himmler (2009), including an indicator of pupils' previous achievement, analyses school-level central exam scores in upper-secondary education and finds that competition, measured as the number of Catholic schools in each municipality, raises achievement in non-Catholic schools: a one SD increase in competition raises achievement by 0.15 SD. The author tests for endogeneity in competition, using Catholic population shares in each education market, but test statistics indicate that it is not a problem. The fixed-effects estimates are not significant, but the author has only access to two observations across time, which makes a zero effect because of insufficient variation more likely. In addition, achievement in Catholic schools is not affected by competition, suggesting that 'the competition effect net of [potential] sorting is supposedly still positive' (Himmler 2009:24). However, competition from non-Catholic schools does not appear to matter for achievement, which has further implications for how we should view Dijkgraaf, Gradus, and de Jong's (2012) study. It may simply be that Catholic schools provide high-quality competition, which the studies above suggest, and this could matter more than the quantity of competition in upper-secondary education. Nevertheless, it is unlikely that current Catholic population shares are valid instruments (see Chapters 2.1 and 2.3), making it difficult to assess the robustness of the findings.

Regarding primary education, and focusing on large towns, Noailly, Vujić, and Aouragh (2012) analyse pupil-level standardised test scores and find positive effects of competition, measured as the number of schools within a designated area, on achievement. Using the distance between the school and the town centre as an instrument for competition (with the assumption that pupils living farther away from the town centre face higher travelling costs to attend schools other than the one closest to them), they show that a one SD increase in competition raises achievement by 0.05 to 0.1 SD. They include the ethnic composition at the school level, but no pupil-level background characteristics. Furthermore, it is not clear whether the instrument is valid since people may move closer to the centre to have a larger *choice set* of different good schools nearby (to make sure that there are decent alternatives to overfull popular schools). Again, therefore, the results should be interpreted with caution.

Finally, a novel and important contribution by de Haan, Leuven, and Oosterbeek (2011) traces the impact of a 1992/94 law that increased the minimum primary school size by varying degrees, depending on municipality, between 1992 and 2003. Analysing changes in achievement on standardised tests, the authors find that where there were large increases in the number of schools, this decreased achievement. This negative effect disappears when controlling for school size, making the authors believe that scale economies can outweigh competition effects. But the change in the number of schools caused by the law is unlikely to be a good measure of changes in competition because the smallest schools (presumably the least popular) disappeared. While there was a decline in the quantity of competition, therefore, this may have been offset by an increase in the quality of competition since larger and more popular schools took on more pupils. Furthermore, there is no control for the number of schools governed by the same school board, which would have controlled for the impact of scale economies across schools belonging to the same board. Nevertheless, the study points to the importance of introducing incentives to utilise scale economies as a means to compete for pupils and increase quality.

In sum, therefore, the evidence of the Dutch school choice system, summarised in Table 4, in the Appendix, is mixed. Both independent school and competition effects are ambiguous. However, there is some evidence that specifically Catholic school attendance and competition are positive. It is also important to note the long history of school choice in the country; small gains in the current context could simply display inevitable diminishing returns. As noted in Chapter 1, academic quality is not the only thing that a modern education system is supposed to promote. The Netherlands consistently performs highly in international surveys, displaying the good quality of its education system; in such situations, as Jacob and Lefgren's (2007) research indicates, parents and pupils may also begin to value other school features.

Nevertheless, there are still many problematic features of the Dutch education system affecting the impact of school choice. While de Haan, Leuven, and Oosterbeek (2011:1) argue that, '[t]he primary school system in [the Netherlands] is very close to the system proposed by Friedman', this is far from true. First, entry to the Dutch education market is very restrictive due to quotas along religious lines that were decided as far back as 1917. Schools are not approved unless parents can show that their faith or preferred pedagogical styles are not already catered for by existing schools to a degree that the relevant quota is filled. This is basically impossible to do today (Fält 2011). As Dijkgraaf, Gradus, and de Jong (2012:4) point out, therefore, '[C]ompetition in the Netherlands occurs between existing school sites and not with entrants.' This obviously puts strong limitations on the possibilites for competition to produce higher education quality, for example by stifling innovation and making it difficult for good school boards to scale up and replicate success. And, of course, if there is no/little entry and expansion in the market, it also means that pupil migration from poorly performing schools is unlikely to occur. The severe market entry restrictions are thus clearly a significant flaw in the Dutch system.

Second, and related to the first point, the most market-driven actors, for-profit companies, cannot receive public money. Indeed, religious diversity rather than competition has been the main rationale for school choice in the Netherlands (Fält 2011). It is true that Dutch schools have become larger over time, but this is because of mandated consolidation. The combined effect of the 1992/94 law increasing the minimum primary school size, and the Primary Education Act of 1998, which stipulated that boards should be encouraged to combine their efforts, was that the number of primary school boards decreased from 2,082 to 1,407 between 2000 and 2006. At the same time the number of school boards with one school only dropped from 1,100 to 664, while the number of boards responsible for at least ten schools increased from 180 to 247 (Bal and de Jong 2007:24).

However, legally mandated rationalisation of production is very different from scaling up. It is not clear whether school boards presiding over more schools in the Netherlands utilise scale economies to rationalise and improve the efficiency of education supply; the incentives to do so and reap the benefits of scale economies are not the same as when schools expand naturally to reap the benefits of popularity. The key to taking advantage of scale economies is to ensure that the appropriate incentives are in place for school organisations to benefit. The Dutch school system would therefore be better off allowing profit-making institutions to operate.

A third problem is that schools are over-regulated in terms of their inputs and curriculum. For example, all schools have to offer the nationally determined qualification, with the stipulations that it requires. In addition, they have to hire trained teachers and pay salaries according to national scales, although they do have control over hiring and promotions (CIEB 2012). There have also been overly strict attainment targets and detailed regulations regarding work conditions that all schools need to follow. As de Viljder (2000:2) argues, 'An important consequence of this system was that the "freedom of choice" and the existence of a large number of private schools did not lead to major variety or differences in the quality between schools. Municipal and independent schools had to fulfil the same quality requirements, mainly based on input and process characteristics as proxies for real outcomes.' As argued in Chapter 4, restricting inputs as a proxy for actual quality hampers innovation and competition. The Dutch school system has thus been too regulated in this respect. As noted below, furthermore, the relatively flawed differentiation of funding did not give autonomy to schools to utilise the additional funding as they saw fit.

Nevertheless, today Dutch schools have high operational autonomy in comparison with most other education systems. It is, for example, the only system surveyed in PISA where all schools have budget autonomy, while also having a high degree of personnel autonomy in a comparative perspective (Hanushek, Link, and Woessmann 2012) – suggesting that its flawed choice system has avoided regulatory pressures better than most other countries. It has also begun increasing autonomy to schools, for example by reducing strict attainment targets in many subjects (Eurydice 2008/09), and leaving it up to schools how they use the additional funding they receive because of the differentiated voucher. Nevertheless, it is important to note the way over-regulation can hamper the potential of choice and competition to increase education quality.

Another problem has been the insufficient information provision in the system. There was no way for parents to assess school quality until 1997 when *Trouw*, a small national newspaper, went to court and won the right to publish upper-secondary school quality scores (adjusted for certain pupil background characteristics), which research shows induced schools to improve performance. The short-term effect of receiving the most negative ranking amounts to an increase in exam grades the next year by 0.10 to 0.30 SD, with the medium- and long-term effects within a similar range (Koning and van der Wiel 2012). Additionally, another study shows that pupils responded directly to the publication of these quality scores by applying to the better schools. Although having a relatively small impact overall, academic-track schools that receive the highest score saw an increase in the pupil inflow by more than 20% (Koning and van der Wiel 2010). This indicates that a new competitive environment is emerging due to *Trouw*'s actions.

However, there is much that the Netherlands could do to improve the quality and supply of information about school performance. As yet, there is still no value-added measure that takes into account prior ability, which could be important for inducing parents to choose schools based on how effective they are at raising quality. And at the primary level there are as yet no publicly available quality indicators (Noailly, Vujić, and Aouragh 2012), although the government stipulates that schools should publish prospectuses for parents, which set out the objectives of the schools and results achieved (Eurydice 2008/09). Furthermore, other types of information, discussed in Chapter 4.14, are also important for raising overall education quality. Clearly, on the whole, the Dutch education system still suffers from a lack of easily accessible and developed quality indicators.

Finally, although the voucher has been differentiated since the 1980s, it has not been differentiated enough. Up until 2006, the weighting scheme gave 25% extra to native pupils with low-educated parents, and 90% extra to children of low-educated immigrant parents, with the money given to the school board rather than to the individual school *per se*.[29] In addition, schools did not get the additional funding if their pupil bodies were not made up of at least 9% of pupils who were eligible for additional funding. And even if that was the case, they only got additional money for the number of pupils above this threshold. This means that most pupils have not been given additional funding at all: in 2005/06, 77.45% of pupils received the regular rate. Meanwhile, 10.2% received the 0.25 weighting and 12.1% received the 0.9 weighting. It also means that many disadvantaged pupils did not receive any additional funding even though they should have according to the general differentiation classification (Ladd and Fiske 2011). As argued in Chapter 4.5, it is important that the voucher is differentiated systematically along the lines of background and/or ability to ensure a level playing field and induce schools to compete for pupils from all backgrounds. This should apply to all pupils, not only if the number of pupils of these profiles reaches a certain threshold in a school. This has not been done in the Netherlands, although its system has been better than countries such as Sweden and Chile. Furthermore, until 2006, schools were given the additional funding for enrolling more disadvantaged pupils in the form of personnel units and money earmarked for materials and supplies, with the government paying all additional salaries based on the national salary scales. Supplying the

---

29 There were two other categories: 40% extra was given to children of shippers who live away from their families in children's homes or with foster families, and 70% extra to children of traveller families. Yet these groups appear to comprise a tiny proportion of the total population (0.3% in 2005/06), making the impact of this funding negligible for the overall dynamic of the education landscape.

additional funding in this prescriptive way gave schools little autonomy with which to allocate resources to the greatest benefit of their pupils.

Since 2006, the above scheme has been phased out in favour of a system where children of low-educated parents get an additional 30%, and pupils with very low-educated parents receive 120% (Ladd and Fiske 2011). This is unlikely to be fine-grained enough, but at least school boards now receive the additional funding in the form of lump sum grants, which gives them more freedom to use the money as they see fit. The government also lowered the threshold at which schools qualify to receive additional funding to 6%, which was a good, though not sufficient, step.

The main lessons English policymakers should learn from the Netherlands are that:

1. cumbersome restrictions regarding market entry can stifle competitive incentives;
2. it is important to ensure that benefits of scale economies and competition are reconciled;
3. information is important for creating a competitive dynamic; and
4. it is important to differentiate funding properly and not in too complex a way.

2.2.4 Denmark

Like the Netherlands, Denmark's independent schools have a long history of receiving public funding (for over one hundred years). Today, the funding amounts to 75% of municipal schools' per-pupil expenditure, with the remaining 25% being covered by parents. Independent compulsory schools must ensure the same quality of education. They are also free to select pupils (Anderson 2008; Shewbridge et al. 2011). Apart from having to guarantee teaching in English, Danish, and mathematics, there are few requirements (Rangvid 2008). Interestingly, in spite of the legal requirements regarding quality, the government is not responsible for holding independent schools to account. Instead, parents are responsible for ensuring that this is the case, and they should report any inadequacies to the Ministry of Education. There is consequently little direct state accountability among the Danish independent schools (Ministeriet for Børn og Undervisning 2013).

In upper-secondary education, however, independent schools are subject to the same regulations as municipal schools. Despite the long history of allowing school choice, only 6% of upper-secondary school pupils and 14% of compulsory school pupils attend independent schools today (Ministeriet for Børn og Undervisning 2013). In 1982, the figure for compulsory school pupils was 8% (Ekholm 2004), displaying very small enrolment growth in the past decades.

The Danish school choice system has been subjected to relatively little scrutiny; the author of this book was able to unearth only seven studies analysing Denmark's compulsory school sector. Analysing total years of schooling for a sample of pupils born between 1965 and 1973, Rangvid (2003) finds no differences between independent and municipal schools in terms of years of schooling after controlling for selection bias, while including detailed background controls. However, the instrument used is the interaction between pupil and peer backgrounds, which is unlikely to be valid. Using data from 2002, and controlling for selection bias, Andersen (2008) finds that independent schools do not improve central exam scores. In oral exams, the effect is actually strongly negative (0.64 SD), although he cautions that these scores are generally considered less objective than the written ones because they are not standardised and are also conducted in the presence of external examiners chosen by the schools themselves. Nevertheless, the instrument used for independent school attendance is a measure of dispersion of education levels in the municipalities, which is unlikely to be valid. At the same time, independent schools with high average levels of pupil socio-economic status improve achievement for disadvantaged and advantaged pupils alike, while achievement falls in independent schools with low average levels of pupil socio-economic status. For the latter findings, however, the author does not attempt to deal with selection bias. Since the instrument is also unlikely to be valid, as noted above, it is important to view the study's overall conclusions with caution.

Neglecting to control for selection bias, Rangvid (2008) uses data for the years 1985–92 and finds that Catholic and grammar schools improve attainment, although the effect size is small (about 0.08 SD). Other types of independent schools, however, are not related to better results, with negative estimates for some of them (e.g. 0.15 SD for free schools in terms of years of schooling). Christoffersen and Larsen (2010a) do not control for selection bias, and find that Danish independent schools have slightly higher achievement and lower cost.[30] Dronkers and Avram (2010a), on the other hand, utilise propensity score matching and find no effects of Danish independent schools on PISA reading test scores. Of course, it is important to point out that independent schools appear to receive about 12% less in total per-pupil funding, even after taking into account parental fees in independent schools (Christoffersen and Larsen 2010b). Zero estimates might thus still indicate that independent schools are more efficient, although some estimates above indicate that the effect is negative. Most important, in general, the studies on choice/school effects in Denmark are problematic from a methodological standpoint and should thus be interpreted with caution.

Regarding competition effects, focusing on the period 1999–2002, Nannestad (2004) finds no positive impacts of independent school competition on municipal school exam achievement. Yet his estimation strategy does not take into account selection bias and endogeneity in competition across municipalities. Andersen and Serritzlew (2007), in turn, analyse data from 2002 and find no effects of independent school competition on municipal school achievement, except that it raises per-pupil costs. For example, the existence of one independent school in the municipality raises costs by 0.33 SD in one model. However, the authors do not control for selection bias in independent schools and endogeneity. They argue that endogeneity in levels of competition is not a problem since independent school enrolment shares barely changed during the 1990s – yet this overlooks the fact that the enrolment shares have long historical roots that may explain achievement or funding differences across municipalities today.

Despite the methodological shortcomings in many of the above studies, summarised in Table 5, in the Appendix, it should be acknowledged that there is little evidence of positive competition or consistently positive choice/independent school effects in Denmark. Given the system's flaws, this is unsurprising. First, municipal schools get more funding per pupil, with parents being forced to pay extra for a place in an independent school. This increases the marginal cost of attending an independent school significantly,

---

30   It is not possible to calculate effect sizes since the authors do not provide descriptive statistics.

which in turn decreases competition significantly. It is not surprising that overall independent school enrolment remains marginal. Since the independent school voucher is not systematically differentiated along the lines of ability or background, differential funding for municipal and independent schools may also have contributed to the segregation effects along ethnic lines that have been found (Rangvid 2010).[31] Furthermore, while 'the [independent] school sector in Denmark is governed by a *de facto* voucher system … the [municipal] school sector [is] to a large extent governed by a traditional politico-administrative system' (Andersen 2008:51). That is, the voucher system does not apply to municipal schools. Indeed, research suggests that while municipalities tend to pay lip service to let money follow pupils, municipal school budgets often do *not* follow enrolment as in independent schools, especially when the number of pupils decreases (Serritzlew 2006). Competition becomes something of a paper tiger in terms of improving education quality in this system.

Second, up until 2005, after which no study has used data to evaluate the system, parents could not choose among municipal schools but were assigned to one of the municipal schools in their residential area (Andersen 2008). This in turn meant that there has traditionally been little competition among municipal schools. The only alternative to a local municipal school was to attend independent schools, the supply of which remains severely restricted. Indeed, despite a long history of vouchers, independent school competition has failed to increase significantly. In combination with differentiated funding of municipal and independent schools, which generates higher costs to attend the latter, it is clear that competitive incentives in the Danish school choice system have been very weak during most of its existence.

Third, not only are for-profit schools banned, but no school board is allowed to own more than one school (Fält 2011). While the ban on for-profit schools reduces incentives among providers to expand and take advantage of scale economies, which would increase competition significantly, the one-school-only rule has ensured that any remaining incentives to do so are entirely abolished. In Denmark, independent schools are small-scale, non-profit providers that have freedom to adopt different approaches to education, representing a release valve

---

31   Compensation is to a certain extent differentiated since schools with pupils with learning disabilities and other special needs are given additional 'special grants' (Ministeriet for Børn og Undervisning 2013).

for the municipal school sector rather than a tool to raise the overall level of competition in the system. In this respect, they are more similar to American charter schools (discussed in Chapter 2.3) than Chilean, Dutch, or Swedish independent schools.

Fourth, the system lacks good information, which also stifles accountability. Publication of exit exam results was prohibited until 2001 (Patrinos 2001); from 2002, results from upper-secondary school exams have been published on the Ministry of Education's website and all schools are required to make their results publicly available (Shewbridge et al. 2011). It should be noted that all studies use data from 2002 or earlier, which reduces their value in this respect. Furthermore, raw test scores are currently the only available quality indicator in upper-secondary school, which is problematic since such scores also measure pupil background and ability rather than school quality *per se* (see Chapters 1 and 4.14). In compulsory education, the Centre for Political Studies has published test scores adjusted for socio-economic background since 2007, and there is some evidence that this induced schools to improve (Christoffersen and Larsen 2012). Again, however, simple adjustments are unlikely to provide valid estimates of school quality. In 2010, new national standardised tests, administered at different points in compulsory education, were introduced to increase accountability in the municipal school sector, and these could be used to design value-added measures. Independent schools, however, do not have to participate in the new accountability regime (Shewbridge et al. 2011). Furthermore, such tests are still subject to manipulation and 'teaching to the test', and, as Chapter 4.14 discusses, it is important to use different types of information in order to incentivise schools and parents to focus on broader quality. Up until 2006, municipalities were not even required to produce quality reports covering municipal schools. Exacerbating this further, '[m]unicipal approaches and capacity to undertake school evaluation vary considerably and central expertise on school evaluation is limited to the private sector' (Shewbridge et al. 2011:38). Poor information and accountability, therefore, undermine the Danish school choice system.

The Danish school choice system, then, has failed to increase the right competitive incentives. Only recently have important changes been made, and it will take years before it will be possible to evaluate whether or not these will make a difference. The main lessons English policymakers should learn from the Danish system are that:

1. municipal schools must be forced to compete on equal terms with independent schools;
2. there must be incentives in place to increase the number of independent schools; and
3. high-quality information is necessary to provide accountability and allow parents to make wise school choices.

2.3 Evidence from other countries, with a particular focus on the impact of small-scale reforms

Having delved deeper into four large-scale national choice programmes, it is also important to look at studies of countries with less systematic approaches to school choice, as well as smaller-scale programmes. The distinct advantage of analysing smaller-scale local reforms is that there is often opportunity to improve the methodology significantly. However, there is also a limit to what can be learnt from these programmes. First, it is doubtful whether targeted and small-scale programmes can be of use in predicting the outcomes of large-scale programmes. Second, the reforms and systems under scrutiny rarely generate more than marginal competition, making it more difficult to assess the impacts of choice. Nevertheless, a wide range of studies is discussed below, with a focus on the most recent research.[32]

2.3.1 *Randomised studies*

Randomised studies are often referred to as 'gold standard' evaluations as the problem of endogeneity can be entirely circumvented. Most randomised studies have evaluated choice and school effects by comparing samples of pupils who have won or lost choice lotteries to gain admission to over-subscribed schools (Wolf 2008). Provided that admission to the school truly is random, this ensures the internal validity of these studies, which means that we can be sure that they do identify causal effects among pupils in the sample analysed. External validity,

---

32 For a review of the international evidence dating from the 1980s, see Coulson (2009). Those studies generally find positive independent school effects, but, as noted, there are significant differences in the quality of the research.

however, remains a concern since effects cannot be extrapolated to pupils who differ significantly from applicants, or to schools that are not over-subscribed (Betts and Atkinson 2012; Tuttle, Gleason, and Clark 2012). It is also possible that the competition introduced by allowing choice raises quality in all schools, which may render the effect of attending a choice school insignificant (Hoxby 2008). There is to date only one, unpublished study, discussed below, that utilises a research strategy that takes into account the latter. Yet, despite the limitations, randomisation is a powerful tool with which to estimate the causal effects of exercising choice.

The large American literature using this technique displays mostly positive effects, but primarily for disadvantaged pupils. In Chicago, public high school choice appears to be unrelated to, or even negative for, achievement. It appears, however, that attending a school with a high value-added score lowers crime and self-reported disciplinary incidents somewhat (Cullen, Jacob, and Levitt 2006).[33] Public school choice at the primary level in Chicago does not appear to have positive effects for pupil achievement either (Cullen and Jacob 2009), though primary charter school choice does among pupils who have spent at least two years in such a school (Hoxby and Rockoff 2005). Public school choice, however, is related to higher short- and long-term performance in Charlotte-Mecklenburg, but only when pupils attend better schools compared to the neighbourhood school to which they otherwise would have been assigned (Deming et al. 2011). Hastings, Kane, and Staiger (2006), however, only find positive effects among pupils whose parents base their choices on school quality. Hastings and Weinstein (2008) find that parents in Charlotte-Mecklenburg who receive information about school quality are significantly more likely to choose higher-performing schools. The results suggest, in turn, that attending a school with scores that are one SD higher as a result of receiving this information increases pupil achievement by about 0.40 SD. This is larger than other findings in the literature, indicating that information is an important ingredient in making wise school choice decisions. In New York City, Hoxby, Murarka, and Kang (2009) also report positive effects of charter school choice on test scores. In San Diego, public school choice through open enrolment does not appear to

---

33 Pupils did not generally choose schools based on value added but rather average test scores. Yet this is not surprising since the latter metric was available to the public while the former was not.

be positive, and is in some cases negative, for achievement (Betts et al. 2006). In Connecticut, Bifulco, Cobb, and Bell (2009) find that high school magnet school attendance boosts reading achievement by 0.28 SD and mathematics achievement by 0.14 SD.[34] Bui, Craig, and Imberman (2011), on the other hand, find no general effects of choosing and attending a magnet school with special programmes geared to gifted children in a large urban school district in the American Southwest. The exception is that lottery winners perform 0.28 SD better in science compared to lottery losers.

Yet the evidence does display heterogeneous effects. A recent study analyses data from 36 middle schools in 15 states and finds positive effects of charter schools serving underprivileged children, but negative effects of charter schools serving more advantaged children (Gleason et al. 2010). This corroborates findings that choice has an especially positive effect among African Americans. Indeed, there is a growing body of evidence to suggest that charter schools generally are positive in urban settings and mostly for disadvantaged, low-performing, and special education pupils (Angrist et al. 2010; Abdulkadiroğlu et al. 2011; Angrist, Pathak, and Walters 2011; Curto and Fryer 2011; Dobbie and Fryer 2011a; Angrist et al. 2012). The findings display gains of up to 0.80 SD. These advantages appear to result from these schools subscribing to the 'No Excuses' paradigm, including selective recruitment of teachers, longer school days and years, and a marked focus on high behavioural standards (Angrist, Pathak, and Walters 2011). Additionally, Hastings, Neilson, and Zimmerman (2012) find that both choosing to attend a magnet school, with a high value-added score, and general charter school attendance in a low-income urban district, improve attendance rates as well as test scores. At the same time, there is little evidence that pilot schools in Boston – which have some autonomy but are still bound by certain provisions of collective bargaining agreements – increase achievement (Abdulkadiroğlu et al. 2011). This hints at the importance of autonomy if school choice is to function properly.

US randomised evidence, therefore, indicates that choice programmes can be very beneficial for underprivileged pupils. It also suggests that choice enables schools to experiment with different approaches to teaching, which can lead to

---

34 A magnet school is a US public school that offers special curricula and that draws pupils from across school district borders. Magnet schools have been used as a tool to reduce racial school segregation.

improved performance and later replication by other schools. Nonetheless, the results can only tell us something about the effects of attending schools that are over-subscribed, since it is only in these circumstances that lotteries are used, and more research is certainly necessary on the impact of choosing and attending under-subscribed schools.

What is the impact of pupils using vouchers to attend otherwise fee-paying private schools? The evidence suggests generally positive effects, but again mostly among underprivileged children. Some findings from Milwaukee displayed null effects (Witte 1997), but two newer studies find small positive effects (Rouse 1998; Greene, Peterson, and Du 1999). In Cleveland, there is also some evidence of a small positive impact in language and social studies, following seven years of voucher use from kindergarten through sixth grade. There are no effects, however, in mathematics, reading, and science compared to rejected applicants (Plucker et al. 2006).[35] In Charlotte, vouchers also appear to improve achievement (Greene 2001; Cowen, J. M. 2008). In Washington, DC, however, there are no significant positive effects of using a voucher on mathematics test scores, but there is a small positive impact on reading test scores and quite large effects on high school graduation rates. Vouchers also raised parents' satisfaction scores, while not having any impact on pupils' ratings (Wolf et al. 2013). In New York and Dayton, there are positive effects on test scores, but some research finds this impact to be significant only among African-American pupils (Howell et al. 2004; Peterson and Howell 2004). Krueger and Zhu (2004) argue that the effects in New York are not robust, but Peterson and Howell (2004) show that this appears to be due to incorrect specifications. This interpretation is buttressed by other research from New York, which also finds an especially positive impact among African Americans, as well as among other ethnicities if they apply from schools with test scores lower than the city median (Barnard et al. 2003). A recent study evaluated long-term effects in the US, and found that private school vouchers improved African Americans' overall college enrolment rates by 24% and increased the enrolment rate in selective colleges by over 100%, with no effects among other

---

35   In Cleveland, Belfield (2006) was only able to evaluate effects up through fourth grade. The research found evidence of negative effects in mathematics and reading in second grade, and no effects in fourth grade. These effects are discussed in Rouse and Barrow (2009), but they fail to mention that Belfield finds a positive impact in fourth grade language tests. (He does not analyse social science scores.)

groups (Chingos and Peterson 2012). Again, this displays that pupils from disadvantaged backgrounds may benefit from choice especially.

Randomised studies on school choice have not been carried out outside the US, with three important exceptions. Created in the early 1990s, Colombia's PACES programme was one of the world's largest targeted voucher schemes for low-income pupils before it was phased out in 1998. Vouchers, assigned by lotteries, covered about half the cost of attending a private upper-secondary school and were renewable conditional upon satisfactory academic progress. Studies analysing this programme find that lottery winners performed better in university entrance exams, with an effect size of up to 0.73 SD, while also being less likely to repeat grades and more likely to finish high school. In the case of pupils in vocational education, this is despite being surrounded by less advantaged peers and less educated teachers than lottery losers (Angrist et al. 2002; Angrist, Bettinger, and Kremer 2006; Bettinger, Kremer, and Saavedra 2010).

It is intriguing that lottery winners attended schools with less advantaged peers and less educated teachers and still ended up benefiting. This may suggest that the positive effect is partly due to the fact that pupils only kept their vouchers if they progressed to the next grade, which produced incentives to work harder (Bettinger 2011). It may simply also be that peer effects and teacher qualifications were not that important for educational outcomes – which is consistent with the available mixed research (Sacerdote 2011; Hanushek and Rivkin 2012). It may also be that choice and school effects, as discussed in Chapter 1, were more important. Indeed, a clearly important factor for pupils in vocational schools was that private schools offered training for which there was greater demand from students and the labour market than the training offered at government schools. This may indicate an advantage of private schools in that they appear more responsive to pupil and labour market needs (Bettinger, Kremer, and Saavedra 2010). Regardless of the mechanism, however, it seems clear that the Colombian voucher programme was beneficial for the pupils who utilised it.

In China, on the other hand, Zhang (2012) uses lotteries to analyse the effects of attending a magnet-type middle school, finding no impact on test scores or the likelihood that pupils gain admission to better high schools. The author also finds that parents choose schools with high average test scores rather than schools with high value added. This may explain the null findings. One plausible explanation is that parents could not observe schools' value added, and that they used average test scores as a proxy. But this is a poor proxy since average test scores are largely uncorrelated with value added. In general, therefore, the research displays the importance of good information to enable parents to choose schools based on quality.

The third randomised study in the developing world analyses primary school pupils in rural India. Muralidharan, Kremer, and Sundararaman (2013) present results from a two-stage experiment of a school-voucher programme that randomised the offer of vouchers both across villages as well as across pupils. This design allows the authors to study the direct effects on pupils of winning a voucher and moving to a private school as well as the spill-over effects on non-participants. The private schools that received voucher pupils could not select them (lotteries were to be used in the case of over-subscription) and could not charge top-up fees on the voucher. Preliminary results reported after four years of the programme display positive effects of winning a voucher on Hindi test scores, but no impact in other subjects. The causal effect of attending a private school appears to differ depending on medium of instruction: Telugu-medium private schools generally improve pupil performance in all subjects, while the effectiveness of English-medium private schools is more mixed. These results suggest that private schools may be more productive if pupils do not have to switch their medium of instruction from their native Telugu to English, which may be costly for them. Since the value of the voucher was 40 per cent of the average per-pupil cost in government schools, and since private schools on the whole display similar results in mathematics and Telugu despite devoting less instructional time to these subjects, the results suggest that the private schools are more productive and cost effective than government schools (although it is worth noting that previous government investments in education might be important for why private schools can be so efficient, as noted in Chapter 2.3.2).

In addition, the authors find no spill-over effects among pupils in government schools or pupils who attended private schools without a voucher, indicating that the voucher system did not create any losers. On the other hand, there is also no evidence of positive competition effects on the government schools, though there is some evidence that the voucher programme was more effective in settings where winners had a greater number of private schools to choose from. In general, however, analysing competition effects after four years of the programme is far from ideal since it takes time before competition matures. Furthermore, since money does not necessarily follow pupils in government schools, it is not clear that these schools had any competitive incentives to improve. Finally, since the programme was implemented in rural villages only, it can tell us little about how competition would function in a system that includes urban areas where opportunities for choice are generally much greater. Overall, therefore, while the research indicates that vouchers can successfully raise school productivity, it is doubtful that it can tell us much about how large-scale choice programmes may function in the developed world.

2.3.2 *Non-randomised studies of choice and school effects*

Apart from the 'gold standard' studies, there is a large body of non-randomised evidence of varying methodological quality. Again, the results are somewhat mixed. Using quasi-experimental panel-data techniques, one of the larger studies, examining 14 states and two districts directly, concludes that 19% of charter schools outperform public schools and 22–31% perform worse than public schools (Davis and Raymond 2011). Another recent study focused on evidence from seven states, using similar techniques, and found that pupils generally perform much the same in charter and public schools, but slightly worse in charter schools in Texas and Chicago (Zimmer et al. 2011). The authors also find that attending a charter high school increases the likelihood of graduating by up to 15% in Florida and 32% in Chicago, while increasing the probability of attending college by 18% in Florida and 14% in Chicago (Zimmer et al. 2009). Yet these estimates are based on using proximity to charter schools as instrument, which may be related to pupil performance in other ways than merely through increasing the likelihood of attending a charter school.

At the same time, Bettinger (2005) finds negative effects of charter schools in Michigan, and these negative effects appear also in North Carolina (Bifulco and Ladd 2006). In Connecticut, Bifulco, Cobb, and Bell (2009) find that value-added and fixed-effects estimations replicate lotteries rather well, displaying positive or zero effects of magnet-school choice, depending on grade and pupils analysed. In California, charter schools have uneven effects, sometimes negative and sometimes positive (Buddin and Zimmer 2005; Zimmer and Buddin 2006). In Milwaukee, however, charter schools outperform public schools (Witte et al. 2011), which is also the case in Chicago and Florida (Booker et al. 2011). In Milwaukee, too, voucher schools increase attainment, while also raising test scores significantly among lower-performing pupils. However, they yield only modest, and sometimes negative, effects on test scores among more able pupils (Lamarche 2008; Cowen et al. 2013). Using an IV approach, Özek (2009) finds some evidence of negative effects from opting out of the local public school through open enrolment in Pinellas County, Florida. At the same time, using the same strategy, Nichols and Özek (2010) find positive effects of public school choice in Washington, DC. Yet both studies use proximity to the pupil's house as instrument, which may very well correlate with unobservable background characteristics and thus contaminate the findings. Meanwhile, exam schools in Boston and New York, which require pupils to sit an entrance exam, do not appear to improve achievement despite a significant boost in peer quality that pupils can expect by attending these schools (Dobbie and Fryer 2011b; Abdulkadiroğlu, Angrist, and Pathak 2012). Berkowitz and Hoekstra (2011), however, find that attending a selective private high school increases the likelihood that pupils will attend more selective universities. Figlio (2011), in turn, finds that private school choice in the Florida tax-credit programme has modest positive effects on test scores, which are not always significant, using a regression discontinuity design that makes the estimates reliable.

Using proximity to the closest alternative as instrument, Cullen, Jacob, and Levitt (2005) find that career academies, a specific type of public school, increase the likelihood of graduating, but that other types of public school choice do not. Lauen (2009) uses propensity score matching and catchment area fixed effects, and finds overall positive gains from public school choice in Chicago. In Indianapolis, in turn, Nicotera, Mendiburo, and Berends (2009) find positive achievement effects of charter schools. One study on Catholic schools specifically finds no significant effects of attending such schools (Jepsen 2003). However, a meta-analysis of 90 studies, which includes both randomised and other types of research, finds that while private religious schools increase performance, charter schools on average do not (Jeynes 2012). Unfortunately the methodological quality of the studies included varies significantly, making it difficult to draw any strong conclusions from this exercise. Three more recent studies, using quite rigorous research designs, find that a Catholic education increases years of schooling and college attendance. Again, however, there is no impact on test scores (Altonji, Elder, and Taber 2005b; Cohen-Zada and Elder 2009; Kim 2012). Also, another meta-analysis, including only randomised and more rigorous non-randomised studies, found that charter schools on average outperform public schools marginally in elementary and middle school, while performing no differently from public schools at the high school level (Betts and Tang 2011). Thus, the evidence regarding both private faith schools and charter schools in the US is mixed. It is important to note that expenditure in American fee-paying private schools is about half to two-thirds of public schools, indicating that they have much higher productivity (Peterson 2008). This does not necessarily mean, however, that increasing spending, for example via vouchers, in private schools would automatically generate higher achievement, since there is no simple relationship between resources and achievement (Hanushek 2008).[36]

Nevertheless, it is important to note that little research takes into account (1) maturation effects; (2) the direct impact of pupil mobility; or (3) heterogeneity in performance among charter/private schools. More recent findings from North Carolina suggest that the state's charter schools mature and recover within six years of operation in terms of reading, but not mathematics, achievement (Carruthers 2011). In Texas, Hanushek et al. (2007) also report learning effects while the average effect is negative. Booker et al. (2007), furthermore, find that the overall impact in Texas may actually be positive. This is confirmed in Florida, where, after an initial period, charter schools perform better in reading than public schools and on a par with them in mathematics (Sass 2006). Imberman (2011a), too, finds some positive maturation effects in a one-district study, while the average effect is zero. A similar finding emerges from a study of Utah, in which charter schools perform slightly lower on average, though this negative impact is driven mainly by new charter schools. After a couple of years, charters perform on a par with, and sometimes even better than, regular public schools

---

36   This does not mean that there is always no effect of resources on achievement, but that it has often been found to be quite small (e.g. Holmlund, McNally, and Viarengo 2010; Nicoletti and Rabe 2012).

(Ni and Rorrer 2012). These results suggest that studies not taking into account maturation effects suffer from bias.

Second, it is also important to note that few studies recognise that the direct impact of switching schools may be bad for achievement in the short term, but not necessarily over the long term (e.g. Sacerdote 2012). When using individual-level fixed effects, for example, one is merely analysing the impact of charter schools on switchers, who are more likely to witness a dip in performance. This makes it important to control for pupil mobility when estimating charter school effects (Ni and Rorrer 2012). Furthermore, pupil-level fixed effects only control for time-invariant differences between individuals, but not time-varying differences that may correlate with both the decisions to switch to or from charter schools and achievement. Such quasi-experimental methods thus clearly fall short of proper randomisation.

Third, and unsurprisingly, there are large variations in performance between charter schools. These heterogeneous effects may point to the results of an on-going experimentation process. Charter schools are supposed to experiment in order to find better ways of improving pupil performance, and it is likely that '[t]he finding of considerable heterogeneity … reflects this spirit of innovation and experimentation' (Betts and Tang 2008:28). Of course, it is important to take into account whether charter schools have sufficient autonomy to experiment. Recent research from Milwaukee, for example, suggests that only charter schools with high autonomy are effective (Nisar 2013). Given the theoretical considerations in Chapter 1, this is not surprising. There is also some evidence concerning the policies that make charter schools effective. Dobbie and Fryer (2011c) find that charter schools using five policies that have been suggested as important in qualitative research – frequent teacher feedback, the use of data to guide instruction, increased instructional time, more tutoring, and high expectations of pupils – explain about 50% of school effectiveness across 35 charter schools in New York.

For this reason, it is important that more randomised studies evaluating single schools or chains are carried out so that 'the full promise of the charter school movement – as a generator of new ways of teaching – could begin to be realized' (Betts and Tang 2011:4).[37] While Preston et al. (2012) find some evidence of innovation in charter schools overall, the analysis cannot extend to classroom-level procedures due to a lack of data. Additionally, they do not analyse potential differences between different types of charter schools, such as between those operated by for-profit and non-profit organisations. Private alternatives are not always better than public schools, but allowing for experimentation can potentially crowd in good alternatives and crowd out bad ones over the long term. It is therefore important to note that Hanushek et al. (2007) show that pupils tend to leave underperforming charter schools in Texas, which may suggest that the crowd-in/crowd-out effect is currently underway. Looking at average charter school effects, therefore, may be misleading for estimating long-term impacts on pupil performance.

But are there any differences between for-profit and non-profit charter schools? The evidence from Michigan suggests little difference in terms of achievement, although the methodology utilised is too simple since it does not control sufficiently for selection bias while using school-level data (Hill and Welsch 2009). In Florida, Sass (2006) improves the methodology by analysing pupil value added while controlling for pupil-fixed effects, and finds that for-profit charter schools perform on a par with public schools, while non-profit charter schools perform on a par with or lower than public schools depending on whether they are conversion or new charters and the number of years they have been operating. Meanwhile, there are no significant differences between for-profit and non-profit charter schools. In Philadelphia, however, the evidence is mixed: two studies find no general differences between district, for-profit, and non-profit schools (MacIver and MacIver 2006; Gill et al. 2007), one finds that both for-profit and non-profit schools underperform compared to district ones (Byrnes 2009), and one finds a moderate for-profit school advantage over both non-profit and public schools, although the latter effect is only present in mathematics (Peterson and Chingos 2009). The latter study, however, appears more robust than the other research. This is because it both analyses pupils' achievement gains (rather than merely

---

37　To date, there are only studies on the Knowledge is Power Program (KIPP), Harlem Children's Zone, and SEED school chains. These randomised studies, which are cited above, generally display quite large performance gains (Angrist et al. 2010, 2012; Curto and Fryer 2011; Dobbie and Fryer 2011a).

their levels of achievement) and includes pupil-fixed effects, accounting for all time-invariant unobserved characteristics between pupils. In Arizona, there is non-robust evidence that for-profit schools outperform non-profit schools, but the methodology is very simple. The paper does not take selection bias into account and analyses school-level and cross-sectional data only (King 2007). Overall, however, the US evidence suggests that for-profit schools are at the very least on a par with non-profit schools, and may even be better.

Turning to other industrialised countries, the evidence is also mixed. In Quebec, Canada, switching to a private high school from a public grade school increases mathematics achievement by up to 0.36 SD (Lefebvre, Merrigan, and Verstraete 2011). Another study, using less robust research strategies to deal with selection bias, finds more ambiguous effects of elementary Catholic schools in Ontario, Canada (Davies 2012). In Australia, in turn, there is some evidence of positive private school effects (Le and Miller 2003). Without controlling for selection bias, Hungarian religious schools outperform their government competitors (Dronkers and Robert 2004), but this is not the case in Russia (Amini and Commander 2011). In turn, the evidence from Spain is mixed, and of relatively low methodological quality, with two out of five studies finding positive effects (Salas-Velasco 2006; Albert and García-Serrano 2010; Mancebón-Torrbia et al. 2010; Crespo-Cebada, Pedraja-Chaparro, and González 2011; Perelman and Santin 2011). In Flanders, Belgium, private schools are on a par with public ones when not taking into account selection bias (Cherchye et al. 2010; Verschelde, Hindriks, and Rayp 2011), while there is evidence of positive effects of general school autonomy in both private and government schools (Hindriks et al. 2010). In Japan, meanwhile, there is evidence that vouchers decrease upper-secondary school dropout rates among pupils on vocational tracks (Akabayashi and Araki 2011). In Tel-Aviv, Israel, Lavy (2010), exploiting a law that abolished forced bussing, finds that government school choice is strongly positive for achievement. Since this situation increased choice significantly, albeit only among government schools, it stands in contrast to many US programmes where it is difficult to estimate the baseline degree of choice due to the fact that parents also exercise it by moving house. A couple of studies, in turn, evaluate the impact of choosing and attending a selective/

academic school, finding positive effects in Romania, but no effects in Germany (Pop-Eleches and Urquiola 2011; Dustmann, Puhani, and Schönberg 2012).

Apart from single-country studies, there are also several multi-country analyses of government–independent school differences within countries. Toma (1996), for example, uses a value-added model and finds that private schools outperform public ones in three out of five countries. A more recent study, using propensity score matching techniques and analysing TIMSS scores, finds that private schools outperform government schools in six out of nine countries (Rutkowski and Rutkowski 2010). At the same time, Dronkers and Avram (2010a, 2010b), also using propensity score matching, analyse the effects on PISA reading scores of government-funded and fee-paying private schools separately, and find that the former outperform government schools in ten out of 26 countries while being outperformed by government schools in four countries. Fee-paying private schools, however, only outperform government schools in five out of 25 countries, while decreasing achievement in four countries too. It is important to note, however, that propensity score matching techniques assume that there are no unobserved differences affecting either school choice or achievement (Bryson, Dorsett, and Purdon 2002) – an assumption that is unlikely to hold. Utilising IV and sample selection models as well as propensity score matching, Vandenberghe and Robin (2004) find that private schools outperform government schools in PISA tests in three out of six countries. Like the heterogeneous findings from US research, then, studies evaluating private schools in other industrialised countries suggest that local conditions are important for determining their effect.

What about the developing world? Here studies often indicate positive effects from private, and often privately funded, schools. Muralidharan and Kremer (2007), for example, find a positive association between private school attendance and achievement in India, but they do not attempt to control for selection bias. Using family-fixed effects and IV models, Desai et al. (2009) find a positive private school impact of about 0.25–0.30 SD in India in a sample covering more than 11,000 pupils. However, the instruments used, for example households' social networks, are unlikely to be valid. Goyal (2009) finds positive effects after controlling for observable factors as well as performing a test of the size of selection bias, using Altonji, Elder, and Taber's (2005b) method. Analysing about one million pupils in rural India, using household-fixed effects, French and Kingdon (2010) also find that private schools outperform government schools by up to 0.17 SD. At the same time, Tooley et al. (2011) find no conclusive evidence that private schools outperform government schools in Delhi/Hyderabad, India (and Lagos, Nigeria). In propensity score matching and sample selection models, private schools have generally strong positive effects, but these disappear in the IV models. Furthermore, using propensity score matching, Chudgar and Quin (2012) find no private school impact among about 7,000 pupils in rural India. The authors also focus on explicitly 'low-fee' private schools, again finding null effects vis-à-vis government schools. The different findings in the studies may depend on estimation strategies as well as sample size and grades analysed. In a novel attempt to separate productivity gains from cream-skimming, Tabarrok (2011) finds that the private school advantage in India does not diminish as the private school enrolment share increases in school districts (some of which have private enrolment shares of 70 per cent), which would be the case if cream-skimming were the sole reason why private schools perform better.

The above Indian research, however, is limited by cross-sectional data. Since private schools differ systematically from government schools, and since it is very difficult to convincingly control for this problem, results may suffer due to selection bias. However, a recent study follows the same cohorts of pupils over time, while having access to more detailed background variables as well as previous achievement. This also shows that private schools perform better in some subjects in rural areas, while there are no differences in urban areas despite the raw performance differences that favour private schools. It is conspicuous that the largest private school sectors are in urban areas, where two-thirds to four-fifths of pupils attend private schools, in comparison to the rural private school shares of 25%. At the same time, private school costs are less than one-third of the cost in government schools, displaying that private schools appear to be more productive (Singh 2012). In India, overall, there appears to be a private school advantage in terms of school productivity, but this does not necessarily mean that there is an overall private school advantage in terms of achievement.

At the same time, research from Pakistan suggests that fee-paying private schools outperform government schools by up to a remarkable 1.0 SD (Aslam 2009; Andrabi et al. 2010). Andrabi et al. (2011) also show the importance of methodology. Taking into account **measurement error** in test scores and unobserved differences between pupils, the authors find that Pakistani private schools produce 0.25 SD better scores than government schools each year.[38] A very strong effect size is also found in Kenya (Bold et al. 2011). Although the estimates are smaller, a recent PhD dissertation also displays that private schools outperform government schools in Nepal (Thapa 2011), which also holds true in Venezuela, Sierra Leone, and the Democratic Republic of Congo where research suggests positive faith school effects (Allcott and Ortega 2009; Backiny-Yetna and Wodon 2009; Wodon and Ying 2009). However, the studies evaluating the latter two countries are based on subjective achievement assessments by parents, making the findings less interesting. In ten Latin American countries, meanwhile, there is no difference in achievement between private and government schools having accounted for peer effects (Somers, McEwan, and Willms 2004), but the study fails to take into account selection bias. In Colombia, however, contracting out government schools to private, non-profit operators generated relatively large achievement improvements (Bonilla 2010).

The only negative private school effects in the developing world that the author of this book was able to find were in Indonesia, where government schools outperform private ones (Newhouse and Beegle 2006). In rural Bangladesh, pupils that had attended primary faith schools performed worse on tests in secondary schools compared to pupils who had attended government primary schools. At the same time, there were no differences in achievement depending on which type of secondary school pupils attended (Asadullah, Chaudhury, and Dar 2009). The evidence from developing countries, therefore, mostly suggests positive choice and private school effects on pupil achievement (although there are exceptions). As in

---

38   However, the fact that the over-identification test is often significant indicates that the instruments for lagged change in performance – lagged levels of performance – might not be valid for this exercise.

India, private schools in Pakistan, for example, are also much cheaper, suggesting that they are more cost-effective.[39]

However, it is important to note that an important reason why the fee-paying private schools appear to be so cheap is often that developing countries' governments have invested in education in the first place. For example, Pakistani for-profit private primary schools have low fixed costs, since most are, initially at least, set up in the owner's home. While teachers' wages comprise about 90 per cent of the operational costs, most teachers are local women with at least a secondary education, who have very often been educated in a government school. This means that the government has been resourcing these schools indirectly.

The reliance on female teachers has been absolutely crucial for the development of affordable private schooling. Indeed, Andrabi, Das, and Khwaja (2013) find that the construction of Pakistani government secondary schools for girls has a very strong causal impact on private primary school construction. The argument is that government secondary schools supply private schools with teachers in the years following. The results display that in villages where the former were constructed, private primary schools are three times more likely to emerge. The authors also show that wages are 27 per cent lower in these villages, and that they have more than twice as many educated women, which supports the idea that there is a supply-side response among private schools to open up and hire young female teachers.

Of course, none of this disproves the advantage that private primary schools seem to have, but merely displays that a reason they can be so cheap and cost effective is because the government supplies them with cheap teachers in the form of secondary school graduates. This would also explain why there has not been a significant excursion into the secondary education sector: this would require teachers educated to a higher level, which the government has yet to supply. As Andrabi, Das, and Khwaja (2013:21) put it, 'The evidence of

---

39 Two studies find positive effects on test scores for pupils in parent-funded private schools in India and Indonesia respectively (James, King, and Suryadi 1996; Kingdon 1996). These studies are noted in Chapter 4.1 in the discussion about whether private funding is associated with higher achievement. The main problem is that they suffer from poor methodology, which renders it impossible to determine whether they have identified true causal effects.

crowd-in and supply-side constraints cautions against over-optimism regarding market educational provision and, in doing so, provides a clearer rationale for the public sector's role … [P]rivate schools do not arise in a vacuum. Previous public investments crowd-in the private sector so that government schools are not only contemporaneous substitutes but also temporal complements with private sector provision (Tilak and Sudarshan [2001] confirm a similar complementary relation in India).' Thus, fee-based private schools in the developing world appear to have relied quite heavily on government investments for their very existence.

Having analysed the evidence from non-randomised studies of choice and private school effects in the developing world, it is also worth noting that the research on the impact of general school autonomy displays positive effects on standardised test scores in El Salvador, Mexico, and Nicaragua, but no effects in Brazil and Honduras (Bruns, Filmer, and Patrinos 2011). A study analysing eight Latin American countries finds no effects of school autonomy on test scores, despite controlling for endogeneity (Gunnarsson et al. 2009). However, the instrument is based on country-level rules regarding autonomy, which are unlikely to be exogenous to achievement. Finally, a couple of studies analyse the impact of choosing and attending a selective school, with positive effects on test scores in China, Mexico City, and Trinidad and Tobago. At the same time, the likelihood of taking the college entrance examination in China decreased, and the probability of dropping out of high school in Mexico City increased, as a result of selective school attendance (Jackson 2010; Park et al. 2010; de Janvry, Dustan, and Sadoulet 2012). In Kenya, meanwhile, there is no impact at all of attending the most selective schools (Lucas and Mbiti 2012).

In general, it is important to note that much research from the developing world is of limited usefulness because of methodology. For example, in some developing countries, such as Indonesia, more low-performing pupils tend to attend private schools (Newhouse and Beegle 2006). If this is not controlled for sufficiently, estimates might be biased in favour of government schools. On the other hand, in Pakistan and India, private schools enrol pupils from higher socio-economic backgrounds on average (Andrabi et al. 2011; Chudgar and Quin 2012), making it likely that the private school effect is overestimated unless all variables are controlled for.

2.3.3 *Non-randomised studies of competition effects*

Turning to competition effects, Belfield and Levin (2002) review the evidence from US studies carried out between 1972 and 2001. The studies mostly evaluate private school competition and different forms of district choice. The authors find that 33% of the estimations in relation to academic outcomes, 42% of those in relation to attainment, and 66% in relation to efficiency find positive effects. A tiny minority find negative effects. Unfortunately, the methodological quality varies strongly between studies reviewed.

One of the most highlighted papers focuses on Tiebout competition, which, as noted above, means that parents move house to get their children into the public school of their choice. This kind of choice has of course long been a feature of the education landscape, and as such can pick up long-term system-level effects in a way that studies of the effects of recent reforms cannot. However, in such a system there are only weak incentives to improve as compared to the potential of choice programmes (provided they are well designed). This makes it unlikely to be a good proxy for the true potential of choice and competition. Nevertheless, Hoxby (2000) finds that greater opportunity for Tiebout choice in the US increases achievement and decreases spending moderately, thus raising overall productivity significantly. However, this study has been criticised by Rothstein (2007) for being sensitive to the construction of instruments, although Hoxby (2007) has provided a rejoinder dealing with this critique. Hanushek and Rivkin (2003) have also displayed positive findings from Texas, but only in larger areas. In addition, they display that Tiebout competition increases teacher quality, thereby uncovering an important mechanism through which competition's effect on achievement might operate. Overall, therefore, the evidence from Tiebout competition appears to be positive but still somewhat mixed.

Another way of estimating long-term achievement gains in the US is through the competition effect provided by fee-paying private schools. A couple of relatively recent papers find mixed evidence depending on methodology. Hoxby (2003a) finds that fee-paying private school shares, instrumented with Catholic population shares in 1950, while holding current shares constant, improve achievement in public schools but have no impacts on costs. This is similar to West and Woessmann's (2010) results in an international context, although they also find that private school competition drives down costs. A difference is that the latter's results are also based on government-funded private schools, which are likely to provide stronger competitive incentives than private-funded schools since the former extends choice to more pupils. Greene and Kang (2004) analyse data from New York, using current Catholic population shares as an instrument, and find positive effects of private school competition on mathematics and science Regents exam scores, as well as on high school completion rates.[40] However, there is also an overall negative effect on the share of pupils receiving a Regents diploma. In addition, public school competition is negative in general. In Georgia, Geller, Sjoquist, and Walker (2006) use an instrument set that includes current Catholic population shares, and find no conclusive effects of private school competition. Some estimates are negative, some are positive, and some are insignificant. At the same time, Cohen-Zada (2009) uses Catholic population shares from 1890 as instruments and finds no evidence of any positive effects of private school competition in the US context. He also finds evidence that using current Catholic population shares as instrument biases estimates upward, which makes it important to interpret findings from studies using this instrument with caution.

A recent paper, instead, uses Catholic sex abuse scandals as instruments for Catholic enrolment shares in US dioceses. The idea is that sex scandals will decrease the Catholic school enrolment rate, because of fears of child molestation, and thus also decrease Catholic school competition. The authors find that a higher degree of Catholic school competition raises fourth grade math test scores, but not reading test scores, in regular public schools (Carattini et al. 2012). A concern with this instrument is that pupils opting for traditional public schools after a sex scandal differ systematically from those who remain in or choose a Catholic school. If so, the quality of pupils in public schools may improve as a result. If this is the case, achievement in public schools may rise simply because better pupils remain in these schools. In another study, Misra, Grimes, and Rogers (2012) use an alternative, more refined measure of private school competition that each

---

40   Regents examinations are standardised tests, administered by the New York State Education Department, which function like high school exit examinations.

Mississippi public school faces, finding small positive effects on efficiency. Yet the study does not take into account the endogeneity of competition. In general, therefore, results from research on private school competition in the US are mixed.

Many of the more recent contributions focus on choice programmes that seek to decouple choice from residence and income. These are likely to provide stronger competitive incentives than Tiebout choice or competition from fee-paying private schools. Hoxby (2003b) reports that charter school competition improves public school achievement in Arizona and Michigan, while voucher school competition improves public school achievement in Milwaukee. Chakrabarti (2008) confirms the findings regarding Milwaukee, highlighting that when parochial schools were allowed to participate and financial incentives to compete increased in 1998, competition increased and raised achievement quite significantly. Carnoy and Adamson et al. (2007), on the other hand, show more mixed evidence in the same city, depending on the methods utilised. They do, however, find positive gains from the policy change in 1998. At the same time, a new study indicates that only charter schools sponsored by non-district (private) authorisers have positive competition effects on public schools in Milwaukee (Nisar 2012). Positive effects of charter/voucher school competition on public school achievement are also detected in Ohio, New York, Florida, and Texas (Greene and Kang 2004; Sass 2006; Booker et al. 2008; Winters and Greene 2008; Figlio and Hart 2010; Carr 2011; Winters 2011; Gray 2012). In North Carolina, however, the evidence suggests positive, null or negative effects depending on methodology (Holmes, DeSimone, and Rupp 2003; Bifulco and Ladd 2006; Jinnai 2011), while more recent studies of Michigan suggest no effects or negative impacts (Bettinger 2005; Ni 2009), which is also true of California (Zimmer and Buddin 2009; Marlow 2010). In a multi-state study, Zimmer et al. (2009), using pupil-fixed effects models, find no effects of charter school competition on public schools in six states, but a small positive impact in Texas. The authors do not, however, control for endogeneity in charter school competition.

Additionally, a recent one-district study finds some negative effects of charter school competition on public school achievement when using IV models. Nevertheless, the evidence also displays maturation effects of competition, as well as a positive impact on non-cognitive outcomes for public school pupils (Imberman 2011b). It is also worth noting, however, that the instruments in this study – the availability of building space and the number of shopping centres or strip malls – are unlikely to be valid: it might be the case that these are characteristics of poorer neighbourhoods, which in turn are likely to have lower test scores. If so, the instruments are affecting achievement through mechanisms other than charter school competition only. In a review of 19 US studies, some of which are noted above, Forster (2011) displays that 18 of these found at least some positive competition effects on public schools. Again, while a majority of studies find small-to-moderate positive effects, the impact varies across states and districts, suggesting that local conditions and complementary reforms are important for the outcome of competition. It is also important to note that while many studies attempt to control for endogeneity bias, it is difficult to do so in practice and the studies vary in terms of methodological quality.

Turning to other countries, in Tel-Aviv, Israel, government school competition appears to be one explanation for the relatively large positive impact of the choice programme that was implemented in the early 1990s. An important point is that the financial repercussions of losing pupils were palpable in this programme, which ensured that failing schools either worked to improve or suffered the consequences in terms of declining pupil rolls. The methodology is good since it uses both a **difference-in-difference** approach and a regression discontinuity design, exploiting that some districts departed from bussing earlier than others (Lavy 2010). The evidence also suggests positive effects on performance or productivity of different forms of competition in Canada, the Czech Republic, Germany, Italy, Norway, and Poland (Bonesrønning and Naper 2005; Agasisti 2008, 2011; Chan 2009; Card, Dooley, and Payne 2010; Woessmann 2010; Agasisti and Murtini 2011; Bukowska and Siwinska-Gorzelak 2011; Ponzo 2011; Caldas and Bernier 2012; Filer and Münich 2012; Haraldsvik 2012; Høiseth Brugård 2012). In Japan, increased competition appears to affect achievement positively in government schools but negatively in private schools (Akabayashi 2006), and in New Zealand, Ladd and Fiske (2003) find negative effects of government school choice. The latter findings, however, are based on teacher/principal surveys, not objective achievement data, making the results rather dubious. For the developing world, the author of this book was able to unearth only three studies, which display positive competition effects in India and Nepal (Pal 2010; Tabarrok 2011; Thapa 2011).[41] One should note that, as in the case of the US research, the quality of methodologies utilised varies strongly, but that the effects in other countries appear to be positive either way. Nevertheless, there is thus far little research displaying very large gains.

Few studies, however, separate (1) choice from competition, and (2) competition quality from quantity. But there are exceptions. Bayer and McMillan (2010) show that competition is a robust determinant of performance in San Francisco elementary schools when isolating schools' responsiveness to parental demand shifts due to changes in school quality. At the same time, Millimet and Collier (2008) find that Illinois public school districts become more efficient when their neighbours become more efficient. Also, Cremata and Raymond (2012) find that the quality of charter schools is related to how well public schools are performing in Washington, DC. Competition from above-average quality charter schools produces gains, while the number of competitors has a very small negative effect. In general, clearly, more refined measures of the competition faced by different schools are important for estimating the competition premium adequately (Misra, Grimes, and Rogers 2012). Both the quality and nature of competition matter for outcomes, which most studies fail to recognise. Instead, they often use coarse measures that are unlikely to capture the actual intensity of competition faced by different schools. Future research should thus clearly be more attentive to how competition is measured.

The question, furthermore, is whether research focusing on local reforms can tell us much about the true potential of school competition for raising education quality. For example, almost all charter and voucher programmes in the US target a small group of pupils, and it is unlikely that competition for these pupils has any bearing on schools in general. Indeed, Zimmer and Buddin (2009) display that Californian public school principals feel little competitive pressure from charter schools. Since less than 2 per cent of the state's pupils attend such schools, this should not be surprising. Due to low enrolment shares, charter schools 'may [in fact] act as a release valve rather than [as] a competitive pressure' (Zimmer and Buddin 2010:333). As Hoxby (2000:1210)

---

41   This only holds true when including both government and private schools in the analysis. Yet this is preferable since it is otherwise difficult to disentangle effects from sorting and competition (Hsieh and Urquiola 2006).

argues, 'Until *many* students experience an increased degree of choice, reforms are unlikely to affect public schools much.' Thus, as Rouse and Barrow (2009:38) rightly conclude, 'Unfortunately, results from … small-scale programs cannot be used to test Friedman's hypotheses.' Second, as Merrifield (2008) contends, all local programmes put heavy restrictions on schools, parental choice and competition, making it unlikely that significant changes will occur. Indeed, very few programmes fulfil even the three most essential aspects of a school choice model in Hoxby's (2006) definition, as noted in Chapter 1. With too many restrictions, schools cannot deviate much from the status quo. One should not be surprised, therefore, that the above research mostly displays relatively modest benefits thus far.

Overall, the evidence from small-scale programmes and results from countries other than the ones analysed in Chapter 2.2, summarised in Table 6 of the Appendix, are mixed. It is also important to note that much research suffers from methodological flaws, which can bias the effects either way. Regarding choice and school effects, however, randomised studies clearly display that vouchers and charter schools can benefit underprivileged pupils especially. The non-randomised evidence on choice and independent school effects is also mixed, although many studies analysing data from developing countries imply that independent schools positively impact achievement and productivity. In general, the heterogeneous findings strongly suggest that local conditions impact the effects of choice. Furthermore, it is also important to note that most studies take into account neither learning effects among new autonomous alternatives, nor heterogeneity in private/charter school performance. Naturally, only the schools with sufficient autonomy to experiment could potentially generate gains. One would also not expect all autonomous alternatives to outperform government schools, but that the better ones will crowd out the bad ones over the long term. Regarding competition, the research is mixed, although a significant number of studies find positive competition effects (albeit mostly small to moderate in size). Yet most studies fail to separate choice from competition effects, and consider the quality of competition, thus most often employing coarse measures of competition.[42] Furthermore, most available research focuses on small-scale competition in school

---

42 It should be noted that reviews of the literature rarely take proper account of the above nuances when discussing the overall conclusions that should be drawn from the research. An example of this is Rouse and Barrow's (2009) paper, which focuses on the impact of vouchers in the US context, providing a short discussion also of the evidence of other types of choice.

systems with heavy regulatory burdens, making it doubtful whether these studies can be used to evaluate the possibilities for large-scale school choice to improve quality. Finally, it is important to note that extremely few studies find that competition is bad for pupils, which has important policy implications. It is more likely that more free choice than currently exists would generate more positive gains, *not* more negative effects. In contrast to what many choice opponents argue, therefore, there appears to be little reason to believe that more choice would hurt school productivity.

2.4 Conclusion

The findings of Chapter 2 may be summarised as follows. First, cross-national studies find quite strong independent school competition effects on educational achievement and productivity. This is very important since it displays the long-term, general-equilibrium effects of private school choice, which should be of interest to policymakers in England.

Furthermore, large-scale national choice programmes in Sweden, Chile, the Netherlands, and Denmark have had mixed impacts, depending on the methodology utilised. While there is evidence of at least some positive choice/independent school effects in Sweden and Chile, the effects of competition are more ambiguous in the latter country. The research from Sweden, on the other hand, does display both short-term and long-term achievement and attainment gains from competition. In the Netherlands, however, there is mixed evidence both in terms of choice/school and competition effects. In Denmark, in turn, there is very little evidence of any positive effects at all.

In general, even when positive choice/school and competition effects have been found in the above countries, the effect size has been small to moderate. But this is not surprising given the problematic features of the choice programmes in all four countries, which are rarely discussed by school choice proponents and critics alike. Without improved accountability to credible measures of achievement, high-quality information provision for parents, differentiated funding, unrestricted entry to and exit from the education market, and equal terms of competition for private and public schools, it is unlikely that the right competitive incentives will increase significantly.

Third, evidence from other countries, and in particular from small-scale, local programmes, indicates that choice can be especially important for disadvantaged pupils. Heterogeneous effects among charter schools may simply display market experimentation processes, which over the long term should weed out failing schools. Naturally, also, only the schools with sufficient autonomy to experiment have even a chance to improve performance. The evidence further suggests that it is important to take into account maturation effects, because new independent schools are unlikely to function efficiently in the beginning.

While there is some evidence from developing countries that private schools have positive effects, the evidence in the general research is mixed in terms of whether school choice raises performance, with significant differences in methodological quality between different studies. The impact of competition is also mixed, although a sizeable number of studies find some positive effects. Most research, however, fails to take into account the differences between choice and competition, as well as in the quality of competition. Furthermore, since schools, parental choice, and competition are greatly constrained in most locations under scrutiny, it is questionable whether these studies can serve as guides for future large-scale reforms. Nevertheless, it is worth noting that very few methodologically persuasive studies find negative effects, which is important.

One should be careful in drawing too strong conclusions regarding whether some types of choice programme have been more successful than others. Focusing on the randomised or very good quasi-experimental research, there is, for example, little evidence that US private school effects in voucher schemes or tax-credit programmes (e.g. Peterson and Howell 2004; Figlio 2011) are consistently stronger than charter school effects (e.g. Hoxby and Rockoff 2005; Hoxby, Murarka, and Kang 2009). Nevertheless, as noted, none of the programmes can tell us much about how large-scale programmes, with stronger competitive incentives, are likely to function.

A general lesson from this chapter is that it is evident that the design of choice programmes matters quite a lot for outcomes. It is important, therefore, that policymakers in England considering further market reforms to the British education system pay careful attention to, and learn from, the international research if they are to reap the potential benefits of these reforms.

3 SCHOOL CHOICE AND EDUCATION QUALITY: ASSESSING THE ENGLISH EVIDENCE

H AVING ANALYSED THE GLOBAL literature on the effects of school choice on education quality, this chapter delves deeper into the English research carried out on this topic. Motivated by fears of falling education standards in the 1980s, successive governments have attempted to introduce market incentives into the system with a view to raising performance. The reforms began with the Education Reform Act of 1988. This abolished the automatic assignment of children to schools on the basis of residency and gave parents the right to choose schools. It also linked school funding more closely to the number of pupils enrolled, theoretically increasing incentives for schools to attract additional pupils and expand. At the same time, certain schools were allowed to opt out of local authority control and instead become directly financed by the government, while being given more autonomy.

Despite a general focus on decentralisation, the 1988 Act also introduced a National Curriculum, which significantly reduced school autonomy. Several national tests in primary school were subsequently introduced, the results of which are published in newspapers and on the web. This also applies to GCSE and A-level performance (Hansen and Vignoles 2005).

3.1 Choice and school effects in England

Most of the research has focused on whether competition increases achievement. There are, however, a few studies which analyse choice and school effects. One of the first of these focused on grant-maintained secondary schools, which were given more autonomy compared to other schools. Analysing changes in exam performance between 1991 and 1996 in 300 non-selective schools across six local authorities, Levačić and Hardman (1999) find that grant-maintained schools did not improve GCSE exam performance after controlling for decreasing shares of socially disadvantaged pupils. The authors suggest that this finding may be attributable to the fact that all schools have increased their focus on exam performance since 1991 due to government pressure, and that grant-maintained schools simply did not figure out how to improve achievement more than other schools did. It should be noted, however, that this study relies on a small sample of schools and a methodology that does not take into account selection bias.

Bradley, Johnes, and Millington (2001) analyse efficiency data between 1993 and 1998 from a larger number of schools, and find positive effects of voluntary-aided and grant-maintained schools on efficiency. Again, however, the authors do not control for selection bias. It is also important to note that the output in the efficiency measures is composed of both attendance rates and exam results, and input is measured as pupils' socio-economic background and staff qualifications. These measures are questionable, as the inputs do not only measure costs while attendance rates are not an output measure. Furthermore, neither of these papers takes into account maturation effects of autonomous schools, which might be expected given the US evidence on charter schools.

More recent contributions on the impact of grant-maintained schools improve the methodology significantly. Using a regression discontinuity research design, exploiting the fact that schools had to hold a vote in order to convert to grant-maintained status, Clark (2009) compares schools in which the vote was won with schools in which it was lost. This decreases selection bias, which is a problem if better/worse schools opted to hold an election. The findings indicate that grant-maintained schools increased the fraction of pupils passing five or more GCSE exams by about 0.25 SD after two years of operation. This positive effect remains for at least eight years after the vote took place – while also being robust to analysing average GCSE scores instead of pass rates – and the author estimates that changing pupil composition is unlikely to account for more than half of the medium-term gains and even less for the short-term gains. However, evidence also suggests that grant-maintained schools had about 10–12 per cent more funding than other schools, suggesting that not all of the above can be interpreted as efficiency gains.

A further problem is that Clark focuses not on the schools where the vote was narrowly won and lost, but rather on all schools that held a vote. This undermines the validity of his methodology. Indeed, the point about regression discontinuity design is to remove unobservable differences between schools by comparisons of schools within a narrow bandwidth of the relevant threshold. Using the whole range of data produces a risk that the treatment group (schools that won the vote) and the control group (schools that lost the vote) differ on important observable and unobservable characteristics that in turn could affect achievement. Kawakita and Sullivan (2011) use Clark's data and show that there are indeed significant differences between schools that won and lost the vote. Within a certain bandwidth, winning schools have higher pass rates and lower shares of pupils on free school meals before the vote compared to schools in which the election was lost. This indicates that schools with landslide election outcomes should not be included in the analysis, and that Clark's methodology may actually overstate the gains from grant-maintained schools.

Furthermore, new evidence suggests that the effects of grant-maintained conversion are insignificant over the long term. Allen (2012a) utilises a similar methodology as Clark, focusing on the impact of grant-maintained conversion on exam scores in 2007 among the schools that later became foundation schools after the Labour government abolished the grant-maintained programme.[1] In contrast to Clark, she finds no impact of grant-maintained conversion, concluding 'that the introduction of grant-maintained status may have led to quite substantial improvements in pupil achievement in the short term, but these have not persisted to today' (Allen 2012a:15). In the light of Kawakita and Sullivan's findings, these results should of course be interpreted with caution as well. It is also important to note that Allen fails to analyse whether there are any differential effects among grant-maintained schools; early converters may perform better than later ones. Another important issue is that the change from grant-maintained to foundation status forced the schools to have more governors appointed by the local authority. Indeed, Gibbons, Machin, and Silva (2008) include foundation schools in the 'non-majority controlled' category because governance is shared more between

---

1   She uses data that are more narrowly distributed around the cut-off point of a 50% vote share (15–85%). This is far from ideal, but necessary given that there were very few schools that were within a very narrow range from the 50% threshold.

different stakeholders, making it more difficult to change school practices considerably. And in Machin and Vernoit's (2011) classification, foundation schools have little overall autonomy. Thus, the change to foundation status may very well have diluted potential long-term gains from grant-maintained conversion.

Analysing the effect of attending faith schools, Gibbons and Silva (2011b) first find small gains: attending a faith school between ages 7 and 11 increases achievement by up to 2.7 percentile points (0.10 SD) in the test score distribution. This gain, however, is linked to autonomous admissions and governance school structures, not religion. Secular foundation and voluntary-aided schools show similar gains, while faith schools under closer control of local authorities show no gains. However, pupils who attend autonomous primary schools, but afterwards proceed to non-autonomous secondary schools do not perform better at age 11 compared to pupils who attend non-autonomous primary schools, but later go on to autonomous secondary schools. This indicates that the autonomous schools' performance advantage in primary school is probably due to unobservable differences between pupils attending the more autonomous schools at *any* point in their educational career and those who do not, rather than that the schools themselves actually hold higher quality. Nevertheless, it is problematic to bunch together foundation and voluntary-aided schools, since the former are not majority controlled and may very well be less able to innovate and change practices in order to produce higher achievement (Gibbons, Machin, and Silva 2008).

The question, however, is whether any of the above studies analyse schools with sufficient autonomy to alter their behaviour significantly. The most significant reform in this respect was the 1997 English academies programme, which was 'far more radical [than the grant-maintained programme]' (Allen 2012a:25). Indeed, Machin and Vernoit (2011), obviating selection bias by comparing academies with schools that became academies after the period under study ended (2008/09), find that academy conversion increases pupil performance. However, improvements are only significant among early converters, defined as those schools that converted between 2002/03 and 2006/07. The results indicate that these academies increased the proportion of pupils achieving five or more GCSEs with at least a C grade by 0.18 SD. This reflects an improvement of 16 per cent compared to the average pre-conversion baseline for these schools.

Furthermore, the authors show that academies with the largest increase in autonomy after conversion generate the greatest performance increase due to such conversion. These results suggest that significant autonomy can produce higher achievement and that it takes a couple of years before this effect kicks in.

Finally, one study that analyses fee-paying independent schools in different countries, using propensity score matching, finds that such schools do not outperform state schools in England in terms of PISA reading results (Dronkers and Avram 2010b). It should also be noted that per-pupil spending in independent schools is on average much higher than in state schools (Sibieta, Chowdry, and Muriel 2008), which indicates that the former are actually less efficient than the latter. The value added of fee-paying schools in terms of achievement might therefore actually be quite low (though it should be noted that this has only been analysed in terms of PISA reading achievement, and has yet to be replicated on other performance measures).

Overall, therefore, the evidence on choice and school effects in England is mixed. While the research on grant-maintained and faith schools is inconclusive, academies in England, the most autonomous alternatives, at least appear to have improved exam achievement. A perhaps more surprising finding is that fee-paying independent schools are comparatively less efficient than state schools in terms of increasing PISA results. Again, however, before these results have been confirmed on other metrics, one should also interpret them with caution.[2]

3.2 Competition effects in England

Turning to competition effects, the evidence depends strongly on the methodology utilised. Studies analysing the quality of competition generally find positive effects. Bradley et al. (2000) show that a 10 percentage point increase in neighbouring schools' GCSE exam performance (measured as the share of pupils achieving five or more GCSEs with at least a grade C) between 1992 and 1997 predicts a 3.3 percentage point rise in schools' exam performance between 1993 and 1998. The authors also

---

2   In addition, there is one study evaluating the impact of attending a grammar school. Clark (2010) analyses data from the East Riding in the 1970s and finds no impact on low-stakes test scores, but quite large effects on the likelihood that pupils take more advanced/academic subjects as well as on university enrolment. However, there was very little choice involved in this system since pupils were generally allocated to the school, grammar or comprehensive, closest to their homes. Consequently, the study provides little evidence on the impact of choice *per se*.

find that a 10 percentage point higher baseline exam performance predicts an increase in school size of about 14 pupils, which, although a rather small effect, they interpret as evidence that good schools crowd out bad ones. In another paper, Bradley, Johnes, and Millington (2001), analysing all secondary schools in England, show that the number of schools in the same area in 1993 predicts small increases in secondary school efficiency between 1993 and 1998. Yet the predictor measuring competition is the initial number of competitors rather than changes over the period, and there is no attempt to deal with potential endogeneity. This makes the results susceptible to bias if unobserved district characteristics spur both achievement and the number of competitors in the area. Furthermore, the problems with the efficiency measure noted in Chapter 3.1 also make this research problematic.[3]

In addition, Bradley and Taylor (2002) find that the effect on exam performance is larger in metropolitan areas: an increase in neighbouring school exam performance by 10 percentage points between 1992 and 1998 predicts a 4.4 percentage point increase in schools' exam performance between 1993 and 1999. This is almost double the effect compared to non-metropolitan areas. Metropolitan areas have a larger degree of school choice, partly because of more developed transport networks, which enable pupils to attend schools in different local authorities. However, in terms of the number of pupils attaining the pass threshold per staff member, they find very similar effects in metropolitan areas as compared to non-metropolitan ones when analysing school efficiency.

It should be noted, however, that the above studies suffer from problematic methodology since it is doubtful whether neighbouring schools' exam performance is exogenous to schools' own performance. In fact, it is endogenous by construction. If grades in surrounding schools affect a school's performance, the same school's performance also affects the surrounding schools. This makes it possible that the findings merely pick up district trends. This is especially problematic since the research design only allows for an investigation of a co-dynamic between quality competition and schools' exam performance, due to the fact that the competition measures are not lagged properly.

In a recent study, Bradley and Taylor (2010) partly address the latter concern by analysing whether changes in neighbouring schools' exam performance, lagged

---

3   When there is no information provided regarding the effect size in terms of SDs, this is because the authors do not supply the necessary descriptive statistics to calculate it.

by one year, affect annual changes in schools' performance. They find that a 10 percentage point increase in neighbouring schools' exam performance predicts a 2 percentage point rise in schools' own exam performance. This impact amounts to about 0.10 SD, which is a small effect. However, the effect increases linearly with a higher number of schools in the district. The largest effect is found in districts with 16 or more schools where it doubles to 3.9 percentage points (0.19 SD), suggesting that competition quantity aids competition quality in raising performance. Similarly, the effect amounts to 4 percentage points (0.19 SD) in districts with the lowest degree of pupil concentration. Competition effects also increase over time, which one would expect as markets evolve. The effect is also strongest among schools with more disadvantaged pupils and ethnic minorities. Finally, the authors also find some evidence of a very small effect of the quantity of competition as measured by the Herfindahl index, which measures market concentrations. It is still, however, questionable whether or not the study merely picks up district trends.

Using a different methodology, Levačić (2004) provides additional evidence pointing in the same direction. Focusing on perceived rather than structural measures of competition, the author shows that having five or more perceived competitors is linked to a 0.3 percentage point annual increase in the share of pupils obtaining five or more GCSEs with at least a C grade between 1991 and 1998. While this supports the case for competition, it is conceivable that headteachers who are motivated by league tables perceive that they are in a more competitive environment, and that this explains the relationship between perceived competition and achievement (Allen 2008). At the same time, structural measures of competition, such as the number of schools and the proportion of grant-maintained schools in the area, are not related to improved performance. Most important, the variables used are rather weak predictors of perceived competition, 'suggesting that other factors, such as the competitive behaviour of the players in the local school markets, which reflects their attitudes and values, are influential' (Levačić 2004:184). Accepting these problems, this might indicate that the actual performance of competitors reflects competitive incentives better than measures of structural competition. This highlights a problem with many studies in that they do not directly measure competitive incentives, but merely presume that such incentives will increase with changes in structural competition.

The problems with structural measures of competition are further reinforced by Burgess et al.'s (2011) study, which shows that parents are greatly constrained in their choice of primary school when estimating *de facto* catchment areas. Only one-third of primary schools within three kilometres of children's homes are accessible to the average child on the basis of historic catchment area data. Choice is more constrained for children from poorer backgrounds. The authors conclude that this 'clearly suggests that using straight line distance to schools as an indicator of whether a child can access that school is extremely problematic' (Burgess et al. 2011:543), providing further evidence that structural measures of competition may not be very useful in the current English context.

It might not be surprising, therefore, that findings from research focused on the quality of competition contrast significantly with findings from research focusing on competition quantity. Burgess and Slater (2006) use boundary changes in Berkshire in 1998, which reduced the number of surrounding schools within the boundary for some schools in the local authority, to estimate the effects of structural competition on achievement. Using schools unaffected by the boundary changes as a control group, the authors find that competition is insignificantly positive for achievement overall. However, the effect on foundation and voluntary-aided schools is significant and very large. The estimates suggest that bringing a single additional school within reach of parents could raise achievement in these schools by 0.56 to 0.82 SD. Although these results are based on only a small number of schools in a single local authority, these findings suggest that more autonomous schools, which are able to react to competitive incentives, benefit more from competition (although the caveats regarding foundation schools noted above still apply). The authors also find overall positive effects in a study of Avon local authority when not using achievement data before the boundary change as a control, but no effects in two other areas. As noted above, however, it is far from clear whether a decrease in the number of schools in the local authority actually captures a decrease in competition. Also, the post-treatment data are from two to four years after the boundary change, and it may take longer for competition to kick in (especially for non-autonomous schools that cannot change their practices as easily or rapidly). This is clear from the study analysing academies discussed below.

In a different approach, Gibbons and Silva (2008) use data covering about 1.2 million pupils and analyse whether school density predicts value-added achievement between primary and secondary school. The authors show that children educated in areas with the most secondary school density gain about 2–3 percentiles in the national test score distribution (about 0.10 SD) compared to pupils educated in areas with the least school density. There is no effect of independent school density, which, however, is not surprising since independent schools generally do not compete on equal terms with state schools due to the high fees charged by the former. The authors interpret the findings as evidence that competition or cooperation between state schools improves achievement. Using IV models with differences in travel costs from home to schools as instrument, the effects are somewhat larger while the estimate becomes insignificant. Nevertheless, the authors argue that the results '[lend] further credence to the idea that a relative increase in [school] density on transition between Primary and Secondary school is linked to small but significant improvement in pupil [achievement]' (Gibbons and Silva 2008:644). While the study cannot separate urban density effects from cooperation and competition effects, it finds a link between a commonly used gauge of structural competition and educational achievement. It is also important to note, however, that travel costs from home to school might not be a valid instrument if families move to school-dense areas to have a larger choice set of different schools nearby.

In another study published the same year, however, the authors come to different conclusions. Separating choice (measured as the number of schools available to pupils) and competition (measured as the number of schools available to pupils at any given school), Gibbons, Machin, and Silva (2008) analyse primary school value-added data, using IV models to correct for endogeneity in competition. They use an instrument based on the distance from pupils' homes to the local authority boundary, a similar approach to the one used by Noailly, Vujić, and Aouragh (2012) in the Netherlands. Using a sample of 200,000 pupils, the authors show that the overall effects of choice and competition are insignificant. The competition impact, however, is heterogeneous depending on school type. The competition effect on non-majority controlled schools is negative: the addition of one more school decreases achievement by 0.10 SD. This makes sense. Unlike majority controlled schools, where one charitable foundation has majority representation on the Governing Body, non-majority controlled schools share governance between different stakeholders, including local authority representatives and teaching staff. This makes it more difficult to implement changes that strongly target education quality, simply because different stakeholders have different goals. In addition, in contrast to majority controlled schools where admissions are handled by the school directly, in most of the non-majority controlled schools (state schools), admissions are handled centrally by local authorities, which may make them disconnected from the process of attracting funding and pupils. In support of the idea that these issues matter, as well as Burgess and Slater's (2006) findings, the effect of competition on majority controlled (voluntary-aided) schools – which enrol about 20% of all primary school pupils and have more autonomy to act upon competitive incentives – is positive: one extra school available to a voluntary-aided school's pupils increases achievement by 0.20 SD. The authors conclude that 'these findings support the existence of a beneficial effect of competition on pupil achievement in a setting in which schools combine more responsive governance … with greater autonomy in admission procedures' (Gibbons, Machin, and Silva 2008:942). This, again, suggests that it is important to give schools autonomy so they can act upon competitive incentives.

There is, however, a problem with the above study, in that the measures of choice and competition are constructed from pupils' revealed school preferences. The idea is to find out how many schools are realistically available to pupils and how many schools are realistically competing with each other. But parents from different backgrounds face vastly different obstacles in their choices; parents from less privileged backgrounds make fewer ambitious choices and their children are less likely to get into good schools than more advantaged pupils (Burgess et al. 2009; Burgess and Briggs 2010; Burgess et al. 2011). In other words, treating pupils as one homogeneous group risks producing bias in the choice and competition measures. Another problem is that the instrument may be endogenous, as discussed in Chapter 2.2.3 in regard to the Netherlands. This is even more problematic in this case since proximity most often serves as a tie-break device in English school admissions – which may induce parents to move to school-dense areas where there are decent choice sets of schools.

Other studies use different structural measures of competition and find similarly mixed results. Using a regression discontinuity approach, and the number of grant-maintained schools as a measure of competition, Clark (2009) does not find that competition spurs neighbouring schools' achievement. First, however, Kawakita and

Sullivan's (2011) findings of imbalance in the treatment and control groups, as noted above, indicate that Clark's methodology is likely to be invalid. Second, although the nature of competition changed with the introduction of grant-maintained schools, it is not clear whether they introduced significant competitive pressures. Again, it is crucial to note that the relationship between the proportion of grant-maintained schools in an area and perceived competition among headteachers is not very strong (Levačić 2004). Third, the author does not investigate whether changes in grant-maintained school performance are related to changes in neighbouring school performance, thus failing to analyse whether the quality of grant-maintained school competition matters. Fourth, grant-maintained schools were only conversions of already existing schools, meaning that the quantity of competition did not increase following their introduction to the market. Overall, therefore, it is difficult to draw strong conclusions from this study.

In yet a different methodological approach, Allen and Vignoles (2010) analyse whether the share of pupils in secondary faith schools impacts GCSE exam achievement in neighbouring schools. Using a sample of over 500,000 pupils, a value-added approach, and IV models with early-to-mid twentieth century levels of Catholic population shares as instruments for Catholic school competition at the county level, the authors find no evidence that Catholic school competition improves achievement, while some results indicate that they increase pupil sorting. When analysing the effect of overall faith school competition without IV models, results are similar. However, the authors do not analyse the impact of faith school competition on different school types, with different levels of autonomy, which Gibbons, Machin, and Silva's (2008) findings suggest might be important.

Finally, in the most recent study, Machin and Vernoit (2011) analyse academies' effect on neighbouring schools. While academy conversions in the area decreased the quality of the pupil intake in neighbouring schools, suggesting cream-skimming effects, this negative effect is entirely offset by the positive impact of competition from early converters: being a neighbouring school to an early converter increases achievement by 0.05 SD. (This effect is also larger, amounting to about 0.10 SD, when focusing on the first three cohorts of converters rather than the first five.) Again, it is also of utmost importance to take into account that it takes time before competition starts working. The positive effect is only detectable among neighbours to early converters; in fact, neighbouring schools to later converters have 0.09 SD lower achievement than the comparison schools. Finally, there is a strong relationship between exam improvements in academies and neighbouring schools, suggesting that the quality of competition also matters. This study, therefore, shows that careful consideration is crucial when estimating the effects of school competition. Nevertheless, given the concerns about grade inflation discussed below and given that the achievement of five or more GCSEs at A*–C is used as the measure of output, it is important to note that the authors do not take sufficient precautions regarding the possibility that academies and schools competing with them began enrolling pupils in easier subjects rather than seeking to increase actual quality. However, the effect is robust to excluding pupils taking 'GCSE equivalents' (vocational subjects deemed equivalent in league tables), which are a key source of such bias.

Overall, therefore, the evidence of school choice in England, which is summarised in Table 7 of the Appendix, is mixed. The most autonomous schools, however, have improved achievement when taking into account maturation effects. Less reliable research indicates that the quality of competition has been linked to secondary school exam scores. The impact of other forms of competition is more mixed. Most studies, however, find that competition in various forms is especially positive for schools that have sufficient autonomy to react to competitive incentives. Furthermore, it should be noted that there is virtually no evidence of negative effects, which is important in its own right.

3.3 What about grade inflation?

Having discussed the evidence of school choice effects in England, it is important to note that none of the studies discuss the problem of grade inflation. The cohort-referenced grading system for O levels was abolished with the new GCSE system in 1988, which introduced a criterion-referenced grading practice. Before 1988, it was impossible to increase the total grade average as the grade distribution was fixed from year to year – 35% of pupils could achieve C grades and above and only 10% could achieve A grades (House of Commons 2003). Since then, however, there has been a tremendous rise in these figures. Here the focus is on GCSE grades, this being the measure generally analysed in the above studies. As Figure 1 shows, between 1988 and 2012, the percentage of pupils achieving A*/A GCSE grades increased from 8.6% to 22.4%, and the percentage of pupils achieving five or more GCSE A*–C grades increased from 42.5% to 69.4%. Between 2011 and 2012, there was a small dip in the figures, but the overall picture remains the same.

It might be the case that these increases were caused by an overall shift to pupils taking easier subjects – but the figures for English and mathematics reflect the same pattern: the percentage of pupils achieving A*/A GCSE grades in mathematics increased from 9% to 15.4% between 1992 and 2012. The percentage of pupils achieving at least a C grade increased from 45.4% to 58.4%. The figures for English display an increase in the share achieving A*/A grades from 9.6% to 15%, while the share of pupils achieving at least a C grade increased from 55.3% to 63.9% (Smithers 2011; JCQ 2012). This indicates that the increase in overall GCSE grades cannot be due to pupils taking easier subjects only. If it were, one would not have expected mathematics and English grades to have increased as much as they have.

Yet, as Figures 2 and 3 show, international tests comparing 13–15-year-olds do not display such huge gains. Disregarding the results in 2003, which should be interpreted with caution because of sampling bias, between 1995 and 2011, England's TIMSS mathematics scores increased by only 1.8% while science scores did not grow at all.[4] In PISA, scores have not increased either. Between

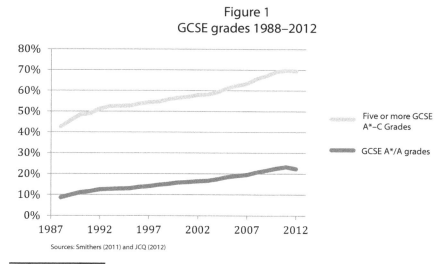

Figure 1
GCSE grades 1988–2012

Sources: Smithers (2011) and JCQ (2012)

---

4   In fourth grade, however, results appear to have increased rather significantly in mathematics since the beginning of 1995. But the results in science have remained very similar too.

Figure 2
TIMSS results for England 1995–2011 (8th grade)

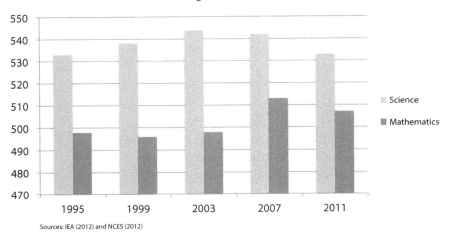

Sources: IEA (2012) and NCES (2012)

Figure 3
PISA results for the UK 2000–09

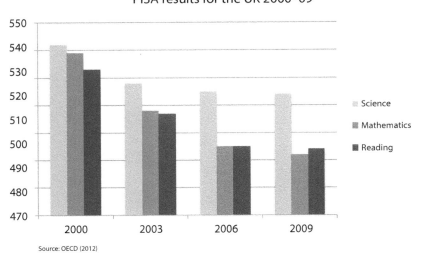

Source: OECD (2012)

2000 and 2009, UK mathematics, science, and reading scores decreased by 3.5%, 7.5%, and 5.9% respectively. Even if we disregard the PISA 2000 and 2003 scores – which are controversial and should be viewed with caution due to sample bias – there were small declines in scores between 2006 and 2009. While it is likely true, therefore, that international tests do not necessarily imply strong declines in knowledge, there is little evidence that there have been gains comparable to those in domestic qualifications.

Similarly, Coe and Tymms (2008:100) use benchmark tests to show that '[GCSE and A-level] candidates of comparable ability are being awarded higher grades each year'. Controlling for ability level based on the benchmark tests, it is clear that pupils of the same ability level are today awarded higher GCSE and A-level grades compared to the mid-1990s and late 1980s. Harris (2008) reports that while pass rates in A levels have skyrocketed, International Baccalaureate grades declined somewhat between 1998 and 2007. In addition, he provides survey evidence indicating that a significant share of British directors do not have confidence in the GCSE/A-level system, and that they believe the qualifications are less demanding than they were in the late 1990s. Additionally, another survey carried out among university admissions tutors also highlights a perception that it is more difficult to select students using only A levels today than previously. Admissions tutors also felt that the quality of new students had declined over the course of their tenure, while those with longer experience also thought the quality of applicants had declined.

Overall, therefore, there is little evidence that the enormous gains in exam achievement over the past decades have been matched by actual gains in knowledge. In other words, there is a strong risk that standard measures used in studies evaluating school choice in the English context suffer from grade inflation. As Coe (2009:365) puts it, '[A]pparent rises [in grades] have been dramatic, though … it seems likely that these substantially overstate any real gains, about which little evidence seems to be available.' This obviously creates serious doubts as to whether the studies discussed above measure actual changes in education quality.

While grade inflation is not likely to have been spurred directly by school choice, since exams are centrally administered, it is still possible that choice has affected inflation indirectly. This is because '[s]everal examination boards compete for schools' business, and a rational choice perspective would suggest that this gives the exam boards an incentive to award higher grades, while the targets facing schools provide them with a clear incentive to use the least demanding syllabuses' (Sullivan, Heath, and Rothon 2011:218). If this is true, increased school competition can provide perverse incentives for exam boards to inflate grades since the stakes for schools are higher when pupils can migrate.

Revelations by *The Daily Telegraph* provided anecdotal evidence for such perverse incentives, disclosing that exam boards provide seminars in which they coach teachers how to perform well in exams. Furthermore, other examiners have boasted how easy their exams are, and it was also disclosed that some teachers clearly engage in rent-seeking behaviour by rationally picking the exam board with the least demanding curricula and grade boundaries (Winnet, Watt, and Newell 2011). The Education Select Committee (2012) also came to the conclusion that competition between boards does create pressures to make exams easier.

Yet there is little rigorous evidence thus far that exam boards actually do compete by making their exams easier (Malacova and Bell 2006). Given that any exam board results that deviate by more than 1 per cent from statistical predictions of grades based on the cohort's and prior cohorts' achievement (across all candidates and exam boards) are heavily scrutinised by the regulator Ofqual, this is not very surprising (CERP 2012). Overall, therefore, it is difficult to see how exam board competition can have increased grade inflation more than marginally.

It is nevertheless important to point out that exam board competition could be problematic in the current context due to the difficulties involved in ensuring accountability in a market where customers receive the same final product (e.g. a GCSE or an A level in English) regardless of what the board assesses; where various curricula offered are viewed as equivalent in the eyes of the government; and where admission to higher education institutions traditionally has been heavily dependent on such grades. The minimum criterion for making exam board competition work is clearly that the government maintains a quality assurance framework that allows boards to differentiate themselves on quality, so that they have to earn the reputation for being the most rigorous on the market. The current framework does not allow for this. If exam boards are to function properly, policymakers must discard the conceptual framework that maintains qualifications should be equivalent, and the apparatus that seeks to guarantee that they are, so that universities and employers have stronger incentives to search for information that distinguishes the best boards from the rest.

While it is unlikely that exam board competition has compounded the problem of grade inflation more than marginally at the most, it might instead be that the weak criterion-referenced grading system, based on statistical predictions from which examiners are allowed to deviate marginally, 'contain[s] an inherent bias that is producing increasing outcomes over time' (Stringer 2011:13). First, since marks in all exams are determined by examiners' judgement, it is impossible to compute the true relative difficulty of any given exam and adjust the grade boundaries accordingly. Further, evidence shows that examiners' judgements are not precise enough to distinguish between scripts within the same range of marks, which is necessary to set grade boundaries. Furthermore, despite the second point, examiners are permitted to deviate from statistical predictions of grade boundaries – based on the cohort's prior achievement and the relationship between a previous cohort's prior achievement and exam performance – within a specific range. In such situations, examiners tend to choose the lower rather than higher possible boundary. All combined, the system is an excellent recipe for grade inflation (Stringer 2011).

Regardless of the causes of grade inflation, it should be noted that studies, such as Gibbons and Silva's (2008) and Bradley and Taylor's (2010), often include **time-fixed effects**. If grade inflation affects all pupils and schools equally, it means that the statistical model cancels out this inflation. Despite the fact that there is little strong evidence that exam board competition is to blame, it is nevertheless unlikely that grade inflation affects all pupils and schools exactly equally. For example, some examiners, such as more inexperienced ones, might simply be more generous in their marking than others. If so, pupils with these examiners will have an advantage and will benefit from grade inflation more than the pupils in the same cohort with less generous examiners. This might be an important issue since, even though the boards are heavily scrutinised if they deviate more than slightly from statistical predictions, '[the] *Code of Practice* allows for considerable variation within and between awarding bodies in terms of the relative emphasis that is placed on statistical and qualitative data' (Stringer 2011:13), and more use of statistical data is shown to provide much more stability in outcomes (Cresswell 2000). Also, although the overall effect might be small, some teachers might engage in more rent-seeking behaviour than others, in accordance with *The Daily*

Telegraph's revelations noted above. Furthermore, since some studies focus on the percentage of pupils obtaining at least five GCSE A*–C grades, many, but not all, are also susceptible to bias since schools simply could have increased the number of pupils taking easier qualifications. This is especially true since vocational grades have been considered equivalent in league tables. It is thus important to interpret all studies on school choice in England with caution, and it is crucial to address the problem of grade inflation for competition to function properly.

3.4 The current English model's shortcomings

The likelihood of grade inflation makes it important to view most studies of English school choice with caution, and further reinforces the interpretation that it has not led to large gains thus far. This is not surprising. First, although the scope for parents to choose schools has widened since the Education Reform Act of 1988, it is still severely constrained. Popular schools are generally over-subscribed, and proximity generally used as the tie-break device. As noted, although most families live within 3 km of about 12 primary schools, only one-third of these are genuinely accessible to the average child. Advantaged pupils benefit more from this system since they tend to live closer to better schools (Burgess et al. 2011), and while 94% of parents gain a place at their preferred school, less advantaged parents make fewer ambitious choices (Burgess et al. 2009). Other findings also show that poor pupils are less likely to get into good secondary schools compared to pupils from wealthier backgrounds. Above all, location is the single most important factor, which is why 'school choice may have an important part to play in narrowing the gap in admission to good schools' (Burgess and Briggs 2010:648).

It is crucial to note that the problem is not that parents do not value good schools in the English context. Indeed, Burgess et al. (2009) show that parents choose schools based on test scores, peer socio-economic composition, and proximity, and that they trade off the latter against their preferences for achievement. Furthermore, these preferences do not differ between rich and poor parents. Similarly, Gibbons and Silva (2011a) find that both school value added and the academic ability of the school intake are related to parental satisfaction with the school. However, value added is a much better predictor of whether parents are satisfied with their children's progress at school and teacher interest compared to the academic ability of the school intake. Research analysing the relationship between school quality and house prices shows that English parents value both initial test scores and value added equally (Gibbons, Machin, and Silva 2013). Regardless, as Allen and Burgess (2010) argue, parents will generally respond to the type of quality information presented, making it important to produce better information, as discussed below. The main problem, therefore, is that proximity remains very important for school assignment, which clearly undermines the effectiveness of school choice in increasing education quality.

The above concern is linked to other flaws in the English system. First, there is no, and has never been, free entry to the market. As Walford (1997:31) argues, 'The 1988 Education Reform Act was central to establishing a quasi-market, but it did little to change the supply side.' In the 1993 Education Act, attempts were made to introduce a new supply-side dynamic by making it possible for new groups to set up grant-maintained schools. Yet due to cumbersome regulations, these attempts failed miserably. Since 2001, some new academies have started, but only twelve of the existing 242 academies in 2008/09 were actually new schools. Furthermore, prior to the Academies Act of 2010, setting up an academy was complicated and needed approval from local authorities to the effect that it was 'seen as the right solution to [their] needs' (Machin and Vernoit 2011:8).

The new free schools programme has also failed to promote new supply effectively. In the first year, 2011, only 24 free schools started, of which five already existed as independent schools (Department for Education 2011). In 2012 an additional 55 free schools started, increasing the total number to a meagre 79 schools (Cox 2012). This is not surprising given the regulatory structures. The review process for new free schools is complex, and is in fact best described as a mixture of procurement, competitive tendering, and allowing independent groups to set up schools. This becomes obvious when looking at the application fact sheet, which provides information on how applications are assessed. The fact sheet lists criteria such as 'the need for more school places in the area', 'the standards of schools in the local area', and 'the level of deprivation in the community the school will serve' (Department for Education 2012b:15). Since the government sets out to provide capital funding for all approved initiatives, all cannot be approved even if these would be perfectly good alternatives. This is far from the liberal establishment rights regime in Sweden, the education system that ostensibly served as the inspiration for the 2010 Academies Act.[5]

Furthermore, current planning restrictions continue to hamper the ability of providers to obtain the appropriate venue and building for schools. For example, there are significant building requirements for schools. There are many ways in which local authorities can effectively render it impossible to set up new schools via planning restrictions. This means that local politicians who are hostile to free schools can ensure that they remain unopened (Fazackerley, Wolf, and Massey 2010). Planning restrictions have most likely ensured that England has had a significantly steeper rise in housing costs and rent compared to most other Western countries (Niemietz 2012). This is likely to deter the supply of new schools too.

The fact that for-profit companies are banned from establishing schools also ensures that the government's sought-after schools revolution is unlikely to materialise. It is conspicuous that it was only when these began entering the Swedish education market that competition increased significantly. For-profit schools have stronger incentives to expand and open new locations in different neighbourhoods. The prospects for producing a strong supply-side dynamic, on which a functioning education market depends, are bleak if profit-making schools continue to be excluded.

So far, therefore, the English school choice model has clearly failed to provide anything close to free entry to the market, and the necessary supply-side dynamic has thus remained conspicuously absent. Parents remain constrained in their choices. As Burgess, Propper, and Wilson (2007:129) argue, '[F]lexibility in the supply of school places is crucial to the success of a policy to extend school choice.' Only a true supply-side revolution will ensure that parents can exercise their now merely legal right to choose schools.

Second, just as it is difficult for new school providers to enter the market, and then to expand, there is no dynamic to force exit. In a competitive setting,

---

5   Surely, at the Swedish upper-secondary school level, 'negative consequences' for the municipality, or neighbouring municipalities, accounted for 75% of all denied new applications in 2009. In 2010, however, the figure was 35%, and in 2011 it was only 23%. At the compulsory education level, on the other hand, it was 7% in 2009 and 2% in 2010 as well as in 2011 (Skolinspektionen 2010, 2011a, 2011b), which indicates that this has not been a problem at the level of education that most of the literature evaluates. Regardless, the Swedish application process for free schools is much smoother and less bureaucratic than the English process.

unpopular schools would be forced to close. Not so in England. As Burgess et al. (2011:532) argue, '[Failing schools] are targeted with a swathe of policies aimed at improving their test results, often with additional financial investment.' This means that competitive incentives are muted. Letting schools go bust is politically difficult, but crucial for an effective education market.

Third, as noted earlier, most schools do not have sufficient autonomy to respond to competitive incentives. For example, apart from among academies and free schools, the national government and teachers unions determine teachers' pay and conditions. In general, headteachers face severe obstacles in rewarding good teachers and firing bad ones. For example, salaries mainly depend on years of tenure rather than effectiveness, as a result of national pay scales, and there is evidence from England suggesting that centralised collective bargaining for teachers is directly harmful for pupils in terms of performance (Propper and Britton 2012). Furthermore, '[w]hile disciplinary procedures exist … for the removal of poorly-performing teachers, they cost so much in terms of time and effort that [headteachers] almost never invoke them' (Muriel and Smith 2011:196). This is especially concerning since both international and English evidence displays the importance of teachers for achievement (e.g. Hanushek and Rivkin 2010; Chetty, Friedman, and Rockoff 2011; Slater, Davies, and Burgess 2011; Jackson 2012), suggesting that incentives to improve teaching can yield better scores. To illustrate just how important teachers can be, Hanushek (2011) calculates that replacing the bottom 5–10 per cent of teachers with merely average ones would raise America's international test scores from below the developed country average to the level of top performers, such as Canada and Finland. Similarly, no schools apart from academies and free schools have the ability to offer alternative qualifications.

Finally, the lack of good quality information for parents has been and remains problematic. Although research suggests that league tables have improved achievement and reduced educational inequality in the English context (Burgess, Wilson, and Worth 2010), they have been far from ideal. The present measures are overly focused on raw test score data, and even this information has been steadily undermined by the likelihood of grade inflation. In 2002, regular value-added measures were added to the raw test score results, and from 2005, a contextual value-added indicator was published also. Contextual value added is supposed to take into account both pupils' prior ability and background characteristics, but there were significant problems with the measure introduced, which led the government eventually to abolish it and revert to only reporting raw scores and regular value added (Stewart 2011).

In fact, both value-added measures utilised, regular and contextual, have thus far proved poor predictors of future school performance (the relevant measure when parents and pupils choose schools), suggesting that such information does not provide a good enough guide for parents seeking to choose a good school for their children (Leckie and Golstein 2009, 2011a, 2011b). In addition, the contextual value-added metric used suffered from a lack of data regarding family composition, income, and parental education, which research shows generated bias in the school rankings (Dearden, Miranda, and Rabe-Hesketh 2011).

In general, furthermore, up until 2012, league tables only reported the average of outcomes among all pupils, thus ignoring that school effectiveness differs between pupils depending on prior ability (Dearden, Micklewright, and Vignoles 2011). Although the evidence suggests that parents making choices based on raw average test scores and contextual value added have been better off than parents choosing schools randomly, the measures are still not very good at predicting which school will improve the achievement of pupils of varying ability and backgrounds the most (Allen and Burgess 2011). Better-designed measures are clearly necessary. These measures also have to be adapted to fit a system that allows for more qualifications autonomy, which, as argued in Chapter 4.9, is important for allowing competition among different types of education.

3.5 Conclusion

Having analysed the evidence on English school choice, this chapter can be summarised as follows. While the overall evidence is mixed, there is evidence of some positive school and competition effects. First, the best evidence – primarily that which takes into account maturation effects – suggests that academies improve achievement. This also indicates that studies not taking maturation effects into account could suffer from bias. Second, there is a clear difference between competition based on quality and structural competition, with the former being consistently linked to higher achievement. This may suggest that quality competition is important, as has also been found in the US context (as noted in Chapter 2.3.3). It is nevertheless important to view the effects of quality competition in the English context with caution due to the fact that the studies' methodologies are far from ideal. On the other hand, there are consistent findings displaying that more autonomous schools raise achievement as a response to competition. This is not surprising since autonomy is key for any school choice programme. Academies competition also seems to raise achievement, but only when this competition has matured. Faith school competition, however, does not seem to improve pupil performance, although this research does not take into account that the impact may differ depending on the level of autonomy in schools.

While there is evidence of some positive choice and competition effects, therefore, the overall conclusion from the available research is still that any gains thus far have been small at best. Given how the English school choice model functions however, this is not surprising. In practice, parental choice in the system remains severely constrained. This arises because of the lack of supply-side flexibility in the schools sector. Due to constraints at the point of entry, and local authority admissions and funding mechanisms that prop up failing schools, there has been nothing even resembling free entry to and exit from the market, meaning that new school start-ups are rare and closures of failing schools even more so. Similarly, good schools do not expand, which depends on the dominant public ownership structure and strong hurdles that have strangled the establishment of new schools. Furthermore, the great majority of schools do not have sufficient autonomy in terms of personnel and qualifications, making it difficult to ensure high-quality teaching and qualification innovation to reach higher performance. Finally, parents still lack high-quality information with which they can base their school choice. It is clear, therefore, that the English school choice model has failed to live up to the criteria noted in Chapter 1.

It is true that the 1988 Education Reform Act and subsequent reforms have introduced some openness in the centralised English education system, but these reforms have stopped short of producing a fundamental transformation. The challenge for policymakers is thus to learn from earlier mistakes, both in England and around the world, and to produce a well-designed school choice system that gives parents more than just a theoretical right to choose schools. The Academies Act of 2010 was a step forward, but was nonetheless insufficient. The next chapter proposes solutions to the problems discussed thus far.

4 CREATING A FUNCTIONING EDUCATION MARKET IN ENGLAND: AN EXPERIMENTAL APPROACH

HAVING REVIEWED THE GLOBAL and English evidence on school choice and education quality, the key lesson is that programme design is important for outcomes. Although England has had at least an embryo of school choice since 1988, there are significant challenges and problems that need to be addressed if the system is to function properly. As argued in Chapter 3, while there has been some opening up of the education system, there has been no fundamental transformation.

Most choice reforms worldwide have been similarly half-hearted, and have lacked the necessary supporting reforms, and there is no programme that lives up to the criteria listed in Chapter 1. This, in turn, means that there is little reason to be surprised that studies analysing certain reforms often find only small-to-moderate gains. Of course, if no programme has been successful in satisfying the necessary criteria, the question is whether or not it is even possible. There are certainly political hurdles to implementing a coherent reform package designed to change the incentive structure in education, but 'possible' and 'politically viable' are different things. As Hoxby (2008) argues, the main reason for the divergence between the idea and implementation of school choice is legislators' tendency to give in to opponents. Questions regarding the political feasibility of the programme proposed are discussed in the conclusion of this book.

Most importantly, it is crucial to understand that the mere introduction of some more choice in the English education system will not improve quality significantly. Rather, a whole new approach to education is necessary. For school choice to function properly as a mechanism for raising quality, systematic reforms designed explicitly with a view to creating an education market are needed. Policymakers, therefore, should be aware of the importance of producing a coherent reform package that, while increasing scope for the exercise of school choice, also satisfies the criteria listed in Chapter 1.

This chapter applies the lessons learned from both the English and global evidence in order to develop a well-functioning model of school choice. It is important to note that most of the global choice reforms analysed in this book never benefited from such lessons. In that there was little experience or evidence base to draw on, reforms to date have naturally been theory led and ideologically driven, rather than being based on a best-practice approach. This being the case, it was inevitable that mistakes would be made along the way. However, there is now a vast body of evidence that can aid our understanding of how choice reforms should be designed. These are the measures that are necessary for the creation of a functioning education market:

1. Introduce a voucher system – but implement it gradually for scientific purposes
2. Make the education quasi-market less quasi
3. Ensure generally equal public funding and treatment
4. Facilitate closure of failing schools
5. Differentiate funding
6. If top-up fees are allowed, discourage cream-skimming by other means
7. Allow policy experiments with selection practices
8. Introduce lotteries as the default tie-break device
9. Increase autonomy for all schools
10. Allow bona fide for-profit schools to set up shop
11. Further stimulate supply
12. Avoid counterproductive anti-trust laws
13. Reform the national exam system – but rely less on it
14. Improve the information and accountability system.

As discussed below, while these measures would generally benefit from being as simple and comprehensive as possible, it might be preferable to settle the details of some of them in an experimental fashion. In general, a gradual process of implementation across different regions is to be preferred for evaluation purposes – as long as these are sufficiently large to produce competitive incentives in schools.

4.1 Introduce a voucher system – but implement it gradually for scientific purposes

First, the English model should be national and universal in nature. Although an important goal of school choice is to raise achievement and attainment levels among disadvantaged pupils, who are unable to access fee-paying independent schools or move houses in order to attend better state schools, successful competition demands universal access. This is because small, targeted programmes are unlikely to create competitive incentives to any significant extent, as indicated by the evidence from the US. When all pupils are able to choose schools more freely, competition among schools will be much stronger. This does not mean that all pupils should be given the same amount or even that all pupils should get any public funding, as noted in Chapter 4.5, but merely that the system must ensure that all pupils have the financial means necessary to attend the school of their choice.

In England, there is currently no voucher system by which parents are able to choose between state and independent providers. Currently, the funding system for existing English state schools amounts to something similar to a *de facto* voucher, since it is largely pupil led, but the system is complicated and non-transparent, which is very different from a voucher scheme (Sibieta, Chowdry, and Muriel 2008; Chowdry, Greaves, and Sibieta 2010). Furthermore, minimum income guarantees for schools still apply, which, as argued in Chapters 3.4 and 4.3, makes it significantly different from a bona fide voucher system.

In comparison to the current English funding system, a national voucher policy is at least theoretically straightforward. Implementation would involve the following steps:

1. determine the voucher value;
2. approve eligible independent schools;
3. issue the vouchers;
4. let parents choose schools;
5. determine the tie-break device in case schools are over-subscribed; and
6. monitor the system.

While some questions arise in regard to these issues, which are discussed in the following sections, a national voucher system would be much simpler and more transparent than the status quo.

Proposing a universal voucher system in the English context may appear radical, but it is not that radical if one looks at previous promises. It would merely realise the aims of the Education Reform Act of 1988, which were that: (1) money should follow pupils; and (2) parents should be given choice. If there is anything that previous school choice reforms have shown, it is that half-hearted measures will generate little more than small-to-moderate gains. The reason for this is that such measures generally fail to increase the right competitive incentives. As long as the system is well designed and monitored, there is little reason to fear increased parental choice. Indeed, despite the problematic features of most reforms, the evidence on school choice and education quality is rarely negative. It is absolutely crucial, however, that a voucher system is not viewed as an isolated measure, but rather as the cornerstone of an entire reform package designed to generate an education market. Without accompanying reforms, the likelihood of a voucher system generating large efficiency gains is slim.

Nevertheless, this book strongly suggests that the government should take this opportunity to do something no other government has done: implement a universal voucher programme gradually across different regions. A key problem with large-scale voucher reforms in most countries is that the implementation has been far from optimal from a research perspective. Since the growth of competition is likely to be endogenous geographically, it has proven very difficult to separate cause and effect in research analysing choice reforms (Hoxby 2008). It would be highly desirable, therefore, if the government rolled out the programme gradually over different regions. It should be borne in mind when deciding what regional level is most appropriate for this type of programme that markets must be large enough, and cover more or less all pupils in those markets, in order to increase competitive incentives significantly. In order to facilitate the evaluation of these programmes, the assignment should be strictly randomised, and the programme should be designed and evaluated by education economists as well as other experts in the field.

4.1.1 *Why not tax credits?*

Some argue that vouchers are not the optimal mechanism for stimulating the right kind of school choice. Proponents of an alternative approach, the education tax credit, claim that the way this reform mimics personal parental financial responsibility for their children's education is important for ensuring wise school choice decisions (e.g. Coulson 2001, 2011a; Schaeffer 2007).

First, it should be noted that there is, in effect, little actual difference between a tax credit and a voucher. In a tax-credit system, people get money back on the amount that they have spent on private education, whereas in a voucher system the government gives a voucher of the same amount to parents who then pay the school they would like their children to attend. The result in both cases is that the government covers the costs of education. If parents are rational, they should not view a tax credit any differently than a voucher since the additional amount that they spend on education under the tax-credit scheme is taken off their tax bill later. Since behavioural economics has established that framing is often important for outcomes (see Greene et al. 2010), however, tax credits may have some additional advantage over vouchers in this respect. Parents could become more cautious when choosing schools, simply by virtue of having to pay up front.

Yet the advantage is small compared to a voucher programme's advantages in terms of increasing competitive incentives in all schools. This is because vouchers apply to both state and independent schools, which forces changes in the incentive structure also in the former. And this is important. For example, in Sweden, where the evidence is the least mixed in terms of outcomes compared with other national voucher programmes, the strongest positive effects on education quality are due to the impact of free school competition on all schools, not that free schools are much better than municipal schools (see Chapter 2.2.1). The same applies to the best cross-national research, which indicates that the main benefit of independent schools arises from their introducing more competition and forcing all schools to improve (see Chapter 2.1).

If we want to increase competition among state schools in England, it is crucial that the funding and admissions mechanisms are changed in those schools as well in order to induce the financial repercussions and rewards associated with changes in enrolment. Today, state schools are nominally dependent on enrolments for their funding, but they are in practice supported also by additional supply-side transfers and minimum income guarantees that decrease their incentives to compete. Significant system-level competition simply demands that state schools do not operate under soft budget constraints. Vouchers give the same funding to all schools and enable pupils other than those who live close to specific state schools to apply and attend the latter. Tax credits focus on private alternatives, but they do much less to change the incentive structure compared to vouchers. As already noted, restrictions such as proximity and additional funding through minimum income guarantees mute competitive incentives in state schools. Instead of restricting school choice to private alternatives, vouchers also allow parents and pupils to choose between different state schools. In order to spur competition significantly, therefore, state and private schools should be given equal means to compete.

On this level playing field, if the private sector has a considerable advantage, it will gain market share from the state sector anyway as pupils opt out from the latter. In an interview with Pearl Rock Kane, a professor in education at Columbia University, Friedman was asked whether only for-profit schools would exist in his vision of schooling. His answer was: 'No, I see competition. Let parents choose. I would expect an open market where there would be for-profit schools, charter schools, parochial schools, and government schools. Which survived would depend on which ones satisfied their customers' (Friedman 2003:58). This book agrees with Friedman and holds that parents should be given the maximum degree of choice between all schools, including state ones, and that the market should be left to decide the outcome.

Second, there is little empirical evidence that financial responsibility, which tax credits might mimic somewhat better than vouchers, is crucial for producing higher quality. Some relatively old research finds positive effects of private spending and unaided private schools in a developing country context, but the methodologies utilised are poor, so one cannot draw causal inferences from them (James, King, and Suryadi 1996; Kingdon 1996).[1] It is thus worth

---

1   James, King, and Suryadi (1996) use instruments based on school ownership structure and district characteristics, which are unlikely to be valid. Kingdon (1996), on the other hand, merely attempts to control for selection bias using a Heckman correction model without an instrument. This is a seriously flawed approach that cannot account for selection bias properly (Currie 2003).

noting that studies evaluating international test score data find little reason to conclude that privately funded independent schools produce better outcomes than independent schools funded by the government, or that a higher share of private funding predicts higher achievement (Ryu and Kang 2009; Hanushek and Woessmann 2011). In Chile, for example, there seem to be no differences between free voucher schools and voucher schools that charge top-up fees (Anand, Mizala, and Repetto 2009).[2] In fact, some cross-national evidence indicates that private secondary schools funded by the government might be better than those that are funded privately, although this research does not take into account selection bias (Dronkers and Robert 2008). Finally, as noted in Chapter 2.1, the cross-national evidence suggests that the system-level effects of independent school competition are not dependent on private funding to those independent schools.

Other research, which uses propensity score matching to deal with selection bias in private schools in each country separately, displays only a small advantage of fee-paying private schools over government schools in some countries and no or even negative effects in other countries. In England, the evidence displays no differences between state schools and fee-paying independent schools. In the developing world, where regulations might be less stifling and one might thus perhaps expect a larger impact, the effects are not consistent either. In Mexico and Thailand, there are negative effects, while there are no effects in Colombia, Indonesia, and Uruguay, but positive effects in Peru and Brazil (Dronkers and Avram 2010b). In England, finally, it should be noted that spending per pupil is higher in fee-paying schools than in state schools (Sibieta, Chowdry, and Muriel 2008), which implies that that the former are less efficient than the latter.

As noted in Chapter 2.3, other evidence from developing countries, such as Pakistan and India, sometimes displays quite strong effects of fee-paying private schools. It seems to be the case, at the very least, that private schools in these countries are more cost effective (although the evidence also suggests this is partly due to their benefiting from previous government investments in education). Yet the randomised

---

2   Mizala and Torche (2012) find no effects of fees among eighth graders in Chile, and only a small effect among fourth graders, and then only for fees of 9–17 dollars per month. Fees of 17–68 dollars per month are insignificant then too. Nevertheless, the authors do not control for selection bias as their primary focus is not fees. This means that the results should be interpreted with caution.

research from India has also found similar effects when analysing pupils who attend such schools with vouchers, suggesting that third-party payments are not necessarily a problem. Overall, this indicates that parental funding at the very least does not seem crucial for academic success.

Another case in point is private tutoring, which might be more akin to a free market in education. Yet it is important to note that the private tutoring industry closely *follows* the public education system, since it is supposed to prepare pupils for national, public examinations (Bray and Lykins 2012). Most importantly, the evidence from private market tutoring systems does not give a very positive picture of private spending on education either. While some research indicates positive effects in Vietnam and Japan (Dang 2007; Ono 2007), it is difficult to draw strong conclusions from it since the instruments are unlikely to be valid (see Ryu and Kang forthcoming). Also, Ono (2007) does not control for family background, school, or community characteristics, which might bias the estimates considerably. Again, methodology is crucial for drawing valid conclusions. In addition, there is evidence of negative effects in Turkey (Gurun and Millimet 2008), while there are generally no or very small effects in Korea, Ireland, and China (Kang 2007; Smyth 2008, 2009; Zhang 2013; Ryu and Kang forthcoming).[3] Overall, therefore, there is no strong evidence that more private spending in any given system, or more private tutoring, produces higher achievement.

This raises an important question. Despite the light regulation, and despite the fact that most agencies are for-profit, parents are apparently prepared to spend often considerable sums of money – total expenditure which rivals public education spending in some countries – even though it has not been proven to help their pupils achieve higher examination results. Why? Again, information asymmetries are endemic as parents have few ways to assess whether the agencies'

---

3   Another study does find some positive effects of private tutoring, rather than spending, in Korea on PISA scores (Choi, Calero, and Escardíbul 2011). Yet the study uses the time spent on private tutoring in other subjects as instruments. This is not a valid strategy due to spill-over effects between subjects and the strong potential for correlation with omitted family-background variables. Other studies using too simple a methodology include Briggs (2001), Mischo and Haag (2002), Ireson and Rushforth (2005), and Cheo and Quah (2005), which show different effects of private tutoring. Again, methodology is key to reliable estimates in the economics of education.

promises actually hold true. Better information for parents, discussed in Chapter 4.14, is clearly very important for ensuring a functioning market in education.

The most important argument in favour of tax credits, then, does not seem to be crucial for the argument in favour of school choice and competition. Little good evidence, as of now at least, suggests that fee-paying private schools consistently are better than government-funded private schools, or that higher shares of private expenditure on education or private tutoring in Asia, Turkey, and Ireland produce higher achievement.

Of course, there are other arguments in favour of tax credits than a somewhat better mimicking of first-party payments. For example, Coulson (2010) finds that whereas US voucher programmes correlate with increased private school regulation, tax-credit programmes do not. The argument is that whereas tax credits do not constitute government money, vouchers do. This, in turn, would increase pressure for regulation in the case of the latter, but not in the case of the former. In addition, proponents argue that since vouchers constitute government money they also compel people to support ideas of schooling to which they are opposed, which increases social tension. Tax credits on the other hand supposedly do not (Coulson 1999).

First, it is questionable whether the regulatory effect does not apply to entirely privately funded schools, and whether social conflict stems only from government involvement in funding different types of education. This arises at a more basic level by reason of the fact that people have different ideas about what type of education children should receive generally. On the regulatory question, in England all privately funded schools have to obtain approval for opening by the state regulator, Ofsted, or by an alternative body licensed to perform the same function. Furthermore, schools are inspected on a regular basis by either the state regulator or these alternative bodies. In order even to be able to register, the school has to conform to regulations stipulated in the Education Act of 2002 regarding, for example, the quality of education provided, the social, cultural, and moral development of pupils, and the suitability of staff (Department for Education 2012a). That private schools are robust to regulatory pressures on the type of education they provide, due to their being privately funded, is simply not true.

And even though there are fewer regulations on privately funded schools compared to publicly funded ones in many countries, it does not follow that this is because of how they are funded. Correlation is not causation. Another reason why the government regulates privately funded schools less than publicly funded schools is probably because the former have been considered a small non-profit alternative to the mainstream. If most pupils were educated in for-profit fee-paying schools, it does not follow that regulations would remain the same as they are today. Extrapolating a situation where about 10% of pupils attend a non-subsidised, non-profit education sector to a situation where 70% attend a non-subsidised for-profit sector is not feasible. It is thus not necessarily the case that private funding would eschew regulatory pressures in education.

Second, in regard to Coulson's (2010) study, it is important to note that there is a strong risk of endogeneity. Politicians may very well opt for vouchers if they want more regulation and tax credits if they want less regulation, especially given the historical legal rulings in the US that tax credits pass constitutional requirements. Indeed, there are US legal differences between vouchers and tax-credit programmes, which may make it easier to pass the latter without a heavy regulatory burden there. But this is less relevant in a European context. It may also very well be the case that lawmakers perceive it to be easier to pass unregulated tax-credit programmes because the American people have yet to grasp the similarities between tax credits and vouchers. This, however, may change in the future as the former gets more attention and is linked more strongly to wider arguments in favour of market reform of education (Huerta and d'Entremont 2007). Coulson's study establishes a correlation between vouchers and a regulation index, but it is not sufficient to establish a causal link running from the former to the latter.

Third, the argument that tax credits are not government money is purely technical and has little practical relevance. The idea is that since in this framework the government does not explicitly fund types of education that some parents may find morally problematic, such as religious schools, there is less threat of social conflict (Coulson 1999). But any tax credit for *any* activity amounts to preferential treatment. Families who do not favour other families' education choices will pay for them anyway, albeit indirectly. Any money that the government grants as a tax credit could have been spent on other public services that would have benefited all taxpayers. This is no different in practice from collecting the money and then granting a voucher for the same amount. The idea that tax credits offer a neutral way to ensure that taxpayers do not have to support every type of school eligible for tax-credit funding is illusory, since they are forced to do so indirectly via distortionary tax incentives. The only neutral treatment of education would be to argue for no special treatment *at all*, and instead advocate radical tax decreases for all families. As Hoxby (2006) argues, any school choice plan that involves any form of public money is an intervention in the marketplace. This includes tax-credit interventions.

Furthermore, there is a case for minimum requirements for any school obtaining government funding, or funding via tax incentives granted by the government, because of the reasons noted in Chapter 1. There are, for example, spill-over effects for wider society, and information asymmetries between parents and schools that are exacerbated by the fact that quality in education is difficult to contract. The government does have a role to play in education, just as Friedman (1962) suggested, although it ought to be significantly more focused than it is today.

For these reasons, therefore, this book prefers a voucher system to tax credits. One could technically envisage two parallel systems, in which vouchers apply to government schools and tax credits to private schools. Yet this would involve higher costs and more bureaucracy than a simple, one-system voucher would require. These costs could only be justified if there is any evidence that tax-credit systems consistently produce higher quality than voucher systems. There is no evidence of this to date.[4]

Yet it is also of utmost important to ensure that the state's involvement in the voucher system does not translate into too detailed, cumbersome regulation regarding how schools should operate and what they should teach. Some rules regarding what type of qualifications should be offered should be in place, but without detailed prescription of how they prepare young people for those qualifications. Chapter 4.9 discusses what is meant by autonomy in more detail.

The question, of course, is whether this vision is politically possible, which is something that is discussed in the book's conclusion, together with a radical proposal for addressing political interference in, and over-regulation of, the education sector.

---

4   Florida's and Ontario's tax-credit systems, for example, do not indicate superior effects compared to voucher programmes for participants or those who are left in state schools (e.g. Chakrabarti 2008; Wolf 2008; Chan 2009; Figlio and Hart 2010; Figlio 2011; Böhlmark and Lindahl 2012a).

By itself, of course, a universal voucher programme would not move England much closer to a functioning education market. Rather, this also depends on the system's design and accompanying reforms. How should the voucher system be designed in practice? And what accompanying reforms are necessary? The rest of the chapter is devoted to these issues.

4.2 Make the education quasi-market less quasi

As noted in Chapter 1, there are important differences between education and other goods and services, which make it difficult to replicate regular, entirely free markets fully. The aim, however, should be to do so as much as possible. First, in contrast to existing universal programmes, an English voucher scheme should replicate the most advantageous aspect of the education tax-credit proposal, engaging parents in both the choice of school and the financial transaction involved in paying that school. This could work in a variety of ways, but an electronic solution would be the easiest and cheapest option. This is to be preferred to parents merely choosing schools, which the government then pays. Although this might seem to be an unimportant detail, engaging parents in actual financial transactions in which they 'pay' schools for their services, although spending public money designated for a specific purpose, would make sure that parents are more aware of their responsibility to ensure a good choice for their children. While the evidence does not support the argument that direct financial responsibility would induce significantly stronger achievement, there is no harm in nudging parents to take even more care when making their choices with a third-party funded voucher.

Another important mechanism to introduce, which mimics regular markets, is to make it mandatory to choose. In practice, this means that the voucher model should not include a default school to which pupils are assigned if their parents do not choose any school. The problem with using the local state school as the default option is that people often stick with the status quo if this is an alternative despite the fact that they would choose something else if they had to (Greene et al. 2010). This may be especially the case among low-educated parents since one might expect them to care less about education than more educated parents. Indeed, research from Milwaukee suggests that low-educated parents and parents who display little interest in their children's education are less likely to apply to a private voucher school in the first place, regardless of their level of income (Chakrabarti 2013). The aim of the voucher system is to create an education market. In regular markets, consumers do not get anything unless they actively buy it. This mechanism should be replicated as far as possible in an education voucher system. Chapter 4.6 considers the case for top-up fees separately, a supplementary mechanism with potential to make the education market more market-like through the introduction of a price mechanism.

4.3 Generally equal public funding and treatment

As stipulated in Chapter 1, it is absolutely crucial that an incentive framework focused on education quality is in place. This entails a level playing field for competition between government and independent institutions: in other words, all schools, whether government or independent, must be treated equally. This principle must be applied to the funding system also, which as Lewis and Patrinos (2011:7) argue, 'must fund equally or close to parity'. In other words, all eligible schools should receive the same public funding per equivalent pupil. This is very important to point out since the research displays that government schools often get additional supply-side transfers on top of the per-pupil funding, which ensures that competitive incentives do not emerge (see Chapters 2 and 3).

In contrast to the relatively simple funding model outlined, the English funding formula is complex and non-transparent (Chowdry, Greaves, and Sibieta 2010). As Allen and Burgess (2010:23) point out, '[Local Authorities] are [able] to subsidise small schools, but this would not be possible with direct funding of schools.' In a functioning voucher system, all public funding should be tied to the value of the voucher. This does not mean that all pupils necessarily should receive vouchers with the same value, but that public funding for schools should solely come from the voucher. As the Chilean case specifically, and most universal voucher schemes generally, have shown, government schools operating within soft budget constraints strongly discourage competitive behaviour. In order to increase efficiency significantly, an English school choice model must therefore ensure that all schools that are approved are eligible for the same level of government funding.

The only exception to this rule is that it might be beneficial to increase the per-pupil funding for popular and high-performing schools. Mechanisms to this effect would enable schools to expand and encourage schools to focus on raising education quality. To incentivise growth among high-quality schools, funding might partly be based on application figures, since over-subscribed schools correspond directly to parental preferences. Some of the additional funding could perhaps be targeted to allow for expansions, or the opening of new schools in other neighbourhoods. It could also be tied to various performance measures, but this would require high-quality information (which is discussed in more detail in Chapter 4.14). A transparent performance-related funding system for schools would strengthen supply-side drivers of quality, thus complementing and speeding up the market process through parental choice. Done right, parents and pupils would have access to a strong, simple quality indicator, which schools would be likely to emphasise in their marketing.

While one could certainly envisage decreasing funding among failing and unpopular schools directly, such a mechanism might be difficult to put into practice because of its consequences for pupils attending those schools. However, it can be countered that if parents were free to choose, the sight of other schools succeeding, and being rewarded accordingly, would be likely to induce pupils and parents to migrate to those schools. It would also induce new schools to start up in competition with failing schools especially. As noted in Chapter 4.4, therefore, a performance-related pay system that to a certain extent rewards good schools would also facilitate the closure of bad ones.

Were all schools funded on the same basis, English vouchers could be used to finance pupils' education at existing fee-paying independent schools as well, which would increase competitive pressures among state schools further. While these schools have the ability to become free schools, there is no reason why they should have to change status in this way in order to be eligible for public funding. Allowing existing independent schools to participate in the English voucher scheme would ensure greater access to them, while at the same time injecting more independent school competition into a state-dominated education system. This would clearly be a significant step forward given the cross-national research displaying the advantages of independent school competition. Whether selection practices in these schools should be allowed, however, is not straightforward and is discussed in Chapter 4.7.

It is important that the voucher is national in the sense that the rules and regulations apply equally regardless of local authority. In Sweden, as discussed in Chapter 2.2.1, a problem has been that municipalities often try to stifle parental choice. This has led to regional inequalities in terms of opportunities for school choice; it is important that all state schools run by local authorities are directly financed in a national system. Such a policy would ensure that the funding of schools is removed from those managing and running publicly operated schools, which otherwise might be favoured in practice.

Private education providers should be expected to raise up-front capital in order to start new schools. What about up-front capital requirements for new state schools? First, it is not necessarily the case that new state schools should be started in the first place. If private school growth is sufficiently large, it would be redundant. Second, if there are very strong reasons for starting new state schools, exceptions could be made. Naturally, if the performance-related funding system is implemented, the increase in funding would also apply to good state schools, and thus enable these to expand and open new sites. The main point is that in almost all cases, the voucher should represent all the public funding schools receive.

4.4 Succeed or go bust: facilitate closure of failing schools

A related issue, and perhaps the most problematic feature of most voucher programmes, is that failing schools, especially schools run or managed by public authorities, rarely close. Although closing down failing schools is politically difficult, it is necessary in order to raise education quality. Indeed, research indicates that significant turnarounds of very bad schools are rare. While pouring money into such schools and combining it with various intervention strategies may improve them a little, it is extremely unlikely to bring about significant improvement (Gross, Booker, and Goldhaber 2009; Stuit 2010). Indeed, research suggests that when bad schools do improve significantly, it is due to radical changes to the school's staff (Dee 2012), which in practice emulate actual school closure.

To a large extent, tying school funding solely to the voucher would solve the problem. Without additional supply-side transfers to prop them up, unpopular schools would simply run out of resources. Thus, as Allen and Burgess (2010:23) argue, 'Minimum income guarantees for schools need to be removed to allow excess capacity to be taken out of the system more quickly.' Provided that new schools start in, and expand into, neighbourhoods currently served by failing schools, the market mechanism would force such schools out of business. Naturally, the voucher system would only facilitate closure of failing schools if there are alternatives to which pupils could migrate. For these reasons, it is crucial that new and existing popular schools are given incentives to start in neighbourhoods with struggling schools. This is discussed in more detail in Chapters 4.5 and 4.10.

A performance-related funding system, which rewards successful schools as described in Chapter 4.3, has the added advantage of making it easier for new and existing schools to target failing ones. As a strategy for growth, this obviously makes sense as it is easier to compete with failing schools than with those that have already proven their capacity to improve quality and thus gain additional resources. In other words, competition and choice would increase where it is most desperately needed, giving parents of pupils in failing schools better alternatives. Indeed, research suggests that while changing schools due to closure is often disruptive in the short run, it is not in the long run. Furthermore, moves to better schools as measured on quantitative performance data often generate performance improvements over the long term (e.g. de la Torre and Gwynne 2009; Brummet 2012; Engberg et al. 2012; Özek, Hansen, and Gonzalez 2012; Sacerdote 2012).

In a functioning market, it is expected that most transfers of pupils from failing to new schools would occur before the former go bust. This is especially true if funding is linked to performance. Some pupils – the children of the least informed parents – would remain until the end given the choice; in such circumstances, special assistance may need to be offered to help parents choose schools. Closures should not under any circumstances be delayed, since the damage to pupils' education would be likely to increase the longer they remained in the declining school. Of course, a functioning market would produce surplus capacity, which would ensure that parents had additional schools to choose from in the case of bankruptcy. In the transition period, however, and in unusual circumstances, there might not be schools with surplus capacity in the area, so it may be necessary to bus pupils to schools further afield. Another option might be to allow and fund enrolment in e-learning courses, as discussed below. In most cases, however, it is likely that remaining pupils would be reallocated to other schools with surplus capacity.

Of course, it is naturally the case that some areas with really bad schools might see a slower growth of competition. As argued in Chapters 4.5 and 4.10, it is crucial that new providers and existing schools are given incentives to compete and to scale up their operations in these areas too. Also, in some places there might be relatively little competition simply because there are very few pupils. It could be the case that these areas are characterised by very bad schools. Thus, where there are currently no viable alternatives to persistently low-performing schools, allowing and funding pupils to enrol in e-learning courses could be a method of ensuring more choice and competition. We know little about how online education impacts pupil performance in primary or secondary school since there are no rigorous studies on this topic available. Yet, as Greene et al. (2010:16) argue, 'Even if online education is not as good as the best classroom instruction, it is almost certainly better than very bad education or none at all. And there are many situations where bad or nothing is the only alternative.'[5] Giving parents and pupils the opportunity to opt out of truly bad schools by the means of virtual education would give them choice even if there are no good schools nearby. This means that the worst schools would have to compete for pupils even if there are no other schools available, and even if they are located in areas where the supply of schools is unlikely to change significantly. The argument in favour of online education is discussed further in Chapter 4.11.

4.5 Differentiated funding

As noted in the review of the Chilean voucher reform, it is important to understand that the real cost of educating pupils depends on their ability and background. A privileged/high-achieving pupil is cheaper to educate than an underprivileged/low-achieving one, since more attention and resources must be spent on the latter. As Sapelli (2003:531) argues, 'If the cost of educating students to a certain level is a negative function of the initial human capital of the child (or family income, or parent education), then we should not have a flat subsidy.' Differentiated vouchers

---

5   There is some research on the impact of using a mix of face-to-face and online instruction, which often finds positive effects (Means et al. 2010). Yet it is difficult to rule out that the studies merely analyse the impact of integrating technology with traditional classroom learning.

are clearly preferable. This would also establish stronger incentives among popular schools to expand, since they would be compensated for the decline in their pupils' ability profiles that one would expect to follow (Allen and Burgess 2010).

One alternative would be to differentiate vouchers based on family income, which would enable less privileged pupils to choose schools to a similar extent as parents from more advantaged backgrounds. In this regard, it is noteworthy that the English system does already give significantly more money to children who receive free school meals or who have special education needs, although in a much less transparent way than a differentiated voucher would do. Additionally, the current funding system responds slowly to changes in the pupil composition of schools, meaning that schools taking on poor or special needs pupils must wait several years before this is reflected in their funding (Sibieta, Chowdry, and Muriel 2008; Chowdry, Greaves, and Sibieta 2010). A more systematic approach, with several levels of differentiation, would be preferable. For example, it would be possible to introduce several brackets based on family income, similar to the current progressive income tax brackets. The pupil premium was a step in the right direction, but was not sufficient.

Another alternative is to differentiate the voucher by pupil ability, which might be preferable since present human capital is a more relevant factor when estimating the real cost of educating a pupil. This is because, in the case of a pupil that is behind, 'it relates more directly to the accelerated learning that is required for that pupil to catch up, and also solves a number of practical problems relating to the collection of pupil social background data' (Allen and Burgess 2010:21). Provided that such a system does not produce perverse incentives for children to underperform in whatever performance assessment that determines the voucher value, it would clearly be beneficial for the voucher to be differentiated based on ability. While the practical details have to be worked out, the goal should be that the voucher reflects the cost of educating a pupil, regardless of ability and background.

It is important to note that it is not necessarily the *absolute* levels of funding that matter most for schools' incentives to compete for all pupils, but rather the *relative* levels. That is, schools must be compensated for taking on poor and low-ability pupils in relation to how much they receive for rich and high-ability pupils. For example, if the voucher amount for the richest and most able pupils were £2,000/year, we would not have to spend as much in absolute terms on the poorest and least able pupils as we would if it were £5,000/year. The main challenge, therefore, is to ensure that different types of pupils are priced correctly in relation to each other.

In theory, since it is difficult to differentiate in a way that corresponds perfectly to pupil differences, schools would be able to seek out 'overvalued' pupils who would be cheaper to teach. Differentiating the voucher partly by ability would minimise this problem. High-ability pupils from low-income backgrounds could technically be overvalued with a voucher differentiated solely on family income. In general, the cost of actively searching for overvalued pupils in a well-differentiated voucher system is very likely to be higher than the benefit. Furthermore, one could use the proposed cohort-referenced tests, discussed in Chapter 4.14, to differentiate the voucher, and simply postpone the classification of pupils until after schools have admitted them. Schools would know that they would be compensated for taking on more disadvantaged and low-performing pupils, but they will not be able to seek out the pupils that for various reasons have been wrongly priced. In practice, therefore, this issue is unlikely to be a problem provided that the voucher is differentiated on several levels based on income or ability, or possibly both.

Furthermore, if some pupils have been incorrectly priced in relation to others, it would be possible to spot and remedy this in hindsight. For example, if privately operated schools primarily set up shop in rich (poor) neighbourhoods, it would signal that the voucher amount would have to be increased for disadvantaged (advantaged) pupils or alternatively decreased for advantaged (disadvantaged) pupils. As Hoxby (2006:31) argues, 'While getting the exact prices right is hard, getting the structure approximately right can be reasonably straightforward and the actors' revealed preferences often give us information to adjust prices in the right direction.'

It is important to discuss whether the voucher *itself* should only be provided to children whose parents cannot pay for them. That is, should state funding of education be means tested? One could envisage a mandate which ensures that parents who can in fact fully pay for their children's education are obliged to do so. Again, different bands could apply whereby parents would have to pay less in accordance with their income. Such a mandate would in that case apply regardless of whether parents choose private or state education. This book does not take a strong stance on this issue, as the issue of private funding is probably not very important for achievement (see Chapter 4.1), though it might well be cheaper for the state, and thus for taxpayers, to require that those who can pay do pay for their children's education. Nevertheless, it is important to note that the strong societal spill-over effects might justify at least some public funding for all pupils.

In general, reviewing the evidence of various types of positive externalities, McMahon (2010) suggests that the research indicates that a bit more than 50 per cent of education should be funded publicly to provide for the spill-over effects. Regardless, it is certainly possible to combine a voucher system with direct parental fees for those who can afford it. Top-up fees, which are discussed in the next section, might be a way to ensure both some public funding for all pupils and that wealthier parents pay more for their education. But top-up fees are not necessary to ensure this. Theoretically, the government could set the price level for different pupil profiles, and then mandate specific contributions towards this price depending on parental background. This shows how malleable the voucher solution could be.

4.6 If top-up fees are allowed, discourage cream-skimming by other means

Should schools be allowed to charge top-up fees? On the one hand, top-up fees would force parents to take some financial responsibility over their children's education. Although the evidence is not very supportive of this position as of yet, this could be beneficial because: (1) schools entirely funded by third-party payments may not be as responsive to parental demands; and (2) parents may have stronger incentives to ensure the best possible choice for their pupils. Furthermore, as Sandström (2002) argues, top-up fees would provide a price mechanism that could generate stronger incentives to increase efficiency and quality, which in the future would allow schools to lower the fees and thus attract more pupils. Such a mechanism could also be important for signalling to education providers what type of education families prefer and giving them incentives to provide such education. The overall result over the long term would then be a better education for all.

On the other hand, the evidence from Chile's voucher system, which is currently the only large-scale school voucher system that allows top-up fees, is not very encouraging. As noted in Chapter 2.2.2, an important implication of allowing top-up fees is that schools have greater incentives to select the richest pupils and compete on this basis rather than by raising quality. While this incentive is always present unless the voucher is differentiated (because the real cost of educating pupils from lower socio-economic backgrounds is greater), top-up fees exacerbate it. Indeed, Chilean voucher schools charging fees tend to take more pupils from advantaged backgrounds. Similarly, privately funded schools in Pakistan and India, which are often for-profit, disproportionately enrol pupils from more advantaged backgrounds compared to government schools (Andrabi et al. 2011; Chudgar and Quin 2012). Of course, private tutoring agencies take only those who can pay for lessons, and these tend to be more advantaged pupils in Europe (Bray 2011). Increasing access to schools for the poor is necessary, but if insufficient attention is paid to the fact that the real cost of educating pupils differs according to profile, the incentives to focus on richer pupils may persist. And, again, the evidence presented in Chapter 4.1 does not lend support to the position that more private funding leads to better achievement. Theoretical evidence also appears to suggest that voucher schools must accept only the voucher as payment, rather than charging top-up fees, for producing a healthy incentive structure that targets efficiency gains instead of producing cream-skimming (Epple and Romano 2012). This idea is supported by empirical research from Milwaukee, which suggests that the lack of top-up fees, in combination with random school selection and the covering of transportation costs, may be important for stemming sorting by income (Chakrabarti 2013).

It is thus unclear whether the introduction of top-up fees would make the English education system move closer towards a functioning education market. However, since the main concern is that schools would be able to compete by cream-skimming, a differentiated voucher based partly on family background may counter the problematic features. If top-up fees are allowed, it should most likely be compensated for by a sufficient increase in the voucher value for pupils from families who cannot afford to pay such fees. This might potentially combine the beneficial effects of fees as noted above, while countering the potential problems that could arise. Naturally, however, it might not be affordable if schools set their tuition levels too high, which they would have every incentive to do if the government takes responsibility for topping up funding for those deemed unable to pay. There might consequently be an argument for some cap over which schools must top up poorer pupils' vouchers themselves, in combination with some form of restriction so that schools cannot accept pupils based on their ability to pay the fees. Again, if implementation of the voucher programme were randomised, as advocated in this book, it would be possible to allow some regions to experiment with various measures of top-up fees in conjunction with the implementation of the voucher system.

4.7 Allow policy experiments with selection practices

Another important issue concerns selection practices. Selection practices may be important for diversity in the education system because they allow schools to specialise and tailor their educational offering to suit different types of pupils. They may also enable a better match between pupil and school/teacher. Selection can ensure a more homogeneous ability level in the school, which may generate higher performance. Furthermore, school choice coupled with academic selection methods might also incentivise primary school pupils to increase their efforts in preparation for admission to secondary school.

However, another theoretical possibility is that selection practices allow schools to cream-skim the best pupils without raising quality. It might also be the case that potential peer effects impact certain pupils in different ways, which has implications for the viability of selection practices. For example, if low-achieving pupils benefit more than high-achieving pupils from being surrounded by high-ability peers, a more integrated system may raise overall achievement. And even if all pupils benefit equally from high-ability peers, a more integrated system could still produce higher education equality. This is because the gap between high-achieving and low-achieving pupils could then widen if each group of pupils is separated into different schools. Thus, in their guide to engaging the private sector in education, Lewis and Patrinos (2011) argue that 'mature' education markets with publicly funded private schools should not allow schools to select their pupils.

It is important to note that whether schools in fact build their reputations by increasing quality may be dependent on their not being allowed to select pupils. Some theoretical evidence suggests that this is indeed the case: given the opportunity, schools will attempt to improve their reputation by selecting better pupils (MacLeod and Urquiola 2012b). Interestingly, the difference in this respect between Sweden, where compulsory schools cannot select pupils, and Chile, where they can, has been upheld as a reason why voucher reform appears to have been positive in the former country but not in the latter (Böhlmark and Lindahl 2012a). However, the difference may very well also be due to the Chilean system's combination of selection practices, top-up fees, and an undifferentiated voucher, as well as information provision which conflates school quality and pupil ability. Theoretically, selection in schools can be a useful mechanism, provided that funding is differentiated by pupil ability and schools cannot charge top-up fees. All pupils would then be equally attractive to enrol as there would be little monetary incentive to simply accept high-ability pupils instead of raising quality (Epple and Romano 2012). However, academic selection practices may have other effects in the school system, with or without increased opportunities for school choice. It is thus important to look at the evidence regarding the impact of academic selection in schools in general.

The international evidence investigating the impact of academic selection practices (sometimes referred to as tracking or streaming) on achievement and long-term outcomes is mixed, with some studies finding positive effects on test scores and grades (e.g. Figlio and Page 2002; Ariga and Brunello 2007; Duflo, Dupas, and Kremer 2011; Haraldsvik 2012; Koerselman 2013);[6] some finding negative effects on test scores (e.g. Hanushek and Woesmann 2006; Pekkarinen, Uusitalo, and Kerr 2009); some finding negative effects on years of schooling as well as earnings on average (e.g. Meghir and Palme 2005; van Elk, van der Steeg, and Webbink 2011);[7] and some finding null effects over the long term on earnings as well as years of schooling (e.g. Malamud and Pop-Eleches 2011; Hall 2012; Zweimüller 2012). Moreover, Jakubowski (2010) shows that Hanushek and Woessmann's (2006) findings suffer from flawed methodology. When taking into account pupils' age and grade, the effect of selection on test scores is insignificant. In addition, only when controlling for test scores among pupils who have not yet spent time in the tracked system is the effect negative in Hanushek and Woessmann's (2006) paper. But this is an invalid approach, since the mere existence of tracking increases incentives among younger pupils to

---

6   Haraldsvik (2012) and Koerselman (2013) analyse the effects of tracking and performance-based school choice respectively in the year before pupils are separated into different tracks, thus focusing on the incentive effects that might occur when selection is used.

7   Meghir and Palme (2005), however, find that tracking increases earnings for pupils from high socio-economic backgrounds, but lowers it for pupils from lower socio-economic backgrounds.

perform better in order to gain access to a better track (Vlachos 2011b; Haraldsvik 2012; Koerselman 2013). In general, therefore, the effects of tracking on overall achievement are far from certain (Betts 2011).

What about inequality? Much of the international and country-level research indicates increased inequality in achievement and long-term labour market outcomes, measured as the impact of family background on the outcome variable, due to tracking (Betts 2011). However, there are methodological uncertainties in most of these studies. Waldinger (2007) and Jakubowski (2010) show that cross-country results on inequality are not robust to using different methodologies and taking into account pupils' age and grade. The latter two are most damaging since age and grade naturally are likely to impact achievement. The negative findings in the cross-country studies thus appear to be due to methodological flaws.

Furthermore, in many of the within-country studies cited above, such as those on Scandinavian countries, 'it is difficult to isolate the effect of tracking ... because most of the educational reforms affected both the amount of education and the timing of selection' (Malamud and Pop-Eleches 2011:1539). It is therefore very interesting that a recent Korean study, exploiting a reform that abolished tracking in favour of neighbourhood schooling while not affecting the amount of education, finds that tracking in different schools decreases inequality in achievement and improves achievement among high-achieving pupils from poor backgrounds compared to a system of district assignment (Lee 2012). Additionally, a review of most studies found randomised evidence that displayed positive gains for all pupils, also emphasising that the differences found in international research may very well be due to the academic–vocational divide (Betts 2011). Overall, therefore, the evidence of selection effects on inequality as well as achievement is mixed and sensitive to the methodology utilised.

In England, initial evidence showed positive effects of selective practices in the form of the Eleven Plus achievement test at age 11 for high-achieving pupils, but no effects on other pupils (Galindo-Rueda and Vignoles 2005). A later study concluded that this finding might be due to endogeneity, since selection practices have positive effects even before pupils enter the level of education in which the practices apply, and that methodological concerns make it difficult to estimate selection effects in the English context (Manning and Pischke

2006). Yet Koerselman (2013) argues that this interpretation is incorrect, since selection practices create stronger incentives to work harder so that pupils can enter the selective track. Indeed, he also finds evidence of such effects in the English and international context. Thus, he argues that Manning and Pischke's study is insufficient to claim that the positive effects of tracking are plagued by selection bias. Another study exploits reforms that affected selection processes at age 11 in Northern Ireland but not in England, finding that increasing the number of pupils attending grammar schools improves educational achievement and decreases inequality in terms of GCSE and A-level performance (Maurin and McNally 2007). Finally, Guyon, Maurin, and McNally (2012) show that increasing access to selective secondary schools in Northern Ireland – tantamount to some form of de-tracking – improved the total number of pass rates. Yet it appears as if this is due to the positive effects of attending selective schools, since quality decreased more in non-selective schools after the reform. Pupils could simply benefit from selective education, which is not the same as arguing that the education system would produce better results without any selection at all. It is thus difficult to draw strong conclusions from the Northern Irish research regarding the usefulness of selection practices in general. Overall, therefore, the English research does not display an unequivocally positive or negative picture of tracking in education.

In general, it is clear that the impact of tracking is still very uncertain. As Betts (2011:375) argues, 'In spite of many decades of research, what we do not know about the effects of tracking on outcomes greatly exceeds what we do know.' Given the uncertainty of the empirical evidence in this area, ideally the government should allow policy experiments that could be tracked and evaluated by academic experts. The best approach would be to carefully design experiments involving all types of schools in order to investigate the system-level effects of selection policies. Of course, these experiments should ideally be combined with the randomised implementation of the voucher programme, which would allow careful research into how selection practices work in a universal voucher context.

Further research is also necessary to analyse how selection practices affect pupils in upper-secondary schools. Here, the situation is less contentious since most industrialised countries have some form of tracking in place at this level of education. Randomised evaluation processes might allow certain areas to use selection practices for Sixth Form colleges as well, with other areas making alternative arrangements.

4.8 Introduce lotteries as the default tie-break device

Having argued that academic selection should be allowed only in experimental form for now, what should serve as a general tie-break device in primary and lower-secondary education? As argued in Chapter 3, using proximity dilutes choice from reality to theory, and gives more advantaged pupils readier access to better schools. Clearly, therefore, a school choice policy designed to improve quality rather than to reproduce segregation should abolish this practice. Long term, a dynamic market could solve these problems if better schools expand to meet increased demand. In the short term, however, it is important that parents are given equal opportunities to enter over-subscribed schools. This means that the role proximity plays as an admissions tool should be minimised as far as possible.

What, then, should be the alternative? In Sweden, as noted in Chapter 2.2.1, over-subscribed compulsory free schools are allowed to employ queues. Municipal schools, however, are not, and therefore generally employ the proximity rule. Like proximity-based admissions criteria, queues are likely to benefit more privileged pupils, whose parents can engage in extensive search behaviour.

A better tie-break device would be to use lotteries. Brighton and Hove have already introduced such a system for over-subscribed secondary schools. This reform led to decreased relationship between pupils' prior achievement and school attended, displaying less of a dependence on location. Yet it actually increased segregation in the short term due to a coinciding reform of school catchment areas, which maintained access to the most popular schools for pupils from more advantaged backgrounds (Allen, Burgess, and McKenna 2012). Displaying the dangers of implementing one good reform together with a bad one, it is nevertheless a model that should be advanced under more favourable conditions.

Of course, pupils could not be expected to travel too far in order to get to school. This is particularly the case in rural areas where public transportation is not as good as in urban areas. In a system of free choice, with lotteries as the tie-break device, pupils could technically lose the lottery and be left without a school within a reasonable proximity. However, there is little reason why this would be important in practice, since parents from outside these areas are just as unlikely to choose those schools. Nevertheless, in certain cases, there must be a second tie-break rule, where parents and local authorities can demand that schools should use proximity if it can be shown that pupils otherwise do not have access to a school within a reasonable proximity. These cases, of course, would be exceptions. Another alternative would be to provide school buses for younger pupils to ensure that they do not have to travel too far by themselves to get to school. This would also be beneficial since evidence from Milwaukee suggests that high transportation costs discourage low-income applicants to voucher schools from taking up their places (Chakrabarti 2013). Of course, expanding opportunities for online education, discussed in Chapters 4.4 and 4.11, would also be helpful for ensuring that all pupils have easy access to education.

4.9 Increase autonomy for all schools

Currently, only academies and free schools are allowed significant autonomy over (1) the terms of employment for teachers, and (2) deviations from the National Curriculum. This type of autonomy should ideally be extended to all schools, despite the political difficulties involved in doing so. However, when it comes to autonomy in matters of curriculum, the government must go further and introduce qualifications autonomy. International evidence and research on academies in England indicate that autonomy is important by itself, at least in developed countries (see Chapters 2 and 3), but it is absolutely crucial for a functioning education market since it allows schools to act upon competitive incentives. First, since the research displays the importance of teachers for pupil outcomes, as noted in Chapter 3.4, being able to hire good teachers and fire bad ones is clearly important. And as noted in Chapter 4.3, in order for competition to raise the performance of publicly operated schools, these and privately operated ones should be treated as equals. In December 2011, as part of the government's ongoing public sector pay review, and in response to proposals submitted by the Department for Education, the School Teachers' Review

Body recently recommended that in future progression through the pay scale will depend not on length of service, but on the results of annual appraisals. Although the national pay scales for teachers remain in place, this may have been the first step towards more significant personnel autonomy in schools, which is crucial for a well-functioning education market.[8]

An example of how teacher incentives could be more closely aligned with the goal of increasing education quality is through performance-related pay. There are some randomised studies on the impact of teacher performance pay: the research from the developing world tends to be positive (Glewwe, Ilias, and Kremer 2010; Muralidharan 2011; Muralidharan and Sundararaman 2011), but the research in the US does not generally display positive effects (Springer et al. 2010; Fryer 2011; Goodman and Turner 2011; Springer et al. 2012). An important reason for the differences between the US and the developing world research in general is that 'all incentive schemes piloted thus far in the US, due in part to strong influence by teacher's unions, have been more complex and provided teachers with less agency than incentive experiments in developing countries' (Fryer 2011:6). Nevertheless, there is some evidence from the US that pupil achievement did increase if teachers were paid in advance and then asked to give back the money if their pupils performed poorly. This was in contrast to teachers who were awarded regular bonuses after their pupils had performed well (Fryer et al. 2012).

Non-randomised research, in turn, often finds positive effects as well. In England, for example, Atkinson et al. (2009) analyse a scheme that introduced performance-related pay for teachers who had reached the upper bound of the national pay scale. Using pupil- and teacher-fixed effects models, they find that this improved value-added GCSE exam scores in science and English, but not in mathematics, by 40 per cent of one grade per pupil. Since the scheme was very complex, which can easily muddle incentives, these findings are noteworthy. Similarly, Woessmann (2011) analyses cross-national data and finds that merit pay for teachers raises PISA scores in reading and mathematics by 0.25 SD and science scores by 0.15 SD. Although the study does not deal with omitted variables

---

8   It is also noteworthy that the government has abolished the requirement that teachers have to notify parents 24 hours before they put pupils in detention outside school hours. This will be followed by other similar autonomy measures designed to improve schools' abilities to deal with disruptiveness in classrooms more effectively (Paton 2012).

conclusively, it provides a battery of robustness tests indicating that these do not drive the findings. Additionally, in fact, the great majority of international studies display at least some positive effects of teacher performance pay. While the design of such programmes is clearly important, and something to which researchers should pay greater attention (Neal 2011; Leigh 2012), the evidence suggests at the very least that schools should be allowed to experiment with different pay systems in order to find out what works best.

Second, it is not enough to allow curriculum autonomy as long as schools must offer exactly the same qualifications. Ideally, schools should be able to offer alternative qualifications so that they can accommodate different pupil needs. By allowing universities, and to a certain extent also Sixth Form colleges, to select pupils on whatever qualifications they see fit, this would ensure healthy competition between different education qualifications. British universities are already well equipped to deal with various forms of European qualifications, so a natural starting point would be to allow all schools to offer any qualification that has already been approved by other EU governments. It should not be construed that these qualifications are the only ones that should be approved. New qualifications produced by independent groups, meeting minimum criteria in respect of standards, should also be allowed in the future. Everything, of course, will not be accepted. As Friedman (1962) pointed out, the government's role in establishing minimum standards remains also in a voucher system.

In general, as Chapter 1 outlined, schools should be given as much autonomy as possible in their day-to-day operations. This means that the government should not generally prescribe how schools educate pupils. A well-functioning education market probably requires that we abandon many preconceived notions of how education should be carried out, and about the facilities required, to ensure quality. For example, in Sweden, many free schools attracted criticism for choosing not to provide their own libraries, and the Swedish government recently mandated that all schools need to have one (Skolinspektionen 2011c). But schools should be held accountable for their output, not their inputs. If they perform well without spending money on traditional inputs, this merely means that these schools focus more on other factors that also matter for pupil performance. This is clearly part of a necessary process of experimentation.

The above only serves to underscore the importance of strong accountability focused on schools' educational output. It is only possible to evaluate whether or not practices are successful if there are good gauges with which to measure quality. That is why a functioning education market requires functioning grading and admissions practices, which are discussed in more detail in Chapters 4.13 and 4.14.

4.10 Allow bona fide for-profit schools to set up shop

As Chapter 1 argued, the use of school competition and economies of scale as mechanisms for raising educational standards requires organisations that are willing to expand and replicate success in different markets. For-profit organisations have the strongest incentives to do so. It is therefore conspicuous that such schools are ineligible to receive public money in England. Deputy Prime Minister Nick Clegg has repeatedly stated that for-profit companies are and will remain banned from entering the education market so long as the Liberal Party remains part of the Coalition.

Such a policy is misguided. It stems from (1) ideological opposition to the idea of schools profiting from public money, and (2) the belief that such schools would reduce quality because of their profit-maximising behaviour. As the review of the global evidence displays, however, there is little evidence to suggest that for-profit schools differ significantly from non-profit schools in terms of quality. Indeed, the only available evidence from England indicates that for-profit, fee-paying private schools generally score higher than not-for-profit independent schools in Ofsted and ISI inspections (Croft 2011). Following a best-practice approach, there is thus little research to substantiate fears about the effects of the profit motive on publicly funded education.

Second, if the government is serious about inducing more competition and choice, with the long-term aim of crowding out failing schools, allowing for-profit schools is simply crucial. This is not because for-profit schools are inherently better than not-for-profit schools, but because they generate different incentives. For-profit companies have strong economic incentives to start new schools and capitalise on economies of scale. This would be especially the case if their funding was performance-related and if there was a differentiated voucher based on pupils' ability and background, as proposed. While non-profit schools are often high achieving, there are fewer incentives for them to increase in size and to open new schools to the same extent as their for-profit counterparts. The Swedish experience, from which the English free school model is drawn, indicates that for-profit schools are more likely to open new locations and expand into new municipalities compared to non-profit schools (Sahlgren 2011a). Indeed, 30 per cent of all Swedish compulsory free schools are run by ten large for-profit companies (Vlachos 2011a:80). The corollary is that the beneficial effects of scale economies are unlikely to materialise without for-profit schools.

Third, non-profit education providers have problems finding up-front capital for new schools. For-profit providers, on the other hand, are entrepreneurs who engage in risk-taking behaviour in exchange for future returns. While some non-profit providers may raise the capital required, this is unlikely to be sufficient for competition to increase significantly. Furthermore, being overly dependent on philanthropy is risky since there are no strong incentives for philanthropists to spend their money on the best schools. Indeed, analysing Californian non-profit charter school networks, Coulson (2011b) finds no relationship between the amount of philanthropic funding and educational achievement. For-profit schools seeking investment funding, on the other hand, have to demonstrate the capacity to generate future profits. This is precisely what the evidence from Chile displays: improvements in average test scores, controlling for changes in pupil background, predict increases in enrolment figures in for-profit schools only. In contrast, the best non-profit schools do not grow faster than other non-profit schools (Elacqua 2009c). While this research suffers from potential endogeneity, it is nevertheless important to note the correlations in this respect.

Fourth, it is also important to note that for-profit educators often expand into neighbourhoods that are unlikely to be served by non-profit schools, which are generally started by enthusiastic parents in middle-class neighbourhoods. The corollary is that they serve primarily middle-class pupils. Indeed, this is what the evidence on the English free schools policy suggests to date (Vasagar and Shephard 2011; Shephard 2012). Funded through a differentiated voucher, for-profit schools would be especially incentivised to expand into less privileged areas where parents are less likely to set up new schools. For-profit schools could therefore be instrumental for expanding the degree of choice also in underprivileged neighbourhoods. As Chowdry, Greaves, and Sibieta (2010:28) argue, 'It is possible that some new schools would be established in disadvantaged neighbourhoods [as a result of the current free schools policy], although, without a "for-profit" incentive, it is unlikely that England would see the same level of expansion as other countries.' Similarly, a partly performance-related funding system would strongly induce for-profit education providers to start competing with failing schools given their pecuniary interests to do so. In conclusion, therefore, encouraging for-profit companies to enter the education market would not undermine the policy goal of providing a good education for all. The two are not mutually exclusive.

Finally, as Nick Cowen (2008:80) argues, in pursuit of profit, '[For-profit schools] are more likely to adjust their profiles to exactly what the majority of parents and pupils generally want: safe, high-performing, mainstream-oriented schools.' Non-profit organisations, such as churches, on the other hand, tend to start schools that are 'mission oriented' rather than being focused on providing a general education. Of course, for-profit schools may also cater to particular subsets of the population as well, if they have a comparative advantage there.

All these points also make the current legal framework in England – which allows non-profit owners to outsource the management of their schools to for-profit providers – clearly unsatisfactory. In contrast to the situation in Chile and Sweden, but similarly to America, the English situation means that schools cannot expand due to the profit motive, which is one of the most important reasons for allowing it. Outsourcing the management of a school to an education company may or may not make it more efficient, but it completely obliterates the dynamic impact of the profit motive and does little to solve the issue of up-front capital.

Allen and Burgess (2010:22–23), two of England's leading education economists, give this straightforward assessment:

> We believe that there is a strong case for allowing private for-profit schools, despite public concerns about extracting profits from the provision of schooling. The primary motivation of for-profit schools will be to provide an education that parents desire, and so provided monitoring and regulatory mechanisms are put in place by the State there is no reason why this relationship should be

exploitative ... The experience of Sweden suggests that not-for-profit organisations tend to set up schools that are specific to their 'mission', rather than provide a general education that many parents want ... Allowing for-profit schools [also] solves the problem of financing upfront capital costs since these should be borne by the provider in exchange for the opportunity to generate a future return. These costs might be particularly large in England (compared to Sweden) in order to create secondary schools that are large enough to accommodate the post-14 curriculum choice that parents have come to expect. Of course, for-profit schools will also have the greatest incentive to keep their costs low and may successfully innovate in educational methods in order to do this. Where innovation is successful it can be replicated across government and not-for-profit schools that will have lower incentives to experiment.

Thus, a voucher system without for-profit schools is unlikely to produce the supply-side dynamic necessary to ensure a functioning education market. The policy implication is loud and clear: the government should revoke the ban on for-profit schools as soon as possible. Of course, due to increased economic incentives in for-profit organisations, it is especially important that schools are accountable to credible measures of performance in order to discourage perverse incentives. As explained in Chapter 1, there are significant differences between education and other goods and services, which should be taken seriously. This means, for example, that the information system should be improved significantly, a reform which is discussed in more detail in Chapter 4.14.

It is often argued that all money available should be spent on children's education, making it morally wrong to allow profits in the education system. It is unclear why this logic does not apply in other sectors. Nowadays few would argue that allowing companies to profit from their activities is a waste of resources. By giving strong incentives to educators to set up shop and expand, the profit motive can increase competition, which in turn has the potential to increase overall education quality to levels that would not be possible without those incentives.

4.11 Further stimulate supply

Given the importance of a supply-side dynamic for the functioning of an education market, it is also important to minimise restrictions regarding how schools should be approved and built. As discussed in Chapter 3.4, the application process is currently a strange mix between procurement, competitive tendering, and bona fide school establishment. What should be an invitation to establish schools is in reality an invitation to participate in a competition to be one of the lucky schools to be approved by the government. The application system should be revamped entirely. As long as schools meet minimum requirements, and provide their own capital, free establishment of schools would streamline the bureaucratic process significantly and help produce a much stronger supply-side dynamic than is currently the case. This would be more similar to the Swedish education system in which the free school application process has been much more liberal in respect of the conditions that have to be met for schools to be approved.

Furthermore, picking up on the discussion in Chapter 3.4, reforms to the planning system are an important complement of a voucher system, since they could stimulate a significant increase in supply. As Fazackerley, Wolf, and Massey (2010) argue, the 'big bang' approach would be to exempt new schools from all local planning investigations to ensure that local authorities cannot use them to bar competition. If this is not possible, schools could at the very least be exempted from the unnecessary building regulations that currently apply. Providers should be able to set up a new school in different types of property. The Swedish case is again relevant here: organisations can, and do, set up new schools in formerly commercial properties. Furthermore, thorough liberalisation of the planning system would lead to lower housing costs, which in turn would make it cheaper to set up new schools.

Finally, it would be highly desirable to expand the opportunities for online education in areas where supply is unlikely to increase radically, even with for-profit schools and a more liberal application/planning structure. Since we know little from rigorous research about the impact of online education on learning in primary or secondary education, it is important to use this alternative carefully. Rigorous evaluation of pilots should decide whether the government should use online education as an alternative to schools on a larger scale. As argued in Chapter 4.4, however, online education could be a wholesale option today if there are no other alternatives to low-performing schools. The minimum rules regarding learning and accreditation would apply to online learning facilities, and the approval and accreditation of such schools would be similar too.

But online education is not only a potential alternative to schools, but also a complement for pupils who attend schools that do not offer specific qualifications. For example, pupils who want to take advanced Latin could be given the opportunity to do so through online education, if the school does not offer it. The funding could be appropriately increased for the online educator and removed from the school the pupil attends, which is currently the practice in Florida for instance. As Greene et al. (2010:17) argue, 'Theoretically, there is a strong incentive for the local district and high school to compete with [the online educator] by making the brick and mortar experience superior to the online experience.' Opportunities for online education would thus clearly induce more competition and liberalise supply to an extent beyond that which might be achieved via traditional methods of schooling alone.

4.12 Big is beautiful: why anti-trust laws are counterproductive

Having argued that the goal should be a voucher system in England designed specifically to ensure that schools compete in terms of quality, it is important to consider whether the state should regulate the market to ensure a minimum number of suppliers. Lewis and Patrinos (2011:6) claim that 'while the public sector can be viewed as a monopolistic supplier of education provision, the same could be true of any private provider'. The authors also refer to the Netherlands in which state authorities seek to ensure that private monopolies do not replace public monopolies by capping the number of schools controlled by any school board at 50 per cent of all schools in one market. In a system with a virtual public monopoly in schooling, this idea is certainly attractive: such a policy would break up the current monopoly in the name of competition. However, setting aside estimates of the impact of online education (which would probably ensure that such a monopoly never emerged), while the above policy certainly conforms to anti-trust regulation in other sectors, it would be counterproductive for the purpose of increasing education quality.

First, assuming that parents choose schools based on quality, which the evidence at least partly suggests is true in the current English context (Burgess et al. 2009; Burgess and Briggs 2010; Gibbons and Silva 2011a; Gibbons, Machin, and Silva 2013), there is no reason why we should prohibit parents from choosing school suppliers simply because they are popular. Indeed, a key argument for school choice is that good alternatives crowd out bad ones; banning suppliers that are best at raising pupil performance from scaling up would be a strange policy. Thus, there is little reason to ban education suppliers from expanding indefinitely.

Second, Lewis and Patrinos (2011) do not find any fundamental difference between government and private monopolies in education: while the former traditionally emerges because of regulation, which perpetuates inefficiencies in large-scale production, the latter is generally a transitory phenomenon reflecting entrepreneurial success in a dynamic competitive process (Schumpeter 1994). Entrepreneurs must constantly satisfy demand, or else other producers will enter the market and compete. For these reasons, schools will face competition from both existing competitors and those which do not yet exist. The best way to ensure healthy competition, therefore, is simply to ensure free entry to and exit from the market.

Furthermore, capping enrolment or placing a ceiling on the number of schools held by any given supplier would dilute the prospects of improving education through scale economies. Indeed, the case for why it is possible to reconcile competition and scale economies depends on the fact that schools face competition from actors outside existing market structures, both from potential new schools and from school suppliers operating in other markets. Only on a static, rather than dynamic, view of competition is there a trade-off between scale economies and competition. If a ceiling is placed on school expansion, we would essentially produce such a trade-off ourselves.

4.13 Reform the national exam system – but rely less on it

As mentioned in the review of the English evidence, the country's education system appears to suffer from grade inflation. There is simply no reason to believe that the huge increases in exam achievement since 1988 have been matched by actual knowledge gains. Although competition among exam boards may have contributed to grade inflation marginally, the current type of weak criterion-referenced grading system seems to have an inherent bias towards gains. Thus, abolishing exam competition was never likely to be a panacea for solving the underlying problem.

There are two solutions to the problem of grade inflation within the GCSE/A-level system: either (1) the reintroduction of a strict cohort-referenced grading system; or (2) the introduction of a quasi cohort-referenced system. Yet such a change would only ensure that the English qualification is more comparable from year to year. Since we also want to ensure qualifications autonomy, and thus competition, one of these solutions should be combined with the 'Americanisation' of university (and to a certain extent Sixth Form) admissions, which would promote alternative procedures, while at the same time giving schools greater discretion to opt for alternative qualifications.

Reintroducing a cohort-referenced grading system would ensure strict comparability within school cohorts. This is because a fixed percentage of pupils would receive each grade. Grades would thus only reflect the relative performance of pupils within their cohorts. No more, no less. But since the likelihood of deviations in overall ability between large school cohorts is low, the cohort-referenced system is likely to be highly comparable from year to year also. It should be noted, however, that this solution might still require something to be done about exam board competition in the *same* qualification since 'an easier syllabus in one examining board would have the same distribution of examination results as a harder syllabus in another' (Baird 2007:132).

The problem with a cohort-referenced system is that it cannot be used to measure gains and losses between school cohorts, however unlikely these are. Yet the whole idea of introducing school choice is to increase overall gains in the education system. Given that the current system produces significant grade inflation, however, little suggests that it is any better in terms of detecting performance gains or losses in the education system as a whole. Pupils assessed in years closer to the year in which the new criterion-referenced GCSE exam was introduced were clearly disadvantaged compared to later cohorts, and this effect is replicated every time there is a change to exam specifications. Clearly, comparability in the present system cannot be guaranteed either. It is possible to get around this problem, however, through the use of international surveys, which offer good alternatives for measuring gains and losses. A cohort-referenced system would at the very least ensure that pupils could be compared within any given cohort.

If policymakers are unwilling to reintroduce a fully cohort-referenced system, a 'contextualised' system, suggested by Stringer (2011), could be a compromise. In this model, the grade distribution in core subjects – GCSE English, Mathematics, and Science – would remain fixed from year to year. Candidates' mean achievement in these subjects could then be used to control for the same cohort's entry pattern in other subjects. This means that we allow the grade distribution in subjects other than the core ones to change from year to year, depending on the ability level of the cohort as decided by their performance in the core subjects. If, for example, a higher percentage of pupils taking GCSE French in year 2 are of A* quality, compared to year 1, we would expect this improvement in the entry profile to be reflected in a higher proportion of these pupils obtaining A* in the core subjects in year 2. Consequently, a higher proportion of pupils studying French would be awarded A* in that subject compared to year 1. In essence, one thus uses the core subjects as an anchor to ensure that the grade distribution in GCSE French reflects the ability profile of the pupils taking that subject in any given year. Of course, French is used here only as an example; the same grading system would apply to all other non-core subjects as well.

In the first year of the new system, grades in subjects other than the core ones would be based solely on examiners' judgements, and the proportion of candidates receiving each grade in relation to their mean achievement in core subjects would be recorded. In subsequent years, this information is then used to predict the proportion of pupils that should receive each grade in subjects other than the core ones. The relationship between the concurrent mean achievement in core subjects and grades in other subjects could not change from year to year, but 'outcomes in subjects [other than the core ones] could increase or decrease with the ability profile of the entry' (Stringer 2011:16). This, in turn, would allow use of the mean achievement in all GCSE subjects as a control for the ability profile for A levels. Such a system could thus potentially ensure both comparability and that gains/losses in knowledge are taken into account.

However, the former two proposals are only meant to ensure that schools that opt for English qualifications are compared on an equal basis, while also providing a better foundation for developing valid school choice information. Neither of the above alternatives is a standalone alternative, but should rather be seen as complements to a stronger reliance on institutions when it comes to accepting pupils. On the model of increased qualification autonomy described earlier, universities would also be able to choose pupils taking various other types of qualifications, which would give strong incentives to schools to offer the qualifications that tertiary education institutions prefer. Competition would then ensure that the weakest qualifications are crowded out, but also that admissions requirements reflect the differences in qualifications. This would not be any news to admissions tutors at British universities, who are already well versed in the EU qualifications proposed here as viable alternatives, which could be offered by any English schools in the beginning. This could technically be complemented by the introduction of standardised national admissions tests, as noted in the Sykes Review (Sykes et al. 2010), to be used by universities and to a certain extent also Sixth Form colleges on a voluntary basis.

A series of reforms to the national exam system are necessary to ensure that pupils taking GCSEs and A levels are assessed in a transparent and comparable way, and that there is greater autonomy with respect to schools choosing which qualifications they should offer their pupils. Rather than promoting competition across boards in the same qualification, this alternative would promote strong competition between alternative qualifications. By allowing, as a starting point, English schools to offer other EU qualifications, which have already been approved by other governments, as well as relying upon universities (and to a certain extent also Sixth Form colleges) to determine whether pupils possess the knowledge and skills necessary for their courses, the importance of the national testing system would decline compared to today. Of course, in the future, other qualifications might be admitted, so long as they satisfy the minimum criteria stipulated by governments.

4.14 Improve the information and accountability system

A well-functioning education market needs good quality measures by which parents and authorities can compare schools. As noted in Chapter 1, research from several countries suggests that schools and parents react positively when provided with information regarding how well the former perform. Since school effectiveness differs depending on pupils' varying ability, it is important that the information reflects this in all metrics presented. Indeed, '[i]f schools' performance were presented by prior [achievement] group, they would have an incentive to focus on the performance of all pupils' (Dearden, Micklewright, and Vignoles 2011:243). Although the government began publishing such information in 2012, the average achievement measure is currently based on pupil groups that are too large (Allen 2012b) and the value-added measure remains undifferentiated. In theory, league tables are supposed to help parents choose a school at which their children will improve their achievement the most. Although parents who choose based on average raw test score data and the now abolished contextual value-added indicator have been better off than parents making random choices, Allen and Burgess (2011) show that none of these measures are effective in this respect. While no gauge is perfect, the authors propose using average exam grades at schools within close proximity of each other, and differentiating this measure based on pupils' prior ability. This would give parents more information on the relative effectiveness of the schools they actually choose between, while also taking into account that this effectiveness differs between pupils of varying prior ability. Due to the trade-offs between different metrics, however, 'it would be most valuable to trial different contents and formats of school performance information in field experiments' (Allen and Burgess 2011:260).

Such experiments could of course also be used to evaluate already existing regular value-added metrics or proposals for new contextual value-added measures. Although both the regular value-added and the now abolished contextual value-added metrics have been far too uncertain to be useful (Leckie and Goldstein 2009, 2011b), the aim of isolating school effectiveness from pupil intake should not be abandoned. Rather, it is important to learn from previous mistakes and develop better effectiveness measures. For example, as previously noted, the modelling of contextual value added suffered from a lack of data regarding family composition, income and parental education, which biased the scores; better data should be collected and included in the computation of potential future contextual value-added measures (Dearden, Miranda, and Rabe-Hesketh 2011). Although raw average test scores have turned out to be a decent guide for parental school choice (Allen and Burgess 2011), properly developed value-added gauges would provide even more relevant information regarding the schools at which pupils would be most likely to improve. Indeed, recent research from the US indicates that when controlling for specific background variables, contextual value-added measures do replicate random assignment to both teachers and schools (Kane and Staiger 2008; Deming et al. 2011). One way of producing more valid measures is to evaluate pupils each year, since value added based on yearly data has proven to be less unstable over time (Ferrão 2012). As argued below, however, an experimentation process among independent actors is probably the best way to improve how school effectiveness is measured. One could, for example, foresee research projects that attempt to identify effective schools, just as a recent project set out to identify effective teachers (Kane et al. 2013).

Since qualification autonomy is important, as argued above, it is naturally important to ensure appropriate information in a system that allows several competing types of education. One could release value-added information and other quality measures from different qualifications. In fact, it could technically be possible to use improved value-added measures to calculate changes in achievement based on normalised scores that would be comparable across qualifications. This means that parents would be able to see the percentage increase in school performance across all qualifications (although this would not tell them anything about achievement *per se*, since some qualifications may simply be more difficult at different stages of a pupil's education).

Yet it is important to acknowledge that different types of qualifications have different types of assessments at different points in the education process. In the Swedish education system, for example, teachers set their own grades, which may or may not reflect the actual quality of the school. Another key problem in linking strong incentives to qualifications, the format of which has to be fairly consistent from year to year, is that it creates strong incentives to game the system among schools, and for teachers to engage in 'teaching to the test'. Thus teachers end up coaching pupils for high-stakes tests, while ignoring other important things (see Filgio and Loeb 2011). Of course, this is not *necessarily* the case. As Winters, Trivitt, and Green (2010) show, high-stakes testing policies in Florida generate gains in the high-stakes tests, but also in low-stakes subjects, thus suggesting positive spill-over effects rather than a crowding out effect. Similarly, Chiang (2009) finds that schools responded to high-stakes tests by raising spending on teacher training, instructional technology, and development of curricula, indicating that high-stakes testing can also produce worthwhile changes in school behaviour. Nevertheless, it is clearly important to take these issues into account.

Neal (2010) and Barlevy and Neal (2012) propose a solution to the problem of perverse incentives in terms of teacher performance-related pay and accountability to state officials, which is based on the separation of qualifications from incentives. By introducing a separate set of examinations, which are entirely cohort-referenced and administered continuously throughout the education process, one could change the format from year to year. This would make it impossible to teach to the test, forcing teachers to focus on actual knowledge to improve their pupils' scores. Different pupils would enter different 'contests' based on their initial achievement levels, background, peers, and other important characteristics. They would then be assigned a percentile score relative to other pupils in this contest.

While the authors focus on tying such tests to teacher performance pay and accountability to state officials, they would also be invaluable for information purposes in a system that allows qualifications autonomy. Examinations could be carried out in whatever way possible and would thus allow less theoretical subjects to be tested too. The tests could focus on the minimum required knowledge and skills that the education authorities want all pupils to master. Of course, they could also become more comprehensive quality metrics for all schools if they are devised to incorporate overlaps between different qualifications. Indeed, the TIMSS framework does precisely that by making sure that the exams test knowledge that is overlapping between various education systems. That the tests are cohort-related, which is crucial for allowing the test format to change over time, means that we can only say how well pupils are doing compared to other pupils, but we can track them and see how they move up and down the ranking across different years, which would allow for a specific relative value-added analysis also in the information tests. One can also construct specific sets of pupils according to whose average performance they may be compared to, depending on background and prior ability. This would take into account potential differential school effectiveness among different types of pupils as described earlier. While the regime would not remove all incentives to manipulate results (Figlio and Loeb 2011), it would make it much more difficult for schools and teachers to simply coach pupils for tests without instilling the knowledge required to perform highly on them.

However, it is also important to provide information on school qualities that cannot easily be captured by test scores alone. School inspections are important for this purpose. Furthermore, school inspections could also be used as an additional tool to compare schools offering different qualifications. It has been shown that the grades from Ofsted inspections correlate with pupil satisfaction with teachers as well as parental satisfaction with schools over and above test scores, which indicates that the inspection grades do pick up qualities that are not captured by conventional measures of education quality. Furthermore, the most methodologically sound research shows that inspections do increase achievement and that these gains are not obtained by making pupils study easier subjects (Allen and Burgess 2012; Hussain 2012). Thus, school inspections can clearly be useful and the outcomes of the inspections are valuable information for parents and pupils.

This is not to say that they cannot be more useful and informative. School inspections should be focused on output alone. Current Ofsted inspections are too prescriptive, for example by evaluating teaching styles rather than whether pupils learn as much as possible. As John McIntosh, former head of the London Oratory School who is currently involved in the government's curriculum review, argues, 'Ofsted inspectors need to assess whether a lesson is a good lesson or not and whether it is effective regardless of the style that the teacher has used in teaching the lesson' (quoted in Patton 2012:1). Even though Ofsted inspections have been shown to improve test scores to a certain extent, therefore, they need to be less prescriptive in terms of how schools achieve success.

Furthermore, beyond whether schools fulfil the minimum requirements, the government does not have to be involved in inspections either. Instead, independent organisations could carry out inspections that are more focused on the specific types of qualification the schools offer. If a school offers the French 'Brevet des collèges', which is roughly equivalent to GCSEs, and 'Baccalaureate', which is roughly equivalent to A levels, for example, a third-party organisation that specialises in quality assurance of French qualifications could carry out additional inspections. The same would apply to new qualifications that have yet to be developed.

It would also be preferable if parental and pupil satisfaction scores could be published to give a fuller picture of the quality of the school. While test scores and inspections could provide reasonable indications of overall school quality, parents have access to more fine-grained indicators of pupil needs and how schools meet these needs. Application statistics are also useful, since these indicate parents' preferences clearly. Teacher quality indicators, too, may be very important to publish as accountability information, since the variation in the quality of teachers is much higher than between schools (Marsh et al. 2011). And, finally, statistics from admissions tests, wage premiums, and employment outcomes after school, corrected for prior achievement and background, could be published so parents know which schools are more successful in preparing their children for access to higher education institutions and the labour market. This would ensure that parents and pupils are informed about which qualifications are best for the purposes of reaching their individual goals.

In addition, it is important to learn from behavioural economics when designing the information system to maximise the potential of parents and pupils to become discerning in their choices. For example, the way information is presented can be very important for how choosers value something. Research from health care has displayed that when gains are described in relative terms, they are viewed more positively than in absolute terms. Similarly, research from health care shows that the provision of personalised information aids people in making more discerning decisions. Information, therefore, should be presented in a way that maximises the potential for this (Greene et al. 2010).

Of course, competition between different information providers can also develop, which could spur innovation also in this field while ensuring that providers act as quality checks of each other. For this reason, it is important to also allow diversity in the provision of information. For example, in the Netherlands, the national newspaper *Trouw* began publishing school quality information, which, in turn, produced radical changes in the government's School Inspection Service. It began publishing its own quality information on the internet, and reformulated its remit to include the provision of school quality information to citizens (Meijer 2007). Yet the government could clearly play a more constructive role from the outset: it could set minimum requirements regarding what information schools should provide, for example.

As Greene et al. (2010) argue, governments could assemble and publish the relevant information, and then allow other actors free use of this information in constructing alternative measures. The former has been proposed in England already, with the government producing an overall quality index that gives specific weights to different quality measures (Astle, Bryant, and Hotham 2011). There are various alternatives, but the main point is that competition in this area may very well generate gradual improvements in information supply, which would greatly aid the establishment of a functioning education market.

In general, therefore, a plethora of new information measures would promote healthy incentives among schools to compete along the lines of quality. As the above discussion indicates, choice in itself allows for a much more nuanced approach to accountability than the current state-dominated situation. Indeed, as Neal (2010:130) argues, 'Expansions of parental choice in whatever guise could allow governments to acquire an army of educational performance monitors.' Such educational performance monitors are crucial for promoting a system of choice and competition that raises education quality significantly.

4.15 Conclusion

This chapter has suggested reforms to the current English school choice model which, if implemented, would move the system towards a well-functioning education market. A national voucher scheme should be the goal, but to facilitate proper evaluation the programme should ideally be randomly rolled out across different regions. The system should involve parents both in the choice of school and the financial transactions involved in paying for education. Parents should be directly involved in 'paying' schools with the voucher they have received, and choosing a school should be mandatory. This means that there should be no default school to which pupils are automatically assigned if they do not exercise any other choice.

It is also of utmost importance that all schools, both state and independent, generally are treated equally in terms of funding. This, in turn, makes it necessary to tie practically all school funding to the voucher. Tying school funding to the voucher would also ensure that unpopular schools go bust, which in turn makes it crucial to incentivise new and better schools to start up in these areas.

However, while equality in school funding should be the general rule, a voucher system that increases funding in one way or the other to well-performing and popular schools might be preferable. This would incentivise schools to focus on quality, and spur good schools to expand, while also facilitating the closure of failing schools. To ensure that such schools actually do close, online education should also be a viable wholesale option when there are only low-quality alternative schools available.

Furthermore, since the real cost of educating pupils depends on their ability and background, the voucher should be differentiated based on these features. While strong recommendations on the issue of top-up fees are not made here, it is important that such fees, if they are allowed, are accompanied by other mechanisms that discourage cream-skimming. Gradual implementation of the voucher would leave room for experimentation in this field, as also in respect of ascertaining the effects of widespread selection practices. Other regions would then be allotted to abolish proximity as the tie-break device to primary and lower-secondary schools, and instead introduce lotteries.

Today, only academies and free schools have significant autonomy in hiring and firing practices and in curriculum matters; all schools, state and independent, should be given such autonomy. Nevertheless, curriculum autonomy is not enough. Stronger qualification autonomy should also be allowed. This book argues that allowing English schools to offer any other qualification that has been approved by an EU government would be a good start. This would ensure that schools have the ability to compete by providing significantly different types of education. In the future, however, new qualifications meeting the minimum requirements can be developed by various independent organisations.

In order to create the necessary supply-side dynamic to raise competition significantly, as well as to ensure access to good schools in underprivileged neighbourhoods, it is important to incentivise successful schools to scale up. This makes it crucial to allow for-profit schools to operate. And precisely because these seek to find out what works best and then replicate it, there should be no caps on enrolment or maximum shares per school provider in any given area. Although such regulation would be introduced under the guise of maintaining static competition, it produces a trade-off between scale economies and competition policy.

Since the supply-side dynamic is very important for the success of school choice, it also makes sense to liberate supply further. First, the process should be streamlined and made easier. The free establishment of schools, provided that these meet requirements and raise their own capital, should be the norm. Second, planning laws should be liberalised when it comes to schools especially (and across the board preferably). A radical approach would be to exempt all schools from local planning investigations. If not, the building restrictions should be abolished, and schools should also be able to convert other types of property rather than being restricted to that designated for school use. Third, opportunities for online education should be increased to facilitate choice also in areas where the supply of schools is unlikely to increase rapidly/radically.

Additionally, reforms to the exam and admissions system should be introduced. While some form of cohort-referenced system would be preferable to the current weak criterion-referenced one, it is still desirable, as noted above, to adapt the system to more qualification diversity. Allowing an on-going 'Americanisation' of the admissions system would mean that universities (and to a certain extent also Sixth Form colleges) would rely more on alternative admissions procedures to differentiate between pupils. Alternatively, they might simply set different admissions criteria for pupils taking different qualifications. This would (1) ensure healthy competition between different qualifications; and (2) produce yardsticks for admissions tutors, who can better understand the standard of grades in one qualification when there are other qualifications with which to compare and contrast. Additionally, standardised admissions tests could be introduced, which schools and universities could require applicants to take on a voluntary basis.

Finally, having dealt with the exam system, the information system must be improved to enable parents to make informed school choices based on education quality. This requires quality measures that better reflect pupil heterogeneity/ background and local differences in school quality. Introducing new cohort-related 'information tests' that allow the test format to vary over time would also ensure that teaching to the test becomes impossible. The unpredictability of the tests would encourage schools and teachers to focus on increasing pupils' actual knowledge and skills, equipping them to do well on any type of test, rather than merely coaching them for exams. Furthermore, school inspections also offer valuable information that could capture school quality over and above that which is included in test scores, while also providing an additional instrument with which schools offering different qualifications could be compared. Other measures, such as parental satisfaction scores, should also be available and it would be preferable to allow an open source approach, which would enable third-party groups to produce new information and compete along these lines as well.

The system proposed would require overhaul of many features of the current education system in England. Nevertheless, the gradual implementation would allow researchers to study the effects in a scientific fashion. As the global evidence suggests, half-hearted attempts to introduce choice will not generate large gains, and may in fact produce perverse incentives to compete through other means than by raising quality. In order to reap the benefits of choice, therefore, it is important that it is not seen as a panacea. Rather, as outlined here, in order to increase efficiency significantly, expanded choice requires many other reforms. Creating a well-functioning market demands a coherent approach to changing the overall incentive structure in the education system.

Conclusion

I T HAS NOW BEEN several decades since Friedman (1962) sparked the contemporary school choice debate by proposing vouchers as an alternative way of organising publicly funded education. As this book has shown, there have been several attempts to realise this proposal in one way or the other. Politicians in the latter part of the twentieth century attempted to open up their countries' often heavily centralised education systems to choice and competition in various ways in order to raise quality.

This book has provided a comprehensive analysis of the results of these programmes. The findings, which are summarised in table form in the Appendix, reveal a very mixed picture. On the positive side, some evidence displays large gains, revealing the potential of school choice and competition. There is also very little convincing evidence of negative impacts on pupil performance. On the negative side, however, many choice reforms have not increased education quality significantly. Yet this is not surprising. Politicians have generally been unable, or unwilling, to carry out the measures necessary to create functioning education markets. Competitive incentives have often not arisen, or when they have arisen, they have often targeted other things than quality. Since many reforms were implemented for ideological reasons, it was inevitable that mistakes would be made along the way. Naturally, also, powerful interest groups have often opposed choice programmes, pressuring politicians to hollow out reforms. Furthermore, ironically, advocates of choice might also be partly responsible for this development: overemphasis of the purported benefits of existing programmes, presented without reference to the importance of programme design and complementary reforms, may have encouraged a lack of joined-up thinking. This has often resulted in programmes that lack crucial components, all in the name of increasing choice and competition so marginally that it often does not matter.

As the first opening quote of this book suggests, the key problem today in education is the lack of proper incentives for improving quality. Merely introducing some more school choice is not a panacea for solving this problem. If competitive incentives do not arise as a result of choice, there is no reason to expect improvements in the first place; if competitive incentives are targeted at other things than quality, they will do more harm than good; and if schools cannot act upon incentives, it does not matter if they are appropriate. It is thus absolutely crucial that politicians are aware that the mere introduction of some choice in the current education systems, within which there are very few incentives to raise quality, will not generate large gains. Rather, a thorough and whole-hearted approach requires coherent complementary reforms that support a transformation of education systems to education markets with radically different incentive structures. In other words, a whole new mind-set with respect to education reform is necessary. Unless politicians are willing to implement reforms that harness and direct incentives toward improving quality, school choice will not be successful. Indeed, changing parts of the incentive structure while keeping the overall systems intact may mean that incentives turn perverse. More generally, problems may occur because education is not like any other goods or services on the market. For example, information asymmetries make education markets more complicated. In such markets, perverse incentives can easily arise – which is precisely why there is a need for clear, well-designed rules to shape the incentive structure in such a way as to target quality deficiencies. Suggestions as to how this could be achieved in England have been presented.

It is worth highlighting that laissez-faire solutions to the problems in education have not been advocated. The role of government in education should be *changed* and *reduced*, but *not abolished* entirely. Instead, general rules have been proposed within which choice and competition should be allowed to operate. Is this tantamount to central planning? Certainly not. As Nobel Prize winning economist Al Roth (2013:1) puts it, 'Organized markets inevitably have rules, which establish the playing field rather than determine outcomes, which is what makes market design different from, say, central planning.' Indeed, as noted by Hayek (2001) in the second opening quote to this book, the fundamental principle that one should resort to spontaneous orders must not be interpreted as a strict rule. It is certainly not a coincidence that strong advocates of vouchers and school choice, such as Friedman (1962) and Hoxby (2006), do propose a larger role for the government in education than they would probably do in other fields.

Naturally, a note is also required on the political possibilities for implementing the proposed programme. The voucher programme and its complementary reforms might not be possible simply because it is a radical departure from the status quo. However, even if we ignore Pigou's (1935) warning in the third opening quote to this book, adapting the proposals to what is politically palatable would be risky. As emphasised, one of the reasons why choice and competition often have not been as successful as some would have hoped is because the programmes have been watered down for the sake of political expediency. As noted below, however, ideas change politics, and what is not politically possible today might be so tomorrow. It is thus a mistake to adapt policy proposals too much to present estimations of what is politically viable.

What is important to note is that once choice is implemented, it is very difficult to roll it back. This is because parents generally value the choices that are available. It is clear that there is a 'negativity bias' in politics, which means that people tend to be very risk averse and oppose challenges to the status quo (e.g. Pierson 1996). Once the changes have been made, however, the situation is changed for ever. If choice is made the new status quo, this becomes very difficult to change. This is what the evidence from most choice systems suggests, since parents normally value the right to choose schools. One example is in Sweden, where 76% of the population claim that parents should have the right to choose schools, while 23% say that it is better that the municipality allocates pupils to schools (Demoskop 2011). Thus, once more choice is instilled in the system, it is very difficult to pull back.

Of course, even if the changes were implemented as suggested, the situation might change with time and the political dynamic. By proposing a role, albeit limited, for the government in education, for example, one might increase the risk of regulatory capture from producers that lobby for entry restrictions and more regulations to serve their own interests, and at the expense of pupils. Even if some intervention might be beneficial, it might not be possible due to political self-interest, as politicians curry favour with special interest groups in their search for vote maximisation. Indeed, this might be what one would expect from public choice theory (Buchanan and Tullock 1962).

First, even *if* a true laissez-faire policy would be preferable, it does not answer the question of how to get education out of politics in the first place. If politicians are self-interested, and there are interest groups that have already hijacked education policy for their own interests, it is unclear why the former would ever vote for reform in the first place. And, if they do vote for reform, it is unclear why they would not regulate the private market just as much as they have regulated the state sector. As noted in Chapter 4.1, if the private school share were to approach something like 70 per cent, it is quite likely that much stronger regulatory pressures would develop even if no government money were involved.

Second, even if one ignores the previous point, it is important to note that this potential problem applies to all types of government involvement in education. Coulson (2011b) argues that tax-credit programmes are different, but as Chapter 4.1 outlines, this is not likely to be the case over the long term and especially not in Europe. Schools and education groups could lobby the government to allow only certain actors to be eligible for tax credits, and teachers unions could lobby the government to set restrictions on teacher conditions just as they might if a voucher programme were to be implemented. Thus, neither complete laissez faire nor education tax credits are necessary or sufficient to avoid regulatory capture and further restrictions.

Instead, just as public choice theory suggests ways of getting around government failure, such as through constitutionally binding rules that put certain matters outside the scope of politicians (Buchanan 1997), it is technically possible to devise rules that put much education policy beyond the scope of politicians. A conspicuous example of a public activity that has been granted much more independence from daily politics in the past decades is that of central banking, in both developing and developed countries (Crowe and Meade 2008). This growing independence is in spite of the importance of central banks for political and economic development, and despite the fact that politicians sometimes use them to serve their own interests (Alpanda and Honig 2009). Maybe one should separate the bulk of education regulation from politicians as well in a similar fashion?

This is a radical idea, but so was central bank independence in some countries once upon a time. As noted in Chapter 2.2.3, the Netherlands enshrined the right to provide privately operated education in its constitution in 1913, with parental choice deriving from this right, which has shaped education policy to this day. In 2006, furthermore, operating authority over the local government schools was 'turned over to independent boards so as to make them more comparable to the privately operated schools and to preclude any temptation by municipalities to favor [municipal] schools' (Ladd, Fiske, and Ruijs 2009:7). In this way, politicians attempted to lift daily politics out of local schools. Of course, the Dutch system was set up primarily to cater for freedom of religion, which manifested itself in the restrictions on the establishment of new schools from the very beginning, via a quota system and other regulatory practices regarding inputs to schools. But one could envisage separating education from daily politics in different ways that cater to the needs of today, after having established the minimum rules that should guide the system and, through a randomised process, having established what features work and what features do not.

Yet even if we ignore the idea of partly separating education policy from politics, government funding and some involvement in education do not necessitate encroachment into detailed policy regulations. This is because the argument that entrenched interest groups run the whole show simply ignores the role of ideas in influencing public policy. Whether vouchers will lead to detailed regulations depends on how the war of ideas plays out. While history suggests that voucher programmes have often been cobbled with regulation, although in different degrees, history is not a strait-jacket. To see why, it is sufficient to look at the growth of the welfare state. While many economic liberals argue for a dismantling of the welfare state, no industrialised country has ever avoided its rise. Does this mean that it is unavoidable? Maybe, but if economic liberals actually believed this to be the case, we would not have classical liberal think tanks advocating lower taxes and less regulation.

Indeed, when analysing broad shifts in countries' strategies, it is important to look beyond immediate interests. The move towards larger central bank independence, noted above, was just a small part of a larger transformation that has occurred over the past decades. For example, Sweden in the 1970s was on the verge of socialising profits, which would have been a major step towards a socialist economy. Two decades later, it had liberalised its welfare system significantly with, for example, an education voucher system that allows for-profit companies to operate. The radical decentralisation that occurred, compared with the previous status quo, highlights the importance of ideas in policymaking rather than interest groups only. Indeed, Swedish policymaking, both when expanding the welfare state as well as when pursuing privatisation and decentralisation, has in fact been guided by the type of social scientific research that was fashionable at the time. In the 1960s, this was statist. In the late 1980s, on the other hand, it began to be guided by liberal economics (Bergh and Erlingsson 2009). Another example could be the major transformations that were implemented by the British Conservative governments in the 1980s, despite strong political resistance from interest groups. All this goes to show that ideas may very well change the political landscape in favour of the proposals put forward in this book, which is first and foremost an account of the ideas that should guide political strategising, rather than an account of political strategising itself.

It is of course true that the future of school choice will not be determined by ideas emanating from academia and policy institutes in the final stages of implementation, but by the dynamics in the political arena. Surely, politicians are fettered by demands from constituencies and interest groups. Those who benefit from the status quo will fight back. Indeed, research shows that American teachers unions have been instrumental in blocking worthwhile education reforms that threaten union prerogatives (Moe 2011). One should be under no illusion that a departure from today's education system will satisfy exactly everybody's desires and interests. But politics cannot deliver utopia. And that is why the creation of a functioning education market at the end of the day requires bold politicians willing to challenge the status quo to improve the overall quality of the system. Certainly, none of the reforms suggested in this book will be easy to implement. This might scare politicians of all parties. But, then again, no great politician has ever settled for the easy tasks.

GLOSSARY

Difference-in-difference (D-i-D) is an econometric technique that can measure the impact of a specific policy change that affects certain units, such as pupils and schools, differently compared to others. For example, if a policy change in education is instituted in one region, but not in an adjacent region, one can analyse how the change affected the treated pupils and schools compared with the control group, consisting of the pupils and schools in the unaffected areas. The strategy requires pre-reform data and that any other changes occurring at the same time as the policy change of interest do not affect pupil performance as well.

Effect size. See 'Standard deviation' below.

Endogeneity means that the variable in question, in this case school choice/competition, is in itself either (1) a product of the level of education quality; or (2) a product of other variables that are important determinants of education quality, but which are not included in the statistical model. The former case means that there is a **reverse causality** problem (e.g. that achievement causes competition rather than vice versa), and the latter case means that there are 'unseen' variables that cause **omitted variable bias** or **selection bias**. For example, regarding (1), policies that advance choice and competition could be a reaction to low education quality. That is, low education quality spurs more competition. If this is not accounted for, one might erroneously conclude that competition is negative for quality. In regard to (2), when analysing school and choice effects, pupils exercising choice may differ significantly from other pupils. They might, for example, have more motivation on average, which is difficult to control for. They could simply be higher-achieving pupils.

    Measurement error is the difference between the true value and measured value (which may give rise to endogeneity bias). For example, no exams can measure a pupil's ability perfectly. Some very high-performing pupils may have a really bad day, while lower-performing pupils may have an unusual good day or simply be lucky when they guess the answers. This gives rise to problems when creating value-added models of achievement. If, for example, a high-achieving pupil has a bad day when first sitting the test, and a good day when sitting the test the following year, the gain over the course of the year will be overstated. On the other hand, if the same pupil had an exceptionally good day the first year and an exceptionally bad day in the second year, his gains would be understated.

Measurement error is also a problem when using data on choice and competition that might have been measured in the wrong way. For example, if an inaccurate number of pupils are counted as attending private schools, and the percentage of pupils in private schools is used as a measure of competition, the latter will contain measurement error. If measurement error is present in the explanatory variable of interest (e.g. either lagged test scores or the relevant variable measuring school choice or competition), its coefficient is biased towards zero.

Fixed-effects model. A statistical tool that removes all variation between the units of analysis, such as pupils and schools, that do not vary over the period analysed. What the model removes depends on what the researcher wants to control for and the available data. (The model requires that one has access to at least two observations of the relevant variable at different points in time.) For example, if one wants to analyse the effects of school competition at the municipality level in Sweden in the period 1992–2012, one may want to remove differences between municipalities that do not change over the period one is studying, but that might both produce higher education quality and higher competition. One such difference could hypothetically be that some municipalities have very apt and politically influential headteachers that retain their jobs under the period of study. If these school leaders both actively promote competition and increase education quality, one might falsely conclude that improvements in education quality are due to competition. By removing such differences between municipalities, the fixed-effects model is a powerful instrument to control for 'unseen' confounding time-constant variables. If one, on the other hand, analyses how competition affects specific pupils over time, the model could remove the constant differences between pupils, such as innate factors that contribute to their performance.

In addition, one can also include **time-fixed effects** to remove common trends in education quality in all locations, which might produce a spurious correlation between increasing choice/competition and lower/higher education quality (depending on whether the trend is negative or positive). Time effects could also remove systemic grade inflation that affects all pupils equally.

Instrumental variable (IV) model. An econometric tool that can potentially solve endogeneity bias as defined above. To do this one must find a specific variable, an instrument, which causes the variable of interest, for example private school attendance or the level of school competition, but is unrelated to educational quality directly. In this case, it is possible to isolate the part of private school attendance or level of school competition, via the instrument, that is not shaped by education quality directly. This solves the problem of reverse causality. If the instrument is also unrelated to any other variable that is not included in the model, for example pupils' motivation, the problem of omitted variable bias is solved too. Finally, by finding an instrument that is correlated with the measured value of a variable, for example test scores, but uncorrelated with the portion in this variable that is due to measurement error, the latter problem can be solved too. In practice, however, it is very difficult to find instruments that satisfy these criteria, especially the second one. If the instrument affects the school choice variable of interest directly, or is related to any other variable that also affects education quality but that is not included in the statistical model, it is not an 'exogenous' (valid) instrument. The assumptions of an instrumental variable are displayed in the figure below.

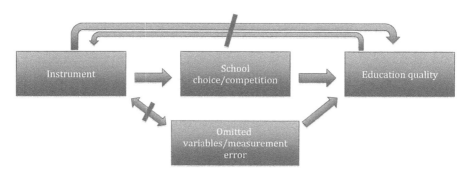

Measurement error. See 'Endogeneity' above.

OLS model. An econometric tool with which researchers can hold constant observable variables that might affect both the variable of interest, such as school choice/competition, and pupil performance. Such observable variables include family background, location characteristics, peer effects, etc. However, the model presumes that all variables that cause both the variable of interest and pupil performance are included in the model, and that pupil performance does not affect the variable of interest. If these assumptions are not met, the model suffers from endogeneity bias.

Omitted variable bias. See 'Endogeneity' above.

Propensity score matching is another technique to deal with endogeneity bias. It means that the researcher matches the units of analysis (such as pupils and schools) that are very similar on observed variables of importance for pupil performance. Such variables include prior ability, background, living situation, etc., but it depends on data availability. By comparing units that are similar on these observed variables, one comes closer to separating causality from correlation when estimating the effects of choice/competition on education quality. Yet this technique is not valid if there are unobserved variables predicting both choice and pupil performance, which is highly likely to be the case without very rich and detailed data.

Regression discontinuity design (RDD) is an econometric method by which one compares only the units, such as pupils and schools, that are within close range on either side of a specific threshold that determines whether or not they are 'treated' in terms of an education policy. For example, English schools were forced to hold an election before converting to grant-maintained status, which granted them more autonomy. By comparing schools in which this election was narrowly won with those in which it was narrowly lost, it is likely that one can compare 'apples with apples' when analysing the impact of grant-maintained status on educational achievement. Provided that there are no unobserved variables that can explain why schools ended up within the narrow range of the threshold, the RDD can estimate causal effects of education policy interventions.

Reverse causality. See 'Endogeneity' above.

Selection bias. See 'Endogeneity' above.

Standard deviation (SD) is a measure of the variation from the arithmetic mean in data. The standard deviation in exam scores, or whatever measure of education quality that is analysed, displays how varied the results are. This, in turn, depends on variation in the exam's level of difficulty and its breadth and scope in terms of what is tested.

Studies evaluating the impact of school choice on educational achievement generally use standard deviations as a reference point for the **effect size** of the policies pursued. The effect size measures the variation in achievement between two groups, such as those attending private schools versus those who attend government schools, or between pupils being subjected to competition and those who are not. There is not one commonly accepted standard for what constitutes small, moderate and large effects. However, a common definition among education researchers in the US is that ±0.1 standard deviations are 'small', ±0.2 to ±0.3 are 'moderate', and ±0.5 or larger are 'large' (e.g. Greene, Peterson, and Du 1997; Rainey 2011).

Value added is a measure of pupil progress that estimates the change in pupils' achievement between two periods. The measure is often preferable when analysing the effects of choice/competition in education since it can ameliorate the endogeneity problems that can occur if pupils engage in choice because of inherent ability and/ or background. It is generally easier to obtain high value added with a low baseline score, since one has much higher potential to improve, and researchers usually control for the baseline score to take differential potentials into account. In itself, however, value added is not sufficient to control for endogeneity since pupils might differ systematically on how fast they progress, for example because of differences in innate ability and background. Value added has been highlighted as a preferable source of information when evaluating school effectiveness. However, due to its volatility from year to year, which partly depends on measurement error as noted above, it has proven quite difficult to construct valid measures.

Appendix

Table 1. Sample of the cross-national research on how school choice affects education quality.

	Method	What is analysed?	Results	Effect size	Comment
Fuchs and Woessmann (2007)	OLS	Independent school effects	Positive	Small-to-moderate	No control for endogeneity
West and Woessmann (2010)	IV	Independent school competition effects	Positive	Small-to-large	Can only analyse competition that stems from Catholic population shares in the 19th century
Hanushek, Link and Woessmann (2012)	Fixed effects	School autonomy effects	Mixed (positive in developed countries + negative in developing countries)	Small-to-moderate	Can only evaluate changes over a short time period

Note: the table summarises some, but not all, of the research cited in Chapter 2.1.

Table 2. Summary of the research on the Swedish school choice system's effect on education quality.

	Method	What is analysed?	
Ahlin (2003)	OLS + IV	Free school competition effects + free school effects	
Sandström and Bergström (2005)	OLS + IV	Free school competition effects	
Björklund et al. (2005)	Fixed effects	Free school competition effects + free school effects	
Skolverket (2005)	OLS	Free school competition effects + free school effects	
Söderström (2006)	D-i-D	Effects of introducing selection by ability in upper-secondary schools in Stockholm	
Böhlmark and Lindahl (2007, 2008)	D-i-D	Free school competition effects	
Waldo (2007)	OLS + IV	Free school competition effects	
Dronkers and Avram (2010a)	Propensity score matching	Free school effects	
Tegle (2010)	IV	Free school competition effects + free school effects	
Lundsten and Löfqvist (2011)	Fixed effects	Private equity buyout effects	
Sahlgren (2011a)	OLS + IV	For-profit/non-profit free school effects	
Vlachos (2011a)	OLS	For-profit/non-profit free school effects	
Vlachos (2011b)	D-i-D	Effects of introducing selection by ability in upper-secondary schools in Stockholm	
Böhlmark and Lindahl (2012a)	D-i-D	Free school competition effects	
Niepel (2012)	D-i-D	Total choice/competition effects	

Results	Effect size	Comment
Mixed (positive competition effects in mathematics, but null in English/Swedish + positive free school effects in mathematics/ Swedish, but null in English)	Zero-to-moderate	Only study that controls for previous achievement. Uses flawed dataset
Positive	Moderate-to-large	Uses flawed dataset + question of instrument validity
Positive	Moderate	Analyses only a few years
Positive	Small	No attempt to deal with endogeneity
Null/negative (upper-secondary school GPA)	Small	Flawed methodology. Controls for ninth grade GPA, ignoring the positive incentive effects that occurred
Mixed (positive short-term gains + no strong evidence of long-term gains	Small	Large, longitudinal dataset. Controls for pre-reform trends. Does not control sufficiently for grade inflation
Null	Zero	Question of instrument validity
Null	Zero	Can only control for observable characteristics
Positive	Small-to-large	Question of instrument validity
Mixed (positive/null in lower-secondary school + null in upper-secondary academic track + negative/null in vocational track)	Small	Analyses school-level data but include background characteristics at the municipal level only
Mixed (Positive non-profit/ for-profit free school effect + no differences between for-profit and non-profit free schools)	Moderate-to-large (no difference between for-profits/non-profits)	Question of instrument validity (comparison between for-profit/ non-profit free schools less likely to be biased), school-level data
Mixed (Positive for ninth grade achievement + negative compulsory school for-profit effect on upper-secondary school GPA)	Small	No attempt to control for endogeneity in ninth grade achievement. Controls for ninth grade GPA in upper-secondary school equations, but no control for endogeneity
Positive (ninth grade achievement)	Small-to-large	Finds evidence of incentive effects of the reform
Positive (short- and long-term gains)	Small	Best study on the free school reform thus far. Might not sufficiently control for other changes that occurred at the same time.
Mixed (positive short-term gains + null/positive long-term gains)	Small	Only study that evaluates total school choice/competition

Table 3. Summary of the research on the Chilean school choice system's effect on education quality.

	Method	What is analysed?	
McEwan (2001)	IV	Private/voucher school effects	
Mizala and Romaguera (2002)	OLS	Private/voucher school effects	
Contreras and Macías (2002)	IV	Total competition effects + private competition effects	
Gallego (2002)	IV	Voucher school competition effects	
Sapelli and Viall (2002, 2003)	IV	Voucher school effects	
Carnoy and McEwan (2003)	Fixed effects	Voucher school competition effects	
Sapelli and Viall (2005)	IV	Voucher school effects	
Auguste and Valenzuela (2006)	IV	Voucher school competition effects	
Gallego (2006)	IV	Voucher school competition effects	
Hsieh and Urquiola (2006)	IV + Fixed effects	Voucher school competition effects	
McEwan, Urquiola, and Vegas (2008)	RDD	Voucher school competition effects	
Anand, Mizala, and Repetto (2009)	Propensity score matching	Voucher school effects	
Contreras and Santos (2009)	Structural switches	Voucher school effects	
Elacqua (2009b)	IV	For-profit/non-profit voucher school effects	
Henríquez, Mizala, and Repetto (2009)	IV	Effects of specific voucher school (SIP)	

Results	Effect size	Comment
Mixed (positive effect of fee-paying school + negative effect of voucher school)	Small-to-large	Question of instrument validity
Positive	Moderate-to-large	Endogeneity is not controlled for
Positive	Small	Question of instrument validity
Positive	Small	Question of instrument validity
Positive	Large (taking into account supply-side transfers to municipal schools)	Question of instrument validity
Mixed (positive in urban areas + negative in rural areas)	Moderate	Cannot control for pre-reform trends in test scores
Positive	Large (taking into account supply-side transfers to municipal schools and fees in voucher schools)	Question of instrument validity
Positive	Small	Question of instrument validity
Positive	Small	Question of instrument validity
Null/negative	Zero-to-moderate	Question of instrument validity + cannot control for pre-reform trends in test scores
Null	Zero	Questions of external validity
Positive	Moderate (and no differences between fee-paying and free voucher schools)	Can only control for observable characteristics
Positive	Small	Can only estimate impact among switchers
Mixed (for-profit independent: lower achievement than the best non-profits and on a par with municipal schools. For-profit franchise: on a par with the best non-profits and higher achievement than municipal schools)	Zero-to-moderte	Question of instrument validity (better for comparing for-profit with non-profit schools)
Positive	Large	Only evaluates one chain + question of instrument validity

Table 3. cont.

	Method	What is analysed?	
Bravo, Mukhopadhay, and Todd (2010)	Mix of empirical + simulations	Effects of voucher reform	
Contreras, Sepúlveda and Bustos (2010)	OLS	Voucher school effects	
Dronkers and Avram (2010a)	Propensity score matching	Voucher school effects	
Dronkers and Avram (2010b)	Propensity score matching	Fee-paying school effects	
Palomer and Paredes (2010)	IV + Propensity score matching	Effects of specific voucher school (SIP)	
Rau, Sánchez, and Urzúa (2010)	Mix of empirical + simulations	Voucher school effects	
Chumacero, Gallegos, Paredes (2011)	IV + Fixed effects	Total competition effects	
Elacqua et al. (2011)	IV	Independent/franchise voucher school effects	
Lara, Mizala, and Repetto (2011)	Structural switches	Voucher school effects	
Henríquez et al. (2012)	Propensity score matching	Effects of specific voucher school (SIP)	
Mizala and Torche (2012)	IV	Voucher school effects	

Results	Effect size	Comment
Mixed (positive effect on attainment + no effect on earnings)	Zero-to-large	Not thoroughly empirical (requires assumptions of how people behave) + other changes not necessarily controlled for
Mixed (positive for voucher schools with moderate-high SES + negative for schools with low SES)	Small	No formal control of endogeneity + bad control (selection methods)
Positive	Moderate	Can only control for observable characteristics
Null	Zero	Can only control for observable characteristics
Positive	Large	Only evaluates one chain + question of instrument validity
Positive	Small-to-large	Not thoroughly empirical (requires assumptions of how parents choose schools)
Positive	Large	Question of instrument validity, poor data
Mixed (null/negative effects of independent voucher schools + positive effects of franchise schools)	Small-to-moderate	Question of instrument validity (better for comparing independent and franchise voucher schools)
Positive	Small	Can only estimate impact among switchers
Positive	Large	Can only control for observable characteristics
Mixed (positive in 4th grade + null in 8th grade)	Zero-to-moderate	Question of instrument validity

Table 4. Summary of the research on the Dutch school choice system's effect on education quality.

	Method	What is analysed?	Results	Effect size	Comment
Levin (2004)	OLS + IV	Catholic school effects	Positive	Moderate	Question of instrument validity
Himmler (2009)	IV + Fixed effects	Catholic school competition effects	Positive/Null	Zero-to-moderate	Question of instrument validity + little data for fixed effects models
Dronkers and Avram (2010a)	Propensity score matching	Independent school effects	Null	Zero	Can only control for observable charcteristics
de Haan, Leuven, and Oosterbeek (2011)	IV	Total competition effects	Null	Zero	Questionable measure of competition
Patrinos (2011)	IV	Independent school effects	Positive	Moderate	Question of instrument validity, but uses bias-correction methods to deal with this
Cornelisz (2012)	IV + Propensity score matching	Independent school effects	Mixed (IV: positive/negative/null. Propensity score matching: null)	Zero-to-large	Little theoretical justification for added variables
Dijkgraaf, Gradus, and de Jong (2012)	IV + Fixed effects	Total competition effects	Negative	Small	Question of instrument validity
Noailly, Vujić, and Aouragh (2012)	IV	Total competition effects	Positive	Small	Question of instrument validity

Table 5. Summary of the research on the Danish school choice system's effect on education quality.

	Method	What is analysed?	Results	Effect size	Comment
Rangvid (2003)	IV	Independent school effects	Null	Zero	Question of instrument validity
Nannestad (2004)	OLS	Independent school competition effects	Null	Zero	No control for endogeneity
Andersen and Serritzlew (2007)	OLS	Independent school competition effects	Mixed (null effects on achievement + increasing costs)	Zero-to-moderate	No control for endogeneity
Andersen (2008)	IV	Independent school effects	Mixed (null in written tests + negative in oral tests)	Zero-to-large	Question of instrument validity
Rangvid (2008)	OLS	Independent school effects	Mixed (positive Catholic and grammar school effects + negative/null effects of other school types)	Zero-to-moderate	No control for endogeneity
Christoffersen and Larsen (2010a)	OLS	Independent school effects	Positive	? (No descriptive data)	No control for endogeneity
Dronkers and Avram (2010a)	Propensity score matching	Independent schools effects	Null	Zero	Can only control for observable characteristics

Table 6. Sample of research from other countries on how school choice affects education quality, with a particular focus on the impact of small-scale reforms.

	Method	What is analysed?	
Hoxby (2000)	IV	Tiebout competition effects	
Cullen, Jacob, and Levitt (2006)	Lottery	Public school choice effects	
Newhouse and Beegle (2006)	IV + Fixed effects	Private school effects	
Rothstein (2007)	IV	Tiebout competition effects	
Chakrabarti (2008)	D-i-D	Voucher competition effects	
Chan (2009)	D-i-D + IV	Tax credit competition effects	
Cohen-Zada (2009)	IV	Private school effects	
Nicotera, Mendiburo, and Berends (2009)	Fixed effects	Charter school effects	
Peterson and Chingos (2009)	Fixed effects	For-profit/non-profit school effects	
Figlio and Hart (2010)	D-i-D	Tax credit competition effects	
French and Kingdon (2010)	Fixed effects	Private school effects	
Gleason et al. (2010)	Lotteries	Charter school effects	
Lavy (2010)	RDD + D-i-D	Public school choice effects	
Abdulkadiroğlu et al. (2011)	Lottery	Charter/pilot school effects	
Andrabi et al. (2011)	IV + Fixed effects	Private school effects	
Bettinger, Kremer, and Saavedra (2010)	Lottery	Voucher school effects	
Davis and Raymond (2011)	Matching + Fixed effects	Charter school effects	

Results	Effect size	Comment
Positive	Small-to-moderate	Question of instrument construction
Mixed (negative or null overall depending on metric)	Small	Randomised + can only estimate effects of over-subscribed schools
Mixed (negative with family-fixed effects + zero with instrument)	Zero-to-moderate	Question of instrument validity
Null	Zero	Question of instrument construction
Positive	Moderate-to-large	Good empirical strategy
Positive	Small	One of two analyses of tax-credit school competition
Null	Zero	Can only estimate private school effects due to historical Catholic shares
Positive	Moderate-to-large	Can only estimate the effects among switchers
Mixed (negative non-profit effect + positive for-profit effect)	Small-to-moderate	Rare study on for-proft/non-profit differences
Positive	Small	One of two analyses of tax-credit school competition. Clean design to estimate short-term competition effects
Positive	Small-to-moderate	Uses family-fixed effects
Mixed (positive among schools serving disadvantaged pupils + negative among schools serving advantaged pupils)	Small-to-large	Randomised + can only estimate effects of over-subscribed schools
Positive	Moderate-to-large	Evaluates change from forced bussing to free choice
Mixed (positive for charter schools + null or negative for pilot schools)	Moderate-to-large (charter), null or small (pilot)	Randomised + can only estimate effects of over-subscribed schools
Positive	Moderate-to-large	Question of instrument validity
Positive	Moderate-to-large	Randomised + can only estimate effects of over-subscribed schools
Mixed (some states positive, some negative)	Small-to-moderate	Can only estimate the effects among switchers or control for observable characteristics

Table 6. cont.

	Method	What is analysed?	
Deming et al. (2011)	Lottery	Public school choice effects	
Imberman (2011b)	IV + Fixed effects	Charter school competition effects	
Lefebvre, Merrigan, and Verstraete (2011)	Structural switches	Private (subsidised) school effects	
Carattini et al. (2012)	IV	Catholic school competition effects	
Hastings, Neilson, and Zimmerman (2012)	Lottery	Charter school and magnet school effects	
Ni and Rorrer (2012)	Fixed effects	Charter school effects	
Singh (2012)	OLS	Private school effects	

Note: the table summarises some, but not all, of the research cited in Chapter 2.3.

Results	Effect size	Comment
Positive	Small-to-moderate	Randomised + can only estimate effects of over-subscribed schools
Mixed (negative for cognitive achievement + positive for non-cognitive outcomes)	Small-to-moderate	Question of instrument validity
Positive	Small-to-moderate	Can only estimate effects among switchers
Mixed (positive in mathematics + null in reading)	Zero-to-small	Question of instrument validity
Positive	Small-to-large (larger for charter schools)	Randomised + can only estimate effects of over-subscribed schools
Mixed (first negative, later positive)	Small-to-moderate	Takes into account maturation effects
Mixed (positive in rural areas + null in urban areas)	Zero-to-moderate	Controls for detailed background variables and prior achievement

Table 7. Summary of the research on the English school choice system's effect on education quality.

	Method	What is analysed?	Results	Effect size	Comment
Levačić and Hardman (1999)	OLS	Grant-maintained school effects	Null	Zero	Small sample, school-level data, no control for endogeneity
Bradley et al. (2000)	Fixed effects	Quality competition effects	Positive	Small-to-moderate	School-level data, no control for endogeneity, might pick up district trends
Bradley, Johnes, and Millington (2001)	Fixed effects	Structural competition effects	Positive	Small-to-moderate	School-level data, no control for endogeneity, might pick up district trends
Bradley and Taylor (2002)	Fixed effects	Quality competition effects	Positive	Moderate	School-level data, no control for endogeneity, might pick up district trends
Levačić (2004)	OLS	Perceived and structural competition effects	Mixed (positive perceived competition effects + null structural competition effects)	Moderate-to-large	Small sample, school-level data, no control for endogeneity
Burgess and Slater (2006)	D-i-D	Structural competition effects	Mixed (null overall + positive for foundation/voluntary-aided schools)	Zero-to-large	Can only estimate short-term change in competition
Gibbons and Silva (2008)	IV + Fixed effects	School density effects	Positive	Small	Effects might not be due to competition, but urban density
Gibbons, Machin, and Silva (2008)	IV	Total choice and competition effects	Mixed (null choice effects + positive competition effects on voluntary-aided schools + negative competition effects on other schools)	Zero-to-moderate	Question of instrument validity

Table 7. cont.

	Method	What is analysed?	Results	Effect size	Comment
Clark (2009)	RDD	Grant-maintained school effects + grant-maintained school competition effects	Mixed (positive grant-maintained school effects + null grant-maintained school competition effects) schoo;lcompetition effect)	Zero-to-moderate	Flawed RDD
Allen and Vignoles (2010)	IV	Faith school competition effects	Null	Zero	Does not analyse effects on different school types
Bradley and Taylor (2010)	Fixed effects	Structural and quality competition effects	Positive	Small-to-moderate	School-level data, no control for endogeneity
Dronkers and Avram (2010b)	Propensity score matching	Fee-paying independent school effects	Null	Zero	Can only control for observable characteristics
Gibbons and Silva (2011b)	Structural switches	Faith school effects	Positive/null	Small/zero	Foundation and voluntary-aided schools form one category, although the latter are majority controlled
Machin and Vernoit (2011)	D-i-D	Academies effect + academies competition effects	Positive	Small-to-moderate	Focuses on pass threshold
Allen (2012a)	RDD	Grant-maintained/ foundation school effects	Null	Zero	Does not evaluate maturation effects + equates grant-maintained and foundation school status

References

Abdulkadiroğlu, Atila, Joshua D. Angrist, Susan N. Dynarski, Thomas J. Kane, and Parag A. Pathak. 2011. 'Accountability and Flexibility in Public Schools: Evidence from Boston's Charters and Pilots.' *Quarterly Journal of Economics* 126(2):699–748.

Abdulkadiroğlu, Atila, Joshua D. Angrist, and Parag A. Pathak. 2012. 'The Elite Illusion: Achievement Effects at Boston and New York Exam Schools.' Discussion Paper No. 6790, Institute for the Study of Labor, Bonn.

Abdulkadiroğlu, Atila, Parag Pathak, Alvin E. Roth, and Tayfun Sonmez. 2006. 'Changing the Boston School Choice Mechanism.' NBER Working Paper No. 11965, National Bureau of Economic Research, Cambridge, MA.

Adnett, Nick and Peter Davies. 2002. *Markets for Schooling: An Economic Analysis*. London: Routledge.

Agasisti, Tommaso. 2008. 'Educational Vouchers in Italy: Theory, Design, Effects.' Unpublished Manuscript, Department of Management, Economics and Industrial Engineering, Politecnico di Milano, Milano.

Agasisti, Tommaso. 2011. 'The Efficiency of Italian Secondary Schools and the Potential Role of Competition: A Data Envelopment Analysis Using OECD-PISA 2006 Data.' *Education Economics* doi:10.1080/09645292.2010.511840.

Agasisti, Tommaso and Samuele Murtini. 2011. '"Perceived Competition" and Performance in Italian Secondary Schools: New Evidence from OECD-PISA 2006.' *British Educational Research Journal* doi:10.1080/01411926.2011.588314.

Aghion, Philippe, Leah Boustan, Caroline Hoxby, and Jerome Vandenbussche. 2009. 'The Causal Impact of Education on Economic Growth: Evidence from the United States.' Brookings Papers on Economic Activitiy, Brookings Institution, Washington, DC.

Ahlin, Åsa. 2003. 'Does School Competition Matter? Effects of a Large-Scale School Choice Reform on Student Performance.' Working Paper, Department of Economics, Uppsala University, Uppsala, Sweden.

Akabayashi, Hideo. 2006. 'Average Effects of School Choice on Educational Attainment: Evidence from Japanese High School Attendance Zones.' Unpublished Manuscript, Faculty of Economics, Keio University, Tokyo.

Akabayashi, Hideo and Hiroko Araki. 2011. 'Do Education Vouchers Prevent Dropout at Private High Schools? Evidence from Japanese Policy Changes.' *Journal of the Japanese and International Economies* 25:183–198.

Albert, Cecilia and Carlos García-Serrano. 2010. 'Cleaning the Slate? School Choice and Educational Outcomes in Spain.' *Higher Education* 60:559–582.

Algan, Yann, Pierre Cahuc, and Andrei Shleifer. 2011. 'Teaching Practices and Social Capital.' NBER Working Paper No. 17527, National Bureau of Economic Research, Cambridge, MA.

Allcott, Hunt and Daniel E. Ortega. 2009. 'The Performance of Decentralized School Systems: Evidence from Fe Y Alegría in República Bolivariana de Venezuela' in Barrera-Osorio, Felipe, Harry A. Patrinos, and Quentin Wodon (eds), *Emerging Evidence on Vouchers and Faith-Based Providers in Education: Case Studies from Africa, Latin America, and Asia*, pp. 81–98. Washington, DC: World Bank.

Allen, Rebecca. 2008. 'Choice-Based Secondary School Admissions in England: Social Stratification and the Distribution of Educational Outcomes.' PhD Dissertation, Institute of Education, University of London, London.

Allen, Rebecca. 2010. 'Replicating Swedish Free School Reforms in England.' *Research in Public Policy* 10:4–7.

Allen, Rebecca. 2012a. 'Measuring Foundation School Effectiveness Using English Administrative Data, Survey Data and a Regression Discontinuity Design.' *Education Economics* doi:10.1080/09645292.2012.687197.

Allen, Rebecca. 2012b. 'Reporting GCSE Performance by Groups is Fraught with Problems.' Blog Post, Personal Blog, http://rebeccaallen.co.uk/2012/01/22/reporting-gcse-performance-by-groups-is-fraught-with-problems/ (accessed 18.02.13).

Allen, Rebecca and Simon Burgess. 2010. 'The Future of Competition and Accountability in Education.' Paper in Public Service Reform Series, 2020 Public Services Trust & Economic and Social Research Council, London.

Allen, Rebecca and Simon Burgess. 2011. 'Can School League Tables Help Parents Choose Schools?' *Fiscal Studies* 32(2):245–261.

Allen, Rebecca and Simon Burgess. 2012. 'How Should We Treat Under-Performing Schools? A Regression Discontinuity Analysis of School Inspections in England.' Working Paper No. 12/287, The Centre for Market and Public Organisation, University of Bristol, Bristol.

Allen, Rebecca, Simon Burgess, and Leigh McKenna. 2012. 'The Short-Run Impact of Using Lotteries for School Admissions: Early Results from Brighton and Hove's Reforms.' *Transactions of the Institute of British Geographers* doi:10.1111/j.1475–5661.2012.00511.x.

Allen, Rebecca and Anna Vignoles. 2010. 'Can School Competition Improve Standards? The Case of Faith Schools in England.' Working Paper No. 09–04, Department of Quantitative Social Science, Institute of Education, University of London, London.

Alpanda, Sami and Adam Honig. 2009. 'The Impact of Central Bank Independence on Political Monetary Cycles in Advanced and Developing Nations.' *Journal of Money, Credit and Banking* 41(7):1365–1389.

Altonji, Joseph G., Todd E. Elder, and Christopher R. Taber. 2005a. 'An Evaluation of Instrumental Variable Strategies for Estimating the Effects of Catholic Schools.' *Journal of Human Resources* 40(4):791–821.

Altonji, Joseph G., Todd E. Elder, and Christopher R. Taber. 2005b. 'Selection on Observed and Unobserved Variables: Assessing the Effectiveness of Catholic Schools.' *Journal of Political Economy* 113(1):151–184.

Amini, Chiara and Simon Commander. 2011. 'Educational Scores: How Does Russia Fare?' Discussion Paper No. 6033, Institute for the Study of Labor, Bonn.

Anand, Priyanka, Alejandra Mizala, and Andrea Repetto. 2009. 'Using School Scholarships to Estimate the Effect of Private Education.' *Economics of Education Review* 28(3):370–381.

Andersen, Simon C. 2008. 'Private Schools and the Parents that Choose Them: Empirical Evidence from the Danish School Voucher System.' *Scandinavian Political Studies* 31(1):44–68.

Andersen, Simon C. and Søren Serritzlew. 2007. 'The Unintended Effects of Private School Competition.' *Journal of Public Administration Research and Theory* 17(2):335–356.

Andrabi, Tahir, Natalie Bau, Jishnu Das, and Asim I. Khwaja. 2010. 'Bad Public Schools are Public Bads: Civic Values and Test-Scores in Public and Private Schools.' Unpublished Manuscript, Population Research Centre, University of Chicago, Chicago, IL.

Andrabi, Tahir, Jishnu Das, and Asim I. Khwaja. 2009. 'Report Cards: The Impact of Providing School and Child Test-Scores on Educational Markets.' Unpublished Manuscript, Poverty Action Lab, New York.

Andrabi, Tahir, Jishnu Das, and Asim I. Khwaja. 2013. 'Students Today, Teachers Tomorrow: Identifying Constraints on the Provision of Education.' *Journal of Public Economics* doi:10.1016/j.jpubeco.2012.12.003.

Andrabi, Tahir, Jishnu Das, Asim I. Khwaja, and Tristan Zajonc. 2011. 'Do Value-Added Estimates Add Value? Accounting for Learning Dynamics.' *American Economic Journal: Applied Economics* 3(3):29–54.

Angrist, Joshua, Eric Bettinger, Erik Bloom, Elizabeth King, and Michael Kremer. 2002. 'Vouchers for Private Schooling in Colombia: Evidence from a Randomized Natural Experiment.' *American Economic Review* 92(5):1535–1558.

Angrist, Joshua, Eric Bettinger, and Michael Kremer. 2006. 'Long-Term Educational Consequences of Secondary School Vouchers: Evidence from Administrative Records in Colombia.' *American Economic Review* 96(3):847–862.

Angrist, Joshua D., Susan M. Dynarski, Thomas J. Kane, Parag A. Pathak, and Christopher R. Walters. 2010. 'Inputs and Impacts in Charter Schools: KIPP Lynn.' *American Economic Review* 100:1–5.

Angrist, Joshua D., Susan M. Dynarski, Thomas J. Kane, Parag A. Pathak, and Christopher R. Walters. 2012. 'Who Benefits from KIPP?' *Journal of Policy Analysis and Management* 31(4):837–860.

Angrist, Joshua D., Parag A. Pathak, and Christopher Walters. 2011. 'Explaining Charter School Effectiveness.' NBER Working Paper 17332, National Bureau of Economic Research, Cambridge, MA.

Antelius, Jesper. 2007. 'Fristående grundskolor och kommunernas kostnader' in Lindbom, Anders (ed.), *Friskolorna och framtiden*, pp. 59–82. Stockholm: Institutet för Framtidsstudier.

Ariga, Kenn and Giorgio Brunello. 2007. 'Does Secondary School Tracking Affect Performance? Evidence from IALS.' IZA Discussion Paper No. 2643, Institute for the Study of Labor, Bonn.

Asadullah, Mohammad N., Nazmul Chaudhury, and Amit Dar. 2009. 'Assessing the Performance of Madrasas in Rural Bangladesh' in Berrera-Osorio, Felipe, Harry A. Patrinos, and Quentin Wodon, *Emerging Evidence on Vouchers and Faith-Based Providers in Education: Case Studies from Africa, Latin America, and Asia*, pp. 137–148. Washington, DC: World Bank.

Aslam, Monazza. 2009. 'The Relative Effectiveness of Government and Private Schools in Pakistan: Are Girls Worse Off?' *Education Economics* 17(3):329–354.

Astle, Julian, Sheree Bryant, and Charles Hotham. 2011. 'School Choice and Accountability: Putting Parents in Charge.' Report, Centre Forum, London.

Atkinson, Adele, Simon Burgess, Bronwyn Croxson, Paul Gregg, Carol Propper, Helen Slater, and Deborah Wilson. 2009. 'Evaluating the Impact of Performance-Related Pay for Teachers in England.' *Labour Economics* 16:251–261.

Auguste, Sebastian and Juan P. Valenzuela. 2006. 'Is It Just Cream Skimming? School Vouchers in Chile.' Fundación de Investigaciones Económicas Latinoamericanas, Buenos Aires.

Backiny-Yetna and Quentin Wodon. 2009. 'Comparing the Performance of Faith-Based and Government Schools in the Democratic Republic of Congo' in Barrera-Osorio, Felipe, Harry A. Patrinos, and Quentin Wodon (eds), *Emerging Evidence on Vouchers and Faith-Based Providers in Education*, pp. 119–136. Washington, DC.

Baird, Jo-Anne. 2007. 'Alternative Conceptions of Comparability' in Newton, Paul, Jo-Anne Baird, Harvey Goldstein, Helen Patrick, and Peter Tymms (eds), *Techniques for Monitoring the Comparability of Examination Standards*, pp. 124–165. London: Qualifications and Curriculum Authority.

Bal, José and Jos de Jong. 2007. 'Improving School Leadership – OECD Review. Background Report for the Netherlands.' Background Report, Directorate for Education, OECD, Paris.

Barlevy, Gadi and Derek Neal. 2012. 'Pay for Percentile.' *American Economic Review* 102(5):1805–1831.

Barnard, John, Constantine E. Frangakis, Jennifer L. Hill, and Donald B. Rubin. 2003. 'Principal Stratification Approach to Broken Randomized Experiments: A Case Study of School Choice Vouchers in New York City.' *Journal of the American Statistical Association* 98(462):299–323.

Bayer, Patrick and Robert McMillan. 2010. 'Choice and Competition in Education Markets.' Economic Research Initiatives at Duke (ERID) Working Paper No. 48, Department of Economics, Duke University, Durham, NC.

Belfield, Clive R. 2006. 'The Evidence on Education Vouchers: An Application to the Cleveland Scholarship and Tutoring Program.' Occasional Paper No. 112, National Center for the Study of Privatization in Education, Columbia University, New York.

Belfield, Clive R. and Henry M. Levin. 2002. 'The Effects of Competition between Schools on Educational Outcomes: A Review for the United States.' *Review of Educational Research* 72(2):279–341.

Bellei, Christian. 2005. 'The Private-Public School Controversy: The Case of Chile.' Conference Paper, Harvard Graduate School of Education, Harvard University, Cambridge, MA.

Bergh, Andreas and Gissur Ó. Erlingsson. 2009. 'Liberalization without Retrenchment: Understanding the Consensus on Swedish Welfare State Reforms.' *Scandinavian Political Studies* 32(1):71–93.

Berkowitz, Daniel and Hoekstra, Mark. 2011. 'Does High School Quality Matter? Evidence from Admissions Data.' *Economics of Education Review* 30(2):280–288

Bettinger, Eric P. 2005. 'The Effect of Charter Schools on Charter Students and Public Schools.' *Economics of Education Review* 24(2):133–147.

Bettinger, Eric P. 2011. 'Educational Vouchers in International Contexts' in Hanushek, Eric A., Stephen Machin, and Ludger Woessmann, *Handbook of the Economics of Education*, pp. 551–572. Amsterdam: North Holland.

Bettinger, Eric, Michael Kremer, and Juan E. Saavedra. 2010. 'Are Education Vouchers Only Redistributive?' *Economic Journal* 120:204–228.

Betts, Julian R. 2011. 'The Economics of Tracking in Education' in Hanushek, Eric A., Stephen Machin, and Ludger Woessmann (eds), *Handbook of the Economics of Education*, pp. 341–381. Amsterdam: Elsevier.

Betts, Julian R. and Richard C. Atkinson. 2012. 'Better Research Needed on the Impact of Charter Schools.' *Science* 335:171–172.

Betts, Julian R., Lorien A. Rice, Andrew C. Zau, Emily Y. Tang, and Cory R. Koedel. 2006. 'Does School Choice Work? Effects on Student Integration and Achievement.' Report, Public Policy Institute of California, San Francisco, CA.

Betts, Julian R. and Emily Y. Tang. 2008. 'Value-Added and Experimental Studies of the Effect of Charter Schools on Student Achievement: A Literature Review.' Report, National Charter School Research Project, Center on Reinventing Public Education, University of Washington, Seattle, WA.

Betts, Julian R. and Emily Y. Tang. 2011. 'The Effect of Charter Schools on Student Achievement: A Meta-Analysis of the Literature.' Report, Center on Reinventing Public Education, University of Washington Bothell, Seattle, WA.

Bifulco, Robert, Casey D. Cobb, and Courtney Bell. 2009. 'Can Interdistrict Choice Boost Student Achievement? The Case of Connecticut's Interdistrict Magnet School Program.' *Educational Evaluation and Policy Analysis* 31(4):323–345.

Bifulco, Robert and Helen F. Ladd. 2006. 'The Impacts of Charter Schools on Student Achievement: Evidence from North Carolina.' *Education Finance and Policy* 1:50–90.

Bishop, John. 2006. 'Drinking from the Fountain of Knowledge: Student Incentive to Study and Learn – Externalities, Information Problems and Peer Pressure' in Hanushek, Eric A., Stephen Machin, and Ludger Woessmann (eds), *Handbook of the Economics of Education*, pp. 909–944. Amsterdam: North-Holland.

Björklund, Anders, Melissa A. Clark, Per-Anders Edin, Peter Fredriksson, and Alan Krueger. 2005. *The Market Comes to Education in Sweden: An Evaluation of Sweden's Surprising School Reforms.* New York: Russell Sage Foundation.

Björklund, Anders, Peter Fredriksson, Jan-Eric Gustafsson, and Björn Öckert. 2010. 'Den svenska utbildningspolitikens arbetsmarknadseffekter: vad säger forskningen?' Report No. 2010:13, Institutet för arbetsmarknadspolitisk utvärdering, Uppsala, Sweden.

Böhlmark, Anders and Helena Holmlund. 2011. '20 år med förändringar i skolan: Vad har hänt med likvärdigheten?' Report, Studieförbundet Näringsliv och Samhälle, Stockholm.

Böhlmark, Anders and Mikael Lindahl. 2007. 'The Impact of School Choice on Pupil Achievement, Segregation and Costs: Swedish Evidence.' IZA Discussion Paper No. 2786, Institute for the Study of Labor, Bonn.

Böhlmark, Anders and Mikael Lindahl. 2008. 'Does School Privatization Improve Educational Achievement? Evidence from Sweden's Voucher Reform.' IZA Discussion Paper No. 3691, Institute for the Study of Labor, Bonn.

Böhlmark, Anders and Mikael Lindahl. 2012a. 'Independent Schools and Long-Run Educational Outcomes: Evidence from Sweden's Large Scale Voucher Reform.' IZA Discussion Paper No. 6683, Institute for the Study of Labor, Bonn.

Böhlmark, Anders and Mikael Lindahl. 2012b. 'Har den växande friskolesektorn varit bra för elevernas utbildningsresultat på kort och lång sikt?' Report No. 2012:17, Institutet för arbetsmarknads- och utbildningspolitisk utvärdering, Stockholm.

Bold, Tessa, Mwangi Kimenyi, Germano Mwabu, and Justin Sandefur. 2011. 'The High Return to Private Schooling in a Low-Income Country.' Working Paper 279, Center for Global Development, Washington, DC.

Bonesrønning, Hans and Linn R. Naper. 2005. 'Does Competition from Private Schools Raise Public Schools' Performance? New Evidence from Norway.' Working Paper, Centre for Economic Policy Research, London.

Bonilla, Juan D. 2010. 'Contracting Out Public Schools for Academic Achievement: Evidence from Colombia.' Job Market Paper, Department of Economics, University of Maryland, College Park, MD.

Booker, Kevin, Scott M. Gilpatric, Timothy Gronberg, and Dennis Jansen. 2007. 'The Impact of Charter School Attendance on Student Performance.' *Journal of Public Economics* 91:849–876.

Booker, Kevin, Scott M. Gilpatric, Timothy Gronberg, and Dennis Jansen. 2008. 'The Effect of Charter Schools on Traditional Public School Students in Texas: Are Children Who Stay Behind Left Behind?' *Journal of Urban Economics* 64:123–145.

Booker, Kevin, Tim R. Sass, Brian Gill, and Ron Zimmer. 2011. 'The Effect of Charter High Schools on Educational Attainment.' *Journal of Labor Economics* 29(2):377–415.

Bradley, Steve, Robert Crouchley, Jim Millington, and Jim Taylor. 2000. 'Testing for Quasi-Market Forces in Secondary Education.' *Oxford Bulletin of Economics and Statistics* 62(3):357–390.

Bradley, Steve, Geraint Johnes, and Jim Millington. 2001. 'The Effect of Competition on the Efficiency of Secondary Schools in England.' *European Journal of Operation Research* 135:545–568.

Bradley, Steve and Jim Taylor. 2002. 'The Effect of the Quasi-Market on the Efficiency-Equity Trade-Off in the Secondary School Sector.' *Bulletin of Economic Research* 54(3):295–314.

Bradley, Steve and Jim Taylor. 2010. 'Diversity, Choice and the Quasi-Market: An Empirical Analysis of Secondary Education Policy in England.' *Oxford Bulletin of Economics and Statistics* 72(1):1–26.

Brandt, Nicola. 2010. 'Chile: Climbing on Giants' Shoulders: Better Schools for All Chilean Children.' Working Paper No. 784, OECD Economics, OECD, Paris.

Brasington, David M. and Donald R. Haurin. 2006. 'Educational Outcomes and House Values: A Test of the Value-Added Approach.' *Journal of Regional Science* 46(2):245–268.

Brasington, David M. and Diane Hite. 2012. 'School Choice and Perceived School Quality.' *Economics Letters* 116(3):451–453.

Bravo, David, Sankar Mukhopadhyay, and Petra E. Todd. 2010. 'Effects of School Reform on Education and Labor Market Performance: Evidence from Chile's Universal Voucher System.' *Quantitative Economics* 1(1):47–95.

Bray, Mark. 2011. 'The Challenge of Shadow Education: Private Tutoring and Its Implications for Policy Makers in Europe.' Report, European Commission, Brussels.

Bray, Mark and Chad Lykins. 2012. 'Shadow Education: Private Supplementary Tutoring and Its Implications for Policy Makers in Asia.' CERC Monograph No. 9, Asian Development Bank, Mandaluyong City.

Briggs, Derek C. 2001. 'The Effect of Admissions Test Preparation: Evidence from NELS:88.' *Chance* 14(1):10–18.

Brummet, Quentin. 2012. 'The Effect of School Closings on Student Achievement.' Job Market Paper, Department of Economics, Michigan State University, East Lansing, MI.

Brunner, Eric J., Jennifer Imazeki, and Stephen L. Ross. 2010. 'Universal Vouchers and Racial and Ethnic Segregation.' *Review of Economics and Statistics* 92(4):912–927.

Bruns, Barbara, Deon Filmer, and Harry A. Patrinos. 2011. *Making Schools Work: New Evidence on Accountability Reforms*. Washington, DC: World Bank.

Bryson, Alex, Richard Dorsett, and Susan Purdon. 2002. 'The Use of Propensity Score Matching in the Evaluation of Active Labour Market Policies.' Working Paper No. 4, Department for Work and Pensions Research, London.

Buchanan, James M. 1997. 'The Balanced Budget Amendment: Clarifying the Arguments.' *Public Choice* 90:117–138.

Buchanan, James M. and Gordon Tullock. 1962. *The Calculus of Consent: Logical Foundations of Constitutional Democray.* Ann Arbor, MI: University of Michigan Press.

Buddin, Richard and Ron Zimmer. 2005. 'Student Achievement in charter schools: A Complex Picture.' *Journal of Policy Analysis and Management* 24(2):351–371.

Bui, Sa A., Steven G. Craig, and Scott A. Imberman. 2011. 'Is Gifted Education a Bright Idea? Assessing the Impact of Gifted and Talented Programs on Students.' NBER Working Paper No. 17089, National Bureau of Economic Research, Cambridge, MA.

Bukowska, Grazyna and Siwinska-Gorzelak. 2011. 'School Competition and the Quality of Education: Introducing Market Incentives into Public Services. The Case of Poland.' *Economics of Transition* 19(1):151–177.

Bulle, Nathalie. 2011. 'Comparing OECD Educational Models through the Prism of PISA.' *Comparative Education* 47(4):503–521.

Burgess, Simon and Adam Briggs. 2010. 'School Assignment, School Choice and Social Mobility.' *Economics of Education Review* 29:639–649.

Burgess, Simon, Ellen Greaves, Anna Vignoles, and Deborah Wilson. 2009. 'What Parents Want: School Preferences and School Choice.' Working Paper No. 09/222, Centre for Market and Public Organisation, Bristol Institute of Public Affairs, University of Bristol, Bristol.

Burgess, Simon, Ellen Greaves, Anna Vignoles, and Deborah Wilson. 2011. 'Parental Choice of Primary School in England: What Types of School do Parents Really Have Available to Them?' *Policy Studies* 32(5):531–547.

Burgess, Simon, Carol Propper, and Deborah Wilson. 2007. 'The Impact of School Choice in England: Implications from the Economic Evidence.' *Policy Studies* 28(2):129–143.

Burgess, Simon and Helen Slater. 2006. 'Using Boundary Changes to Estimate the Impact of School Competition on Test Scores.' Working Paper No. 06/158, Centre for Market and Public Organisation, Bristol Institute of Public Affairs, University of Bristol, Bristol.

Burgess, Simon, Deborah Wilson, and Jack Worth. 2010. 'A Natural Experiment in School Accountability: The Impact of School Performance Information on Pupil Progress and Sorting.' Working Paper No. 10/246, Centre for Market and Public Organisation, Bristol Institute of Public Affairs, University of Bristol, Bristol.

Byrnes, Vaughan. 2009. 'Getting a Feel for the Market: The Use of Privatized School Management in Philadelphia.' *American Journal of Education* 115:437–455.

Caldas, Stephen J. and Sylvain Bernier. 2012. 'The Effects of Competition from Private Schooling on French Public School Districts in the Province of Québec.' *Journal of Economic Research* 105(5):353–365.

Camargo, Braz, Rafael Camelo, Sergio Firpo, and Vladimir Ponczek. 2011. 'Test Scores Disclosure and School Performance.' Working Paper No. 11/2011, Center for Applied Microeconomics, São Paolo School of Economics, São Paolo.

Carattini, Juliana F., Angela K. Dills, Mulholland S. E, and Rachel B. Sederberg. 2012. 'Catholic Schools, Competition, and Public School Quality.' *Economics Letters* 117(1):334–336.

Card, David, Martin Dooley, and Abigail Payne. 2010. 'School Competition and Efficiency with Publicly Funded Catholic Schools.' *American Economic Journal: Applied Economics* 2(4):150–176.

Carlson, Deven E., Joshua M. Cowen, and David J. Fleming. 2012. 'School Choice and School Accountability: Evidence from a Private Voucher Program in Milwaukee, Wisconsin.' Conference Paper, INVALSI Improving Education Conference, Rome.

Carnoy, Martin, Frank Adamson, Amita Chudgar, Thomas F. Luschei, and John F. Witte. 2007. *Vouchers and Public School Performance: A Case Study of the Milwaukee Parental Choice Program*. Washington, DC: Economic Policy Institute.

Carnoy, Martin, Iliana Brodziak, Andres Molina, and Miguel Socías. 2007. 'The Limitations of Teacher Pay Incentive Programs Based on Inter-Cohort Comparisons: The Case of Chile's SNED.' *Education Finance and Policy* 2(3):189–227.

Carnoy, Martin and Patrick J. McEwan 2003. 'Does Privatization Improve Education? The Case of Chile's National Voucher Plan' in Plank, David N. and Gary Sykes (eds), *Choosing Choice: School Choice in an International Perspective*, pp. 24–44. New York: Teachers College Press.

Carr, Matthew. 2011. 'The Impact of Ohio's EdChoice on Traditional Public School Performance.' *Cato Journal* 31(2):257–284.

Carruthers, Celeste K. 2011. 'New Schools, New Students, New Teachers: Evaluating the Effectiveness of Charter Schools.' *Economics of Education Review* doi:10.1016/j. econedurev.2011.06.001.

Chakrabarti, Rajashri. 2008. 'Can Increasing Private School Participation and Monetary Loss in a Voucher Program Affect Public School Performance? Evidence from Milwaukee.' *Journal of Public Economics* 92:1371–1393.

Chakrabarti, Rajashri. 2013. 'Do Vouchers Lead to Sorting under Random Private School Selection? Evidence from the Milwaukee Voucher Program.' *Economics of Education Review* doi:10.1016/j.econedurev.2013.01.009.

Chakrabarti, Rajashri and Joydeep Roy 2010. 'The Economics of Parental Choice' in Peterson, Penelope, Eva Baker, and Barry McGaw (eds), *International Encyclopedia of Education (Third Edition)*, pp. 367–373. Oxford.

Chan, Ping C. W. 2009. 'School Choice, Competition, and Public School Performance.' PhD Dissertation, Department of Economics, University of Toronto, Toronto.

Cheo, Roland and Euston Quah. 2005. 'Mothers, Maids and Tutors: An Empirical Evaluation of their Effect on Children's Academic Grades in Singapore.' *Education Economics* 13(3):269–285.

Cherchye, Laurens, Kristof De Witte, Erwin Ooghe, and Ides Nicaise. 2010. 'Efficiency and Equity in Private and Public Education: A Nonparametric Comparison.' *European Journal of Operational Research* 202(2):563–573.

Chetty, Raj, John N. Friedman, and Jonah E. Rockoff. 2011. 'The Long-Term Impacts of Teachers: Teacher Value-Added and Student Outcomes in Adulthood.' NBER Working Paper No. 17699, National Bureau of Economic Research, Cambridge, MA.

Chiang, Hanley. 2009. 'How Accountability Pressure on Failing Schools Affects Student Achievement.' *Journal of Public Economics* 93:1045–1057.

Chingos, Matthew M., Michael Henderson, and Martin West. 2012. 'Citizen Perceptions of Government Service Quality: Evidence from Public Schools.' *Quarterly Journal of Political Science* 7:411–445.

Chingos, Matthew M. and Paul E. Peterson. 2012. 'The Effects of School Vouchers on College Enrollment: Experimental Evidence from New York City.' The Brown Center on Education Policy at Brookings & Harvard's Program on Education Policy and Governance, Brookings Institution and Harvard University, Washington, DC/Cambridge, MA.

Choi, Álvaro, Jorge Calero, and Josep-Oriol Escardíbul. 2011. 'Hell to Touch the Sky? Private Tutoring and Academic Achievement in Korea.' Working Paper No. 2011/10, Barcelona Institute of Economics, University of Barcelona, Barcelona.

Chowdry, Haroon, Ellen Greaves, and Luke Sibieta. 2010. 'The Pupil Premium: Assessing the Options.' IFS Commentary C113, Institute for Fiscal Studies, London.

Christoffersen, Henrik and Karsten B. Larsen. 2010a. 'Comparison of Cost and Performance in the Private and Public Primary and Lower Secondary Schools in Denmark.' CEPOS Working Paper No. 13, Center for Political Studies, Copenhagen.

Christoffersen, Henrik and Karsten B. Larsen. 2010b. 'Den fysiske tilstand af folkeskoler og privatskolers bygninger.' CEPOS Working Paper No. 7, Center for Political Studies, Copenhagen.

Christoffersen, Henrik and Karsten B. Larsen. 2012. 'Når befolkningen får viden om grundskolernes kvalitet – et studie af forskellen mellem markedsløsninger og politiske løsninger.' CEPOS arbejdspapir nr. 20, Centre for Political Studies (CEPOS), Copenhagen.

Chubb, John E. 2001. 'The Private Can be Public.' *Education Next* 1(1).

Chubb, John E. and Terry M. Moe. 1988. 'Politics, Markets and the Organization of Schools.' *American Political Science Review* 82(4):1065–1087.

Chudgar, Amita and Elizabeth Quin. 2012. 'Relationship between Private Schooling and Achievement: Results from Rural and Urban India.' *Economics of Education Review* 31(4):376–390.

Chumacero, Rómulo A., Juan M. Gallegos, and Ricardo D. Paredes. 2011. 'Competition Pressures and Academic Performance in a Generalized Vouchers Context.' Unpublished Manuscript, Pontificia Universidad Católica, Santiago.

Chumacero, Rómulo A., Daniel Gómez, and Ricardo D. Paredes. 2011. 'I Would Walk 500 Miles (If it Paid): Vouchers and School Choice in Chile.' *Economics of Education Review* 30:1103–1114.

CIEB. 2012. 'Teacher and Principal Quality.' Information Leaflet, National Center on Education and the Economy, Washington, DC. Available at: http://www.ncee.org/programs-affiliates/center-on-international-education-benchmarking/top-performing-countries/netherlands-overview/netherlands-teacher-and-principal-quality/ (accessed 18.02.13).

Clark, Damon. 2009. 'The Performance and Competitive Effects of School Autonomy.' *Journal of Political Economy* 117(41):745–783.

Clark, Damon. 2010. 'Selective Schools and Academic Achievement.' *The B.E. Journal of Economic Analysis & Policy* 10(1):Article 9.

Coe, Robert. 2009. 'School Improvement: Reality and Illusion.' *British Journal of Educational Studies* 57(4):363–379.

Coe, Robert and Peter Tymms. 2008. 'An Academic View: Summary of Research on Changes in Educational Standards in the UK' in Harris, Mike (ed.), *Education Briefing Book 2008*, pp. 86–109. London: Institute of Directors.

Cohen-Zada, Danny. 2009. 'An Alternative Instrument for Private School Competition.' *Economics of Education Review* 28:29–37.

Cohen-Zada, Danny and Todd Elder. 2009. 'Historical Religious Concentrations and the Effects of Catholic Schooling.' *Journal of Urban Economics* 66(1):65–74.

Contreras, Dante, Sebastían Bustos, and Paulina Sepúlveda. 2007. 'When Schools are the Ones that Choose: The Effects of Screening in Chile.' Working Paper No. 242, Department of Economics, Universidad de Chile, Santiago.

Contreras, Dante and Victor Macías. 2002. 'Competencia y resultados educacionales.' Working Paper, University of Chile.

Contreras, Dante and Humberto Santos. 2009. 'Educational Transitions, Voucher and Choice in Chile: Evidence from Panel Data SIMCE 2004–2006.' Working Paper No.13, Centro de Políticas Comparades de Educación, Universided Diegon Portales, Santiago.

Contreras, Dante, Paulina Sepúlveda, and Sebastían Bustos. 2010. 'When Schools are the Ones that Choose: The Effects of Screening in Chile.' *Social Science Quarterly* 91(5):1349–1368.

Cornelisz, Ilja. 2012. 'A Reexamination of Private School Effectiveness: the Netherlands.' Tier Working Paper 12/03, Maastricht University, Top Institute for Evidence Based Education Research, Maastricht.

Correa, Juan A., David Inostroza, Fransisco Parro, Loreto Reyes, and Gabriel Ugarte. 2012. 'The Effects of Vouchers on Academic Achievement: Evidence from the Chilean Preferential Scholastic Subsidy.' Unpublished Manuscript, Ministry of Finance & Ministry of Education (Chile), Santiago.

Coulson, Andrew J. 1999. *Market Education: The Unknown History*. New Brunswick, NJ: Transaction Books.

Coulson, Andrew J. 2001. 'Toward Market Education: Are Vouchers or Tax Credits the Better Path?' Policy Analysis No. 392, Cato Institute, Washington, DC.

Coulson, Andrew J. 2009. 'Comparing Public, Private, and Market Schools: The International Evidence.' *Journal of School Choice* 3:31–54.

Coulson, Andrew J. 2010. 'Do Vouchers and Tax Credits Increase Private School Regulation?' Working Paper No. 1, Cato Institute, Washington, DC.

Coulson, Andrew J. 2011a. 'On the Way to School: Why and How to Make a Market in Education' in Forster, Greg, and C. Bradley Thompson (eds), *Freedom and School Choice in American Education*, pp. 17–46. Palgrave Macmillan.

Coulson, Andrew J. 2011b. 'The Other Lottery: Are Philanthropists Backing the Best Charter Schools?' Policy Analysis No. 677, Cato Institute, Washington, DC.

Cowen, Joshua M. 2008. 'School Choice as a Latent Variable: Estimating the "Complier Average Causal Effect" of Vouchers in Charlotte.' *Policy Studies Journal* 36(2):301–315.

Cowen, Joshua M., David J. Fleming, John F. White, Patrick J. Wolf, and Brian Kisida. 2013. 'School Vouchers and Student Attainment: Evidence from a State-Mandated Study of Milwaukee's Parental Choice Program.' *Policy Studies Journal* 41(1):147–168.

Cowen, Nick. 2008. *Swedish Lessons: How Schools with More Freedom Can Deliver Better Education*. London: Civitas.

Cox, Simon. 2012. 'Many Free Schools "Significantly Under Subscribed".' BBC, 11 October. Retrieved from: http://www.bbc.co.uk/news/education-19909369 (accessed 18.02.13).

Cremata, Edward J. and Margaret E. Raymond. 2012. 'The Competitive Effects of Charter Schools: Evidence from the District of Columbia.' CESifo Area Conference Paper, Stanford University, Palo Alto, CA.

Crespo-Cebada, Eva, Francisco M. Pedraja-Chaparro, and Santín González. 2011. 'The Impact of School Ownership in Spain. A Regional Analysis Throughout Unbiased Parametric Distance Functions.' XVIII Encuentro de economía pública, Presented at Encuentro de Economía Pública, Málaga, Spain.

Cresswell, Mike J. 2000. 'The Role of Public Examinations in Defining and Monitoring Standards.' *Proceedings of the British Academy* 102:69–120.

Croft, James. 2011. 'Profit-Making Free Schools: Unlocking the Potential of England's Proprietorial Schools Sector.' Report, Adam Smith Institute, London.

Crowe, Christopher and Ellen E. Meade. 2008. 'Central Bank Independence and Transparency: Evolution and Effectiveness.' *European Journal of Political Economy* 24(4):763–777.

Cullen, Julie B. and Brian A. Jacob. 2009. 'Is Gaining Access to Selective Elementary Schools Gaining Ground? Evidence from Randomized Lotteries' in Gruber, Jonathan (ed.), *The Problems of Disadvantaged Youth: An Economic Perspective*, pp. 43–84. Chicago, IL: University of Chicago Press.

Cullen, Julie B., Brian A. Jacob, and Steven D. Levitt. 2005. 'The Impact of School Choice on Student Outcomes: An Analysis of the Chicago Public Schools.' *Journal of Public Economics* 89(5–6):729–760.

Cullen, Julie B., Brian A. Jacob, and Steven Levitt. 2006. 'The Effect of School Choice on Participants: Evidence from Randomized Lotteries.' *Econometrica* 74(5):1191–1230.

Cullen, Julie B., Mark C. Long, and Randall Reback. 2013. 'Jockeying for Position: Strategic High School Choice Under Texas' Top Ten Percent Plan.' *Journal of Public Economics* 97:32–48.

Currie, Janet. 2003. 'When Do We Really Know What We Think We Know? Determining Causality.' Washington, DC. Invited paper presented at Work, Family, Health and Well-Being conference, NICHD Administration for Children and Families.

Curto, Vilsa E. and Roland G. J. Fryer. 2011. 'Estimating the Returns to Urban Boarding Schools: Evidence from SEED.' NBER Working Paper No. 16746, National Bureau of Economic Research, Cambridge, MA.

Dang, Hai-Anh. 2007. 'The Determinants and Impact of Private Tutoring Classes in Vietnam.' *Economics of Education Review* 26(6):683–698.

Davies, Scott. 2012. 'Are There Catholic School Effects in Ontario, Canada?' *European Sociological Review* doi:10.1093/esr/jcs065.

Davis, Devora H. and Margaret E. Raymond. 2011. 'Choices for Studying Choice: Assessing Charter School Effectiveness Using Two Quasi-Experimental Methods.' *Economics of Education Review* doi:10.1016/j.econedurev.2011.08.012.

de Haan, Monique, Edwin Leuven, and Hessel Oosterbeek. 2011. 'Scale Economies Can Offset the Benefits of Competition: Evidence from a School Consolidation Reform in a Universal Voucher System.' Discussion Paper No. 5528, Institute for the Study of Labor, Bonn.

de Janvry, Alain, Andrew Dustan, and Elisabeth Sadoulet. 2012. 'The Benefits and Hazards of Elite High School Admission: Academic Opportunity and Dropout Risk in Mexico City.' Unpublished Manuscript, University of California at Berkeley, CA.

de la Torre, Marisa and Julia Gwynne. 2009. 'When Schools Close: Effects on Displaced Students in Chicago Public Schools.' Research Report, University of Chicago, Consortium on Chicago School Research, Urban Education Institute, Chicago.

de Viljder, Frans J. 2000. 'Dutch Education: A Closed or an Open System?' Manuscript, Dutch Ministry of Education, Culture and Science, Hague.

Dearden, Lorraine, John Micklewright, and Anna Vignoles. 2011. 'The Effectiveness of English Secondary Schools for Pupils of Different Ability Levels.' *Fiscal Studies* 32(2):225–244.

Dearden, Lorraine, Alfonso Miranda, and Sophia Rabe-Hesketh. 2011. 'Measuring School Value Added with Administrative Data: The Problem of Missing Variables.' *Fiscal Studies* 32(2):263–278.

Dearden, Lorraine and Anna Vignoles. 2011. 'Schools, Markets and League Tables.' *Fiscal Studies* 32(2):179–186.

Dee, Thomas S. 2004. 'Are There Civic Returns to Education?' *Journal of Public Economics* 88(9–10):1697–1720.

Dee, Thomas. 2012. 'School Turnarounds: Evidence from the 2009 Stimulus.' NBER Working Paper No. 17990, National Bureau of Economic Research, Cambridge, MA.

Deming, David J. 2011. 'Better Schools, Lower Crime.' *Quarterly Journal of Economics* 126(4):2063–2115.

Deming, David J., Justine S. Hastings, Thomas J. Kane, and Douglas O. Staiger. 2011. 'School Choice, School Quality and Postsecondary Attainment.' NBER Working Paper No. 17438, National Bureau of Economic Research, Cambridge, MA.

Demoskop. 2011. 'Ska föräldrar ha rätt att välja skola åt sina barn?' Opinion Poll, Friskolornas riksförbund, Stockholm.

Department for Education. 2011. '24 Free Schools to Open Across England This Month.' Press Release (7th September), UK Department for Education, London.

Department for Education. 2012a. 'Registration of independent schools.' Official guidelines, London. Retrieved from: http://www.education.gov.uk/a009053/registration-of-independent-schools (accessed 18.02.13).

Department for Education. 2012b. 'Free Schools in 2014: How to Apply (Mainstream and 16 to 19 Free Schools).' Fact Sheet, London. Retrieved at: http://www.education.gov.uk/schools/leadership/typesofschools/freeschools/b0074965/apply (accessed 18.02.13).

Desai, Sonalde, Amaresh Dubey, Reeve Vannemann, and Rukmini Banerji. 2009. 'Private Schooling in India: A New Educational Landscape' in Bery, Suman, Barry Bosworth, and Arvind Panagariya (eds), *Brookings-NCEAR India Policy Forum*, pp. 1–58. Washington, DC: SAGE Publications.

Dijkgraaf, Elbert, Raymond H. J. M. Gradus, and J. Matthijs de Jong. 2012. 'Competition and Educational Quality: Evidence from the Netherlands.' *Econometrica* doi:10.1007/s10663-012-9195-6.

Dijkstra, Anne B., Jaap Dronkers, and Sjoerd Karsten. 2004. 'Private Schools as Public Provision for Education: School Choice and Market Forces in the Netherlands' in Wolf, Patrick J. (ed.), *Educating Citizens. International Perspectives on Civic Values and School Choice*, pp. 67–90. Washington, DC: Brookings Institution Press.

Dills, Angela K. and Rey Hernández-Julian. 2011. 'More Choice, Less Crime.' *Education Finance and Policy* 6(2):246–266.

Dobbie, Will and Roland G. Fryer. 2011a. 'Are High-Quality Schools Enough to Increase Achievement among the Poor? Evidence from the Harlem Children's Zone.' *American Economic Journal: Applied Economics* 3(3):158–187.

Dobbie, Will and Roland G. Fryer. 2011b. 'Exam High Schools and Academic Achievement: Evidence from New York City.' NBER Working Paper No. 17286, National Bureau of Economic Research, Cambridge, MA.

Dobbie, Will and Roland G. Fryer. 2011c. 'Getting Beneath the Veil of Effective Schools: Evidence from New York City.' NBER Working Paper No. 17632, National Bureau of Economic Research, Cambridge, MA.

Downes, Thomas A. and Jeffrey E. Zabel. 2002. 'The Impact of School Characteristics on House Prices: Chicago 1987–1991.' *Journal of Urban Economics* 52(1):1–25.

Drago, José L. and Ricardo, D. Paredes. 2011. 'La brecha de calidad en la educación chilena.' *Cepal Review* 104:167–180.

Dronkers, Jaap and Silvia Avram. 2010a. 'A Cross-National Analysis of the Relations of School Choice and Effectiveness Differences between Private-Dependent and Public Schools.' *Educational Research and Evaluation* 16(2):151–175.

Dronkers, Jaap and Silvia Avram. 2010b. 'A Cross-national Analysis of the Relations between School Choice and Effectiveness Differences between Private-Independent and Public Schools.' *Sociological Theory and Methods* 25(2):183–205.

Dronkers, Jaap and Peter Robert. 2004. 'Has Educational Sector any Impact on School Effectiveness in Hungary? A Comparison of the Public and the Newly Established Religious Grammar Schools.' *European Societies* 6(2):205–236.

Dronkers, Jaap and Peter Robert. 2008. 'Differences in Scholastic Achievement of Public, Private Government-Dependent, and Private Independent Schools: A Cross-National Analysis.' *Educational Policy* 22(4):541–577.

Duflo, Esther, Pascaline Dupas, and Michael Kremer. 2011. 'Peer Effects, Teacher Incentives, and the Impact of Tracking: Evidence from a Randomized Evaluation in Kenya.' *American Economic Review* 101:1739–1774.

Dustmann, Christian, Patrick A. Puhani, and Uta Schönberg. 2012. 'The Long-term Effects of School Quality on Labor Market Outcomes and Educational Attainment.' CReAM Discussion Paper No. 08/12, Centre for Research and Analysis of Migration, University College London.

Education Select Committee. 2012. 'The Administration of Examinations for 15–19 Year Olds in England.' Report, Education Select Committee, House of Commons, London.

Ekholm, Mats. 2004. 'Pilot Review of the Quality and Equity of Schooling Outcomes in Danish Basic Education.' OECD National Education Policy Reviews, Directorate for Education, OECD, Paris.

Elacqua, Gregory. 2009a. 'The Impact of School Choice and Public Policy on Segregation: Evidence from Chile.' Working Paper No. 10, Centro de Políticas Comparades de Educación, Universidad Diego Portales, Santiago.

Elacqua, Gregory. 2009b. 'For-Profit Schooling and the Politics of Education Reform in Chile: When Ideology Trumps Evidence.' Working Paper No. 5, Centro de Políticas Comparades de Educación, Universito Diego Portales, Santiago.

Elacqua, Gregory. 2009c. 'Parent Behavior and Yardstick Competition: Evidence from Chile's National Voucher Program.' Working Paper CPCE No. 2, Centro de Políticas Comparades de Educación, Universidad Diego Portales, Santiago.

Elacqua, Gregory. 2012. 'The Impact of School Choice and Public Policy on Segregation: Evidence from Chile.' *International Journal of Educational Development* 32:444–453.

Elacqua, Gregory, Dante Contreras, Filipe Salazar, and Humberto Santos. 2011. 'The Effectiveness of Private School Franchises in Chile's National Voucher Program.' *School Effectiveness and School Improvement* 22(3):237–263.

Elacqua, Gregory and Matías Martínez. 2011. 'Searching for Schools in a Low Quality Market: Evidence from Chile.' Working Paper No. 16, Facultad de Economia y Empresa, Universidad Diego Portales, Santiago.

Elacqua, Gregory, Matías Martínez, Humberto Santos, and Daniela Urbina. 2012. 'School Closures in Chile: Access to Quality Alternatives in a School Choice System.' *Estudios de Economía* 39(2):179–202.

Elacqua, Gregory, Mark Schneider, and Jack Buckley. 2006. 'School Choice in Chile: Is it Class or the Classroom?' *Journal of Policy Analysis and Management* 35(3):577–601.

Engberg, John, Brian Gill, Gema Zamarro, and Ron Zimmer. 2012. 'Closing Schools in a Shrinking District: Do Student Outcomes Depend on Which Schools are Closed?' *Journal of Urban Economics* 71(2):189–203.

Epple, Dennis and Richard Romano. 2012. 'Economic Modeling and Analysis of Educational Vouchers.' *Annual Review of Economics* 4:159–183.

Eurydice. 2008/09. 'Organisation of the Education System in the Netherlands.' European Commission, Brussels.

Fack, Gabrielle and Juliet Grenet. 2010. 'When Do Better Schools Raise Housing Prices? Evidence from Paris Public and Private Schools.' *Journal of Public Economics* 94(1–2):59–77.

Falch, Torberg and Justina A. V. Fischer. 2012. 'Public Sector Decentralisation and School Performance: International Evidence.' *Economics Letters* 114(3):276–279.

Falck, Oliver and Ludger Woessmann. 2011. 'School Competition and Students' Entrepreneurial Intentions: International Evidence Using Historical Catholic Roots of Private Schooling.' *Small Business Economics* doi:10.1007/s11187-011-9390-z.

Fält, Mats. 2011. 'Valfrihetens gränser – friskolors villkor i Danmark, Finland och Nederländerna.' Report, Timbro, Stockholm.

Fazackerley, Anna, Rachel Wolf, and Alex Massey. 2010. 'Blocking the Best: Obstacles to New, Independent State Schools.' Policy Report, Policy Exchange and New Schools Network, London.

Ferrão, Maria E. 2012. 'On the Stability of Value Added Indicators.' *Quality & Quantity* 46:627–637.

Figlio, David N. 2011. 'Evaluation of the Florida Tax Credit Scholarship Program: Participation, Compliance and Test Scores in 2009–10.' Evaluation Report, Northwestern University and National Bureau of Economic Research.

Figlio, David N. and Cassandra M. D. Hart. 2010. 'Competitive Effects of Means-Tested School Vouchers.' NBER Working Paper No. 16056, National Bureau of Economic Research, Cambridge, MA.

Figlio, David and Susanna Loeb 2011. 'School Accountability' in Hanushek, Eric A., Stephen Machin, and Ludger Woessmann, *Handbook of the Economics of Education*, pp. 383–421. Amsterdam: North-Holland.

Figlio, David and Jens Ludwig. 2012. 'Sex, Drugs, and Catholic Schools: Private Schooling and Non-Market Adolescent Behaviors.' *German Economic Review* 13(4):385–415.

Figlio, David N. and Marianne E. Page. 2002. 'School Choice and the Distributional Effects of Ability Tracking: Does Separation Increase Inequality?' *Journal of Urban Economics* 51:497–514.

Filer, Randall K. and Daniel Münich. 2012. 'Responses of Private and Public Schools to Voucher Funding.' *Economics of Education Review* doi:10.1016/j.econedurev.2012.12.004.

Forster, Greg. 2011. 'A Win-Win Solution: The Empirical Evidence on School Vouchers.' Report, The Foundation for Educational Choice, Indianapolis, IN.

Fredriksson, Peter and Jonas Vlachos. 2011. 'Reformer och resultat: Kommer regeringens utbildningsreformer att ha någon betydelse?' Report No. 2011/3, Swedish Fiscal Policy Council, Stockholm.

French, Ron and Geeta Kingdon. 2010. 'The Relative Effectiveness of Private and Government Schools in Rural India: Evidence from ASER Data.' DoQSS Working Paper No. 10–03, Department of Quantitative Social Science, Institute of Education, University of London, London.

Friedman, Milton. 1962. 'The Role of Government in Education' in *Capitalism and Freedom*, pp. 85–107. Chicago, IL: University Chicago Press.

Friedman, Milton. 1997. 'Public Schools: Make them Private.' *Education Economics* 5(3):341–344.

Friedman, Milton. 2003. 'Choice & Freedom: Legendary Economist Milton Friedman Reflects on the Idea He Spawned Half a Century Ago.' *Education Next*, Winter, 57–59. Interview with Pearl Rock Kane.

Friesen, Jane, Mohsen Javdani, Justin Smith, and Simon Woodcock. 2012. 'Does Public Information about School Quality Lead to Flight from Low-Achieving Schools?' *Canadian Journal of Economics* 45(2):784–807.

Friskolornas Riksförbund. 2011. 'Skolpeng på lika villkor - så har det gått och dit vill vi komma.' Report, Friskolornas Riksförbund, Stockholm.

Friskolornas Riksförbund. 2012. 'Branschfakta om fristående förskolor och skolor.' www. friskola.se, Stockholm.

Fryer, Roland G. 2011. 'Teacher Incentives and Student Achievement: Evidence from New York City Public Schools.' NBER Working Paper No. 16850, National Bureau of Economic Research, Cambridge, MA.

Fryer, Roland G., Steven D. Levitt, John List, and Sally Sadoff. 2012. 'Enhancing the Efficacy of Teacher Incentives through Loss Aversion: A Field Experiment.' NBER Working Paper No. 18237, National Bureau of Economic Research, Cambridge, MA.

Fuchs, Thomas and Ludger Woessmann. 2007. 'What Accounts for International Differences in Student Performance? A Re-examination Using PISA Data.' *Empirical Economics* 32:433–464.

Galindo-Rueda, Fernando and Anna Vignoles. 2005. 'The Heterogeneous Effect of Selection in Secondary Schools: Understanding the Changing Role of Ability.' Working Paper, Centre for the Economics of Education, London School of Economics, London.

Gallego, Fransisco A. 2002. 'Competencia y resultados educadivos: teoria y evidencia para Chile.' *Cuadernos de Economía* 39(118):309–352.

Gallego, Fransisco A. 2006. 'Voucher-School Competition, Incentives, and Outcomes: Evidence from Chile.' Working Paper, Centro de Políticas Públicas, Universidad Católica, Santiago.

Gallego, Fransisco A. 2008. 'School Choice, Stratification, and Information on School Performance: Lessons from Chile [with Comments].' *Economía* 8(2):32–42.

Gallego, Fransisco A. and Andrés Hernando. 2009. 'School Choice in Chile: Looking at the Demand Side.' Working Paper No. 356, Instituto de Economia, Pontificia Universidad Catolica de Chile, Santiago.

Gallego, Fransisco A. and Claudio Sapelli. 2007. 'Financiamiento y Selección en Educación: Algunas Reflexiones y Propuestas.' Centro de Estudios Públicos, Santiago.

Gauri, Varun. 1998. *School Choice in Chile: Two Decades of Educational Reform*. Pittsburgh: University of Pittsburgh Press.

Geller, Christopher R., David L. Sjoquist, and Mary B. Walker. 2006. 'The Effect of Private School Competition on Public School Performance in Georgia.' *Public Finance Review* 34(1):4–32.

Gibbons, Stephen, Stephen Machin, and Olmo Silva. 2008. 'Choice, Competition, and Pupil Achievement.' *Journal of the European Economic Association* 6(4):912–947.

Gibbons, Stephen, Stephen Machin, and Olmo Silva. 2013. 'Valuing School Quality Using Boundary Discontinuities.' *Journal of Urban Economics* 75:15–28

Gibbons, Stephen and Olmo Silva. 2008. 'Urban Density and Pupil Attainment.' *Journal of Urban Economics* 63:631–650.

Gibbons, Stephen and Olmo Silva. 2011a. 'School Quality, Child Wellbeing and Parents' Satisfaction.' *Economics of Education Review* 30(2):312–331.

Gibbons, Stephen and Olmo Silva. 2011b. 'Faith Primary Schools: Better Schools or Better Pupils?' *Journal of Labor Economics* 29(3):589–635.

Gibbons, Stephen and Shqiponja Telhaj. 2012. 'Peer Effects: Evidence from Secondary School Transition in England.' Discussion Paper No. 6455, Institute for the Study of Labor, Bonn.

Gill, Brian, Ron Zimmer, Jolley Christman, and Suzanne Blanc. 2007. 'State Takeover, School Restructuring, Private Management, and Student Achievement in Philadelphia.' Monograph 533, RAND Education, RAND Corporation, Pittsburgh, PA.

Gleason, Philip, Melissa Clark, Christina C. Tuttle, and Emily Dwoyer. 2010. 'The Evaluation of Charter School Impacts: Final Report.' IES Evaluation Report, National Center for Education Evaluation and Regional Assistance, Institute of Education Sciences, U.S. Department of Education, Washington, DC.

Glewwe, Paul, Nauman Ilias, and Michael Kremer. 2010. 'Teacher Incentives.' *American Economic Journal: Applied Economics* 2(3):205–227.

Gómez, Daniel, Rómulo A. Chumacero, and Ricardo D. Paredes. 2012. 'School Choice and Information.' *Estudios de Economia* 39(2):143–157.

Goodman, Sarena and Lesley Turner. 2011. 'Does Whole-School Performance Pay Improve Student Learning?' *Education Next*, Spring, 67–71.

Goyal, Sangeeta. 2009. 'Inside the House of Learning: The Relative Performance of Public and Private Schools in Orissa.' *Education Economics* 17(3):315–327.

Gray, Nathan L. 2012. 'School Choice and Achievement: The Ohio Charter School Experience.' *Cato Journal* 32(3):557–579.

Greene, Jay P. 2001. 'Vouchers in Charlotte.' *Education Matters*, Summer, 55–60.

Greene, Jay, Tom Loveless, W. Bentley MacLeod, Thomas Nechyba, Paul Peterson, Meredith Rosenthal, and Grover Whitehurst. 2010. 'Expanding Choice in Elementary and Secondary Education: A Report on Rethinking the Federal Role in Education.' Policy Report, Brown Center on Education Policy at Brookings, Brookings Institution, Washington, DC.

Greene, Jay P., Paul E. Peterson, and Jiangtao Du. 1997. 'The Effectiveness of School Choice: The Milwaukee Experiment.' Working Paper, Program on Education Policy and Governance, Harvard University, Cambridge, MA.

Greene, Jay P., Paul E. Peterson, and Jiangtao Du. 1999. 'Effectiveness of School Choice: The Milwaukee Experiment.' *Education and Urban Society* 31:190–212.

Greene, Kenneth V. and Byung-Goo Kang. 2004. 'The Effect of Public and Private Competition on High School Outputs in New York State.' *Economics of Education Review* 34:497–506.

Grönqvist, Erik and Jonas Vlachos. 2008. 'One Size Fits All? The Effects of Teacher Cognitive and Non-Cognitive Abilities on Student Achievement.' Working Paper 2008:25, Institute for Labour Market Policy Evaluation, Stockholm.

Gross, Betheny, T. K. Booker, and Dan Goldhaber. 2009. 'Boosting Student Achievement: The Effect of Comprehensive School Reform on Student Achievement.' *Educational Evaluation and Policy Analysis* 31(2):111–126.

Gunnarsson, Victoria, Peter F. Orazem, Mario A. Sánchez, and Aimee Verdisco. 2009. 'Does Local School Control Raise Student Outcomes? Evidence on the Roles of School Autonomy and Parental Participation.' *Economic Development and Cultural Change* 58(1):25–52.

Gurun, Ayfer and Daniel L. Millimet. 2008. 'Does Private Tutoring Payoff?' Discussion Paper No. 3637, Institute of the Study of Labor, Bonn.

Guyon, Nina, Eric Maurin, and Sandra McNally. 2012. 'The Effect of Tracking Students by Ability into Different Schools: A Natural Experiment.' *Journal of Human Resources* 47(3):684–721.

Hall, Caroline. 2012. 'The Effects of Reducing Tracking in Upper Secondary School.' *Journal of Human Resources* 47(1):237–269.

Hansen, Kirstine and Anna Vignoles. 2005. 'The United Kingdom Education System in a Comparative Context' in Machin, Stephen, and Anna Vignoles (eds), *What's the Good of Education? The Economics of Education in the UK*, pp. 13–35. Oxford: Princeton University Press.

Hansson, Örjan, Magnus Henrekson, and Jonas Vlachos. 2011. 'Godtyckliga betyg skadar skolan.' *Axess*, 1 May.

Hanushek, Eric A. 2000. 'Incentives: The Fundamental Problem in Education: An Interview with Eric A. Hanushek.' Interview by George A. Clowes. Retrieved from: http://news.heartland.org/newspaper-article/2000/01/01/incentives-fundamental-problem-education-interview-eric-hanushek (accessed 18.02.13). Heartland Institute, Chicago, IL.

Hanushek, Eric A. 2008. 'Incentives for Efficiency and Equity in the School System.' *Perspektiven der Wirtschaftspolitik* 9(Special Issue):5–27.

Hanushek, Eric A. 2011. 'The Economic Value of Higher Teacher Quality.' *Economics of Education Review* 30(3):466–479.

Hanushek, Eric A., John F. Kain, Jacob M. Markman, and Steven G. Rivkin. 2003. 'Does Peer Ability Affect Student Achievement?' *Journal of Applied Econometrics* 18:527–544.

Hanushek, Eric A., John F. Kain, Steven J. Rivkin, and Gregory F. Branch. 2007. 'Charter School Quality and Parental Decision Making with School Choice.' *Journal of Public Economics* 91:823–848.

Hanushek, Eric A., Victor Lavy, and Kohtaro Hitomi. 2008. 'Do Students Care about School Quality? Determinants of Dropout Behavior in Developing Countries.' *Journal of Human Capital* 2(1):69–105.

Hanushek, Eric A., Susanne Link, and Ludger Woessmann. 2012. 'Does School Autonomy Make Sense Everywhere? Panel Estimates from PISA.' *Journal of Development Economics* doi:10.1016/j.jdeveco.2012.08.002.

Hanushek, Eric A., Paul E. Peterson, and Ludger Woessmann. 2012. 'Achievement Growth: International and U.S. State Trends in Student Performance.' PEPG Report No. 12–03, Harvard's Program on Education Policy and Governance & Education Next, Harvard University, Cambridge, MA.

Hanushek, Eric A. and Steven G. Rivkin 2003. 'Does Public School Competition Affect Teacher Quality' in Hoxby, Caroline M. (ed.), *The Economics of School Choice*. Chicago/London: University of Chicago Press.

Hanushek, Eric A. and Steven G. Rivkin. 2010. 'Generalizations about Using Value-Added Measures of Teacher Quality.' *American Economics Review* 100:261–271.

Hanushek, Eric A. and Steven G. Rivkin. 2012. 'The Distribution of Teacher Quality and Implications for Policy.' *Annual Review of Economics* 4:131–157.

Hanushek, Eric A. and Ludger Woessmann. 2006. 'Does Educational Tracking Affect Performance and Inequality? Differences-in-Differences Evidence Across Countries.' *Economic Journal* 116(510):C63–C76.

Hanushek, Eric A. and Ludger Woessmann. 2011. 'The Economics of International Differences in Educational Achievement' in Hanushek, Eric A., Stephen Machin, and Ludger Woessmann (eds) *Handbook of the Economics of Education*, pp. 89–200. Amsterdam: Elsevier.

Hanushek, Eric A. and Ludger Woessmann. 2012. 'Do Better Schools Lead to More Growth? Cognitive Skills, Economic Outcomes, and Causation.' *Journal of Economic Growth* 17(4):267–321.

Haraldsvik, Marianne. 2012. 'Does Performance-Based School Choice Affect Student Achievement?' Unpublished Manuscript, Department of Economics, Norwegian University of Science and Technology, Trondheim, Norway.

Harris, Mike. 2008. 'Education Briefing Book 2008.' IoD Policy Paper, Institute of Directors, London.

Hastings, Justine S., Thomas J. Kane, and Douglas O. Staiger. 2006. 'Preferences and Heterogeneous Treatment Effects in a Public School Choice Lottery.' NBER Working Paper No. 12145, National Bureau of Economic Research, Cambridge, MA.

Hastings, Justine S., Christopher A. Neilson, and Seth D. Zimmerman. 2012. 'The Effect of School Choice on Intrinsic Motivation and Academic Outcomes.' NBER Working Paper No. 18324, National Bureau of Economic Research, Cambridge, MA.

Hastings, Justine S., Richard Van Weelden, and Jeffrey Weinstein. 2007. 'Preferences, Information, and Parental Choice Behavior in Public School Choice.' NBER Working Paper No. 12995, National Bureau of Economic Research, Cambridge, MA.

Hastings, Justine S. and Jeffrey M. Weinstein. 2008. 'Information, School Choice, and Academic Achievement: Evidence from Two Experiments.' *Quarterly Journal of Economics* 123(4):1373–1414.

Hattie, John A. 2009. *Visible Learning. A Synthesis of Over 800 Meta-Analyses*. New York: Routledge.

Hayek, Friedrich A. 1945. 'The Use of Knowledge in Society.' *American Economic Review* 35(4):519–530.

Hayek, Friedrich A. 2001. *The Road to Serfdom*. Cornwall: Routledge.

Henig, Jeffrey R. 1999. 'School Choice Outcomes' in Sugarman, Stephen D. and Frank R. Kemerer (eds), *School Choice and Social Controversy: Politics, Policy and Law*, pp. 68–110. Washington, DC: The Brookings Institution.

Henrekson, Magnus and Henrik Jordahl. 2012. 'Vinster och privatiseringar i landet Lagom.' IFN Policy Paper No. 55, Research Institute of Industrial Economics, Stockholm.

Henrekson, Magnus and Jonas Vlachos. 2009. 'Konkurrens om elever ger orättvisa gymnasiebetyg.' *Dagens Nyheter*, 17 August. Available at: http://www.dn.se/debatt/konkurrens-om-elever-ger-orattvisa-gymnasiebetyg (accessed 18.02.13).

Henríquez, Fransisco, Bernardo Lara, Alejandro Mizala, and Andrea Repetto. 2012. 'Effective Schools Do Exist: Low-Income Children's Academic Performance in Chile.' *Applied Economics Letters* 19(5):445–451.

Henríquez, Fransisco, Alejandro Mizala, and Andrea Repetto. 2009. 'Effective Schools for Low Income Children: A Study of Chile's Sociedad de Instrucción Primaria.' Working Paper No. 258, Centro de Economía Aplicada, Universidad de Chile, Santiago.

Hensvik, Lena. 2012. 'Competition, Wages and Teacher Sorting: Lessons Learned from a Voucher Reform.' *Economic Journal* 122(561):799–824.

Hill, Cynthia D. and David M. Welsch. 2009. 'For-Profit versus Not-for-Profit Charter Schools: An Examination of Michigan Student Test Scores.' *Education Economics* 17(2):147–166.

Himmler, Oliver. 2009. 'The Effects of School Competition on Academic Achievement and Grading Standards.' Working Paper No. 2676, Center for Economic Studies (CESifo), Munich.

Hindriks, Jean, Maijn Verschelde, Glenn Rayp, and Koen Schoors. 2010. 'School Autonomy and Educational Performance: Within-Country Evidence.' Core Discussion Paper 2010/82, Centre for Operations Research, Université catholique de Louvain, Louvain-la-Neuve, Belgium.

Hjalmarsson, Randi and Lance Lochner. 2012. 'The Impact of Education on Crime: International Evidence.' *CESifo DICE Report* 10(2):49–55.

Høiseth Brugård, Kaja. 2012. 'School Choice and Academic Achievement.' Unpublished Manuscript, Center for Economic Research, Norwegian University of Science and Technology, Trondheim.

Holmes, George M., Jeff DeSimone, and Nicholas G. Rupp. 2003. 'Does School Choice Increase School Quality?' NBER Working Paper No. 9683, National Bureau of Economic Research, Cambridge, MA.

Holmlund, Helena, Sandra McNally, and Martina Viarengo. 2010. 'Does Money Matter for Schools?' *Economics of Education Review* 29(6):1154–1164.

House of Commons. 2003. 'House of Commons Education and Skills Third Report 2003.' House of Commons, London.

Howell, William G., Patrick J. Wolf, David E. Campbell, and Paul E. Peterson. 2004. 'School Vouchers and Academic Performance: Results from Three Randomized Field Trials.' *Journal of Policy Analysis and Management* 21(2):191–217.

Hoxby, Caroline M. 1994. 'Do Private Schools Provide Competition for Public Schools?' Working Paper No. 4978, National Bureau of Economic Research, Cambridge, MA.

Hoxby, Caroline M. 2000. 'Does Competition among Public Schools Benefit Students and Taxpayers?' *American Economic Review* 90(5):1209–1238.

Hoxby, Caroline M. 2003a. 'School Choice and School Productivity: Could School Choice be a Tide that Lifts All Boats?' in Hoxby, Caroline M. (ed.), *The Economics of School Choice*, pp. 287–341. Chicago: University of Chicago Press.

Hoxby, Caroline M. 2003b. 'School Choice and School Competition: Evidence from the United States.' *Swedish Economic Policy Review* 10(2):9–65.

Hoxby, Caroline M. 2006. 'School Choice: The Three Essential Elements and Several Policy Options.' Keynote speech delivered 30 June 2005 to the New Zealand Association of Economists 46th Annual Conference 2005, Christchurch, New Zealand, Education Forum, Wellington.

Hoxby, Caroline M. 2007. 'Does Competition among Public Schools Benefit Students and Taxpayers? Reply.' *American Economic Review* 97(5):2038–2055.

Hoxby, Caroline M. 2008. 'School Choice and Competition' in Durlauf, Steven N. and Lawrence E. Blume, *The New Palgrave Dictionary of Economics*. New York: Palgrave Macmillan.

Hoxby, Caroline M., Sonali Murarka, and Jenny Kang. 2009. 'How New York City's Charter Schools Affect Achievement.' The New York City Charter Schools Evaluation Project, Cambridge, MA.

Hoxby, Caroline M. and Jonah E. Rockoff. 2005. 'The Impact of Charter Schools on Student Achievement.' Working Paper, RAND Corporation, Washington, DC.

Hsieh, Chang-Tai and Miguel Urquiola. 2006. 'The Effects of Generalized School Choice on Achievement and Stratification: Evidence from Chile's Voucher Program.' *Journal of Public Economics* 90:1477–1503.

Huerta, Luis A. and Chad d'Entremont. 2007. 'Education Tax Credits in a Post-Zelman Era: Legal, Political, and Policy Alternatives to Vouchers?' *Educational Policy* 21(1):73–109.

Hussain, Iftikhar. 2012. 'Subjective Performance Evaluation in the Public Sector: Evidence from School Inspections.' Discussion Paper No. 135, Centre for the Economics of Education, London School of Economics, London.

IEA. 2012. Data retrieved from reports accessible at IEA's website: http://www.iea.nl/.

Imberman, Scott A. 2011a. 'Achievement and Behavior in Charter Schools: Drawing a More Complete Picture.' *Review of Economics and Statistics* 93(2):416–435.

Imberman, Scott A. 2011b. 'The Effect of Charter Schools on Achievement and Behavior of Public School Students.' *Journal of Public Economics* 95:850–863.

Imberman, Scott A. and Michael F. Lovenheim. 2013. 'Does the Market Value Value-Added? Evidence from Housing Prices after a Public Release of School and Teacher Value-Added.' Unpublished Manuscript, Michigan State University and Cornell University.

Ireson, Judith and Katie Rushforth. 2005. 'Mapping and Evaluating Shadow Education.' ESRC Research Project RES-000-23-0117, Institute of Education, London.

Jackson, C. Kirabo. 2010. 'Do Students Benefit from Attending Better Schools? Evidence from Rule-based Student Assignments in Trinidad and Tobago.' *Economic Journal* 120(549):1399–1429.

Jackson, C. Kirabo. 2012. 'Do High-School Teachers Really Matter?' NBER Working Paper No. 17722, National Bureau of Economic Research, Cambridge, MA.

Jacob, Brian A. and Lars Lefgren. 2007. 'What Do Parents Value in Education? An Empirical Investigation of Parents' Revealed Preferences for Teachers.' *Quarterly Journal of Economics* 122(4):1603–1637.

Jakubowski, Maciej. 2010. 'Institutional Tracking and Achievement Growth: Exploring Difference-in-Differences Approach to PIRLS, TIMSS, and PISA Data' in Dronkers, Jaap (ed.), *Quality and Inequality of Education: Cross-National Perspectives*, pp. 41–81. London: Springer.

James, Estelle, Elizabeth M. King, and Ace Suryadi. 1996. 'Finance, Management, and Costs of Public and Private Schools in Indonesia.' *Economics of Education Review* 15(4):387–398.

JCQ. 2012. 'GCSE and Entry Level Certificate Results Summer 2012.' Joint Council for Qualifications, London.

Jepsen, Christopher. 2003. 'The Effectiveness of Catholic Primary Schooling.' *Journal of Human Resources* 38(4):928–941.

Jeynes, William H. 2012. 'A Meta-Analysis on the Effects and Contributions of Public, Public Charter, and Religious Schools on Student Outcomes.' *Peabody Journal of Education* 87(3):305–335.

Jinnai, Yusuke. 2011. 'Who Benefits from School Choice? School Competition, Student Sorting, and Spillover Effects.' Unpublished Manuscript, Department of Economics, University of Rochester, Rochester.

Jürges, Hendrik, Kerstin Schneider, and Felix Büchel. 2005. 'The Effect of Central Exit Examinations on Student Achievement: Quasi-Experimental Evidence from TIMSS Germany.' *Journal of the European Economic Association* 3(5):1134–1155.

Jürges, Hendrik, Kerstin Schneider, Martin Senkbeil, and Claus H. Carstensen. 2012. 'Assessment Drives Learning: The Effect of Central Exit Exams on Curricular Knowledge and Mathematical Literacy.' *Economics of Education Review* 31:56–65.

Kane, Thomas J., Daniel F. McCaffrey, Trey Miller, and Douglas O. Staiger. 2013. 'Have We Identified Effective Teachers? Validating Measures of Effective Teaching Using Random Assignment.' Reasearch Paper, Bill and Melinda Gates Foundation, Seattle, WA.

Kane, Thomas J. and Douglas O. Staiger. 2008. 'Estimating Teacher Impacts on Student Achievement: An Experimental Evaluation.' NBER Working Paper No. 14607, National Bureau of Economic Research, Cambridge, MA.

Kang, Changhui. 2007. 'Does Money Matter? The Effect of Private Educational Expenditures on Academic Performance.' Working Paper No. 0704, Department of Economics, National University of Singapore, Singapore.

Kawakita, Todd and Colin Sullivan. 2011. 'School Autonomy and Regression Discontinuity Imbalance.' Unpublished Manuscript, Harvard University, Cambridge, MA.

Kim, Young-Joo. 2012. 'Catholic Schooling and Further Education.' *Economics Letters* 114:346–348.

King, Kerry A. 2007. 'Charter Schools in Arizona: Does Being a For-Profit Institution Make a Difference?' *Journal of Economic Issues* 41(3):729–746.

Kingdon, Geeta. 1996. 'The Quality and Efficiency of Private and Public Education: A Case-Study of Urban India.' *Oxford Bulletin of Economics and Statistics* 58(1):57–82.

Koerselman, Kristian. 2013. 'Incentives from Curriculum Tracking.' *Economics of Education Review* 32:140–150.

Koning, Pierre and Karen van der Wiel. 2010. 'Ranking the Schools: How School-Quality Information Affects School Choice in the Netherlands.' Discussion Paper No. 4984, Institute for the Study of Labor, Bonn.

Koning, Pierre and Karen van der Wiel. 2012. 'School Responsiveness to Quality Rankings: An Empirical Analysis of Secondary Education in the Netherlands.' *De Economist* 160(4):339–355.

Krueger, Alan B. and Pei Zhu. 2004. 'Another Look at the New York City School Voucher Experiment.' *American Behavioral Scientist* 47(5):658–698.

Kupiainen, Sirkku, Jarkko Hautamäki, and Tommi Karjalainen. 2009. 'The Finnish Education System and PISA.' Ministry of Education Publications, Finland 2009:46, Ministry of Education, Helsinki.

Ladd, Helen F. and Edward B. Fiske. 2003. 'Does Competition Improve Teaching and Learning? Evidence from New Zealand.' *Educational Evaluation and Policy Analysis* 25(1):97–112.

Ladd, Helen F. and Edward B. Fiske. 2011. 'Weighted Student Funding in the Netherlands: A Model for the U.S.?' *Journal of Policy Analysis and Management* 30(3):470–498.

Ladd, Helen F., Edward B. Fiske, and Nienke Ruijs. 2009. 'Parental Choice in the Netherlands: Growing Concerns about Segregation.' Conference Paper, National Center for School Choice, Vanderbilt University, Nashville, TN.

Lamarche, Carlos. 2008. 'Private School Vouchers and Student Achievement: A Fixed Effects Quantile Regression Evaluation.' *Labour Economics* 15:575–590.

Lara, Bernardo, Alejandro Mizala, and Andrea Repetto. 2011. 'The Effectiveness of Private Voucher Education: Evidence from Structural School Switches.' *Educational Evaluation and Policy Analysis* 33(2):119–137.

Lauen, Douglas L. 2009. 'To Choose or Not to Choose: High School Choice and Graduation in Chicago.' *Educational Evaluation and Policy Analysis* 31(3):215–229.

Lauen, Douglas L. and Michael S. Gaddis. 2012. 'Shining a Light or Fumbling in the Dark? The Effects of NCLB's Subgroup-Specific Accountability on Student Achievement.' *Educational Evaluation and Policy Analysis* doi:10.3102/0162373711429989.

Lavy, Victor. 2010. 'Effects of Free Choice among Public Schools.' *Review of Economic Studies* 77:1164–1191.

Lavy, Victor. 2011. 'What Makes a Teacher Effective? Quasi-Experimental Evidence.' NBER Working Paper No. 16885, National Bureau of Economic Research, Cambridge, MA.

Lavy, Victor, Olmo Silva, and Felix Weinhart. 2009. 'The Good, the Bad and the Average: Evidence on the Scale and Nature of Ability Peer Effects in Schools.' Working Paper No. 15600, National Bureau of Economic Research, Cambridge, MA.

Le, Anh T. and Paul W. Miller. 2003. 'Choice of School in Australia: Determinants and Consequences.' *Australian Economic Review* 36(1):55–78.

Leckie, George and Harvey Goldstein. 2009. 'The Limitations of Using League Tables to Inform School Choice.' *Journal of the Royal Statistical Society* 172:835–851.

Leckie, George and Harvey Goldstein. 2011a. 'Understanding Uncertainty in School League Tables.' *Fiscal Studies* 32(2):207–224.

Leckie, George and Harvey Goldstein. 2011b. 'A Note on "The Limitations of School League Tables to Inform School Choice".' *Journal of the Royal Statistical Society* 174(3):833–836.

Lee, Yong S. 2012. 'Educational Tracking, Residential Sorting, and Intergenerational Economic Mobility: Evidence from South Korea.' Job Market Paper, Brown University, Providence, NE.

Lefebvre, Pierre, Philip Merrigan, and Matthieu Verstraete. 2011. 'Public Subsidies to Private Schools Do Make a Difference for Achievement in Mathematics: Longitudinal Evidence from Canada.' *Economics of Education Review* 30:79–98.

Leigh, Andrew. 2012. 'The Economics and Politics of Teacher Merit Pay.' *CESifo Economic Studies* doi:10.1093/cesifo/ifs007.

Levačić, Rosalind. 2004. 'Competition and the Performance of English Secondary Schools: Further Evidence.' *Education Economics* 12(2):177–193.

Levačić, Rosalind and Jason Hardman. 1999. 'The Performance of Grant Maintained Schools in England: An Experiment in Autonomy.' *Journal of Education Policy* 14(2):185–212.

Levin, Jesse. 2004. 'Differences in Educational Production between Dutch Public and Religious Schools.' Occasional Paper No. 93, National Center for the Study of Privatization in Education, Columbia University, New York.

Lewis, Laura and Harry A. Patrinos. 2011. 'Framework for Engaging the Private Sector in Education.' Report, System Assessment and Benchmarking Education for Results, World Bank, Washington, DC.

Lieberman, Myron. 1993. *Public Education: An Autopsy.* Cambridge, MA: Harvard University Press.

Lindbom, Anders and Ellen Almgren. 2007. 'Valfrihetens effekter på skolornas elevsammansättning' in Lindbom, Anders (ed.), *Friskolorna och framtiden – segregation, kostnader och effektivitet*, pp. 89–188. Stockholm: Institutet for framtidsstudier.

Lucas, Adrienne M. and Isaac M. Mbiti. 2012. 'Effects of School Quality on Student Achievement: Discontinuity Evidence from Kenya.' Unpublished Manuscript, Department of Economics, University of Delaware.

Lundahl, Lisbeth. 2002. 'Sweden: Decentralization, Deregulation, Quasi-Markets – And Then What?' *Journal of Education Policy* 17(6):687–697.

Lundberg, Anders. 2011. 'Hur får vi en riktigt bra skola? Sammanfattning från Timbros skolkonferens 18 november 2011.' Summary from conference, Timbro, Stockholm.

Lundsten, Ludvig and Martin Löfqvist. 2011. 'The Impact of Private Equity in the Swedish Independent School Sector.' Master's Thesis, Stockholm School of Economics, Stockholm.

Machin, Stephen and Sandra McNally. 2008. 'The Literacy Hour.' *Journal of Public Economics* 92(5–6):1441–1462.

Machin, Stephen and James Vernoit. 2011. 'Changing School Autonomy: Academy Schools and their Introduction to England's Education.' Discussion Paper No. 123, Centre for the Economics of Education, London School of Economics, London.

MacIver, Martha A. and Douglas J. MacIver. 2006. 'Which Bets Paid Off? Early Findings on the Impact of Private Management and K-8 Conversion Reforms on the Achievement of Philadelphia Students.' *Review of Policy Research* 23(5):1077–1093.

MacLeod, W. Bentley and Miguel Urquiola. 2012a. 'Competition and Educational Productivity: Incentives Writ Large.' Discussion Paper No. 7063, Institute for the Study of Labor, Bonn.

MacLeod, W. Bentley and Miguel Urquiola. 2012b. 'Anti-Lemons: School Reputation, Relative Diversity, and Educational Quality.' Discussion Paper No. 6805, Institute for the Study of Labor, Bonn.

Malacova, Eva and John Bell. 2006. 'Changing Boards: Investigating the Effects of Centres Changing their Specifications for English GCSE.' *Curriculum Journal* 17(1):27–35.

Malamud, Ofer and Christian Pop-Eleches. 2011. 'School Tracking and Access to Higher Education among Disadvantaged Groups.' *Journal of Public Economics* 95:1538–1549.

Mancebón-Torrbia, María-Jesús, Jorge Calero, Álvaro Choi, and Domingo P. Ximénez-de-Embún. 2010. 'The Efficiency of Public and Publicly-Subsidized High Schools in Spain. Evidence from PISA-2006.' MPRA Paper No. 2235, Munich Personal RePEc Archive.

Manning, Alan and Jörn-Steffen Pischke. 2006. 'Comprehensive versus Selective Schooling in England in Wales: What Do We Know?' IZA Discussion Paper No. 2072, Institute for the Study of Labor, Bonn.

Marlow, Michael L. 2010. 'The Influence of Private School Enrollment on Public School Performance.' *Applied Economics* 42(1):11–22.

Marsh, Herbert W., Benjamin Nagengast, John Fletcher, and Ioulia Televantou. 2011. 'Assessing Educational Effectiveness: Policy Implications from Diverse Areas of Research.' *Fiscal Studies* 32(2):279–295.

Martio, Olli. 2009. 'Long Term Effects in Learning Mathematics in Finland: Curriculum Changes and Calculators.' *Teaching of Mathematics* 12(2):51–56.

Maurin, Eric and Sandra McNally. 2007. 'Educational Effects of Widening Access to the Academic Track: A Natural Experiment.' IZA Discussion Paper No. 2596, Institute for the Study of Labor, Bonn.

McEwan, Patrick J. 2001. 'The Effectiveness of Public, Catholic, and Non-Religious Private Schools in Chile's Voucher System.' *Education Economics* 9(2):103–128.

McEwan, Patrick J. 2003. 'Peer Effects on Student Achievement: Evidence from Chile.' *Economics of Education Review* 22:131–141.

McEwan, Patrick J. and Martin Carnoy. 2000. 'The Effectiveness and Efficiency of Private Schools in Chile's Voucher System.' *Educational Evaluation and Policy Analysis* 22(3):213–239.

McEwan, Patrick J., Miguel Urquiola, and Emiliana Vegas. 2008. 'School Choice, Stratification, and Information on School Performance: Lessons from Chile.' *Economía* 8(2):1–27.

McMahon, Walter W. 2010. 'The External Benefits of Education' in Brewer, Dominic and Patrick J. McEwan (eds), *The Economics of Education*. Oxford: Elsevier.

McMeekin, Robert W. 2003. 'Network of Schools.' *Education Policy Analysis Archives* 11(16). Retrieved from: http://epaa.asu.edu/epaa/u11n16/ (accessed 18.02.13).

Means, Barbara, Yukie Toyama, Robert Murphy, Marianne Bakia, and Karla Jones. 2010. 'Evaluation of Evidence-Based Practices in Online Learning: A Meta-Analysis and Review of Online Learning Studies.' Report, Office of Planning, Evaluation, and Policy Development, U.S. Department of Education, Washington, DC.

Meghir, Costas and Mårten Palme. 2005. 'Educational Reform, Ability, and Family Background.' *American Economic Review* 95(1):414–424.

Meijer, Albert J. 2007. 'Publishing Public Performance Results on the Internet: Do Stakeholders Use the Internet to Hold Dutch Public Services Organizations to Account?' *Government Information Quarterly* 24:165–185.

Merrifield, John. 2008. 'Dismal Science: The Shortcomings of U.S. School Choice Research and How to Address Them.' Policy Analysis No. 616, Cato Institute, Washington, DC.

Metzler, Johannes and Ludger Woessmann. 2010. 'The Impact of Teacher Subject Knowledge on Student Achievement: Evidence from Within-Teacher Within-Student Variation.' Discussion Paper No. 4999, Institute for the Study of Labor, Bonn.

Millimet, Daniel L. and Trevor Collier. 2008. 'Efficiency in Public Schools: Does Competition Matter?' *Journal of Econometrics* 145:134–157.

Ministeriet for Børn og Undervisning. 2013. 'Private Schools.' Fact Sheet, Ministeriet for Børn og Undervisning, Copenhagen, http://eng.uvm.dk/Fact-Sheets/Primary-and-lower-secondary-education/Private-schools (accessed 18.02.13).

Mischo, Christoph and Ludwig Haag. 2002. 'Expansion and Effectiveness of Private Tutoring.' *European Journal of Psychology of Education* 17(3):263–273.

Misra, Kaustav, Paul W. Grimes, and Kevin E. Rogers. 2012. 'Does Competition Improve Public School Efficiency? A Spatial Analysis.' *Economics of Education Review* 31:1177–1190.

Mizala, Alejandra and Pilar Romaguera. 2000. 'School Performance and Choice: The Chilean Experience.' *Journal of Human Resources* 35(2):392–417.

Mizala, Alejandra and Pilar Romaguera. 2002. 'Equity and Educational Performance.' *Economía* 2(2):219–262.

Mizala, Alejandra and Pilar Romaguera. 2005. 'Teachers' Salary Structure and Incentives in Chile' in Vegas, Emiliana (ed.), *Incentives to Improve Teaching: Lessons from Latin America*, pp. 103–150. Washington, DC: World Bank.

Mizala, Alejandra, Pilar Romaguera, and Miguel Urquiola. 2007. 'Socioeconomic Status or Noise? Tradeoffs in the Generation of School Quality Information.' *Journal of Development Economics* 84(1):61–75.

Mizala, Alejandra and Florencia Torche. 2012. 'Bringing the Schools Back In: The Stratification of Educational Achievement in the Chilean Voucher System.' *International Journal of Educational Development* 32:132–144.

Mizala, Alejandra and Miguel Urquiola. 2007. 'School Markets: The Impact of Information Approximating Schools' Effectiveness.' NBER Working Paper No. 13676, National Bureau of Economic Research, Cambridge, MA.

Moe, Terry M. 2008. 'Beyond the Free Market: The Structure of School Choice.' *Brigham University Law Review* 2008(2):557–592.

Moe, Terry M. 2011. *Special Interest: Teachers Unions and America's Public Schools.* Washington DC: Brookings Institution Press.

Muralidharan, Karthik. 2011. 'Long-Term Effects of Teacher Performance Pay: Experimental Evidence from India.' Unpublished Manuscript, Department of Economics, University of California, San Diego, CA.

Muralidharan, Karthik and Michael Kremer. 2007. 'Public and Private Schools in Rural India.' Unpublished Manuscript, Harvard University, Cambridge, MA.

Muralidharan, Karthik, Michael Kremer, and Venkatesh Sundararaman. 2013. 'The Aggregate Effects of School Choice: Evidence from a Two-Stage Experiment in India.' Unpublished Manuscript, University of California, San Diego, CA.

Muralidharan, Karthik and Venkatesh Sundararaman. 2011. 'Teacher Performance Pay: Experimental Evidence from India.' *Journal of Political Economy* 119(1):39–77.

Muriel, Alastair and Jeffrey Smith. 2011. 'On Educational Performance Measures.' *Fiscal Studies* 32(2):187–206.

Nannestad, Peter. 2004. 'Do Private Schools Improve the Quality of Municipal Schooling? The Case of Denmark.' Conference Paper at EPCS Annual Meeting, 15–18 April 2004, Berlin.

NCES. 2012. The National Center for Education Statistics, Institute of Education Sciences, U.S. Department for Education. Data retrieved from the NCES website: http://nces.ed.gov/timss/ (accessed 18.02.13).

Neal, Derek. 2002. 'How Vouchers Could Change the Market for Education.' *Journal of Economic Perspectives* 16(4):25–44.

Neal, Derek. 2010. 'Aiming for Efficiency Rather than Proficiency.' *Journal of Economic Perspectives* 24(3):119–132.

Neal, Derek. 2011. 'The Design of Performance Pay in Education.' NBER Working Paper No. 16710, National Bureau of Economic Research, Cambridge, MA.

Newhouse, Davin and Kathleen Beegle. 2006. 'The Effect of School Type on Academic Achievement: Evidence from Indonesia.' *Journal of Human Resources* 41(3):529–557.

Nguyen-Hoang, Phuong and John Yinger. 2011. 'The Capitalization of School Quality into House Values: A Review.' *Journal of Housing Economics* 20:30–48.

Ni, Yongmei. 2009. 'The Impact of Charter Schools on the Efficiency of Traditional Public Schools: Evidence from Michigan.' *Economics of Education Review* 28:571–584.

Ni, Yongmei and Andrea K. Rorrer. 2012. 'Twice Considered: Charter Schools and Student Achievement in Utah.' *Economics of Education Review* 31(5):835–849.

Nichols, Austin and Umut Özek. 2010. 'Public School Choice and Student Achievement in the District of Columbia.' Working Paper No. 53, Urban Institute, Washington, DC.

Nicoletti, Cheti and Birgitta Rabe. 2012. 'The Effects of School Resources on Test Scores in England.' ISER Working Paper No. 2012–13, Institute for Social and Economic Research, University of Essex, Colchester.

Nicotera, Anna, Maria Mendiburo, and Mark Berends. 2009. 'Charter School Effects in an Urban School District: An Analysis of Student Achievement Gains in Indianapolis.' Working Paper, National Center for School Choice, Vanderbilt University, Nashville, TN.

Niemietz, Kristian. 2012. 'Abundance of Land, Shortage of Housing.' IEA Discussion Paper No. 38, Institute of Economic Affairs, London.

Niepel, Verena. 2012. 'Essays on Skills, School Choice and their Long-Term Consequences.' PhD Dissertation, Mannheim University, Mannheim, Germany.

Nisar, Hiren. 2012. 'Heterogeneous Competitive Effects of Charter Schools in Milwaukee.' Occasional Paper No. 202, National Center for the Study of Privatization in Education, Columbia University, New York.

Nisar, Hiren. 2013. 'Do Charter Schools Improve Student Achievement?' Occasional Paper No. 216, National Center for the Study of Privatization in Education, Columbia University, New York.

Noailly, Joëlle, Sunčica Vujić, and Ali Aouragh. 2012. 'The Effects of Competition on the Quality of Primary Schools in the Netherlands.' *Environment and Planning A* 44(9):2153–2170.

Nordström Skans, Oskar and Olof Åslund. 2010. 'Etnisk segregation i storstäderna – bostadsområden, arbetsplatser, skolor och familjebildning 1985–2006.' Report 2010:4, Institutet för arbetsmarknadspolitisk utvärdering (IFAU), Uppsala.

OECD. 1998. *Education at a Glance: OECD Indicators 1998*. Paris: Centre for Educational Research and Innovation (OECD).

OECD. 2011a. *PISA 2009 Results: What Makes a School Successful? Resources, Policies and Practices (Volume IV)*.

OECD. 2011b. *Maintaining Momentum: OECD Perspectives on Policy Challenges in Chile*. Paris: OECD Publishing.

OECD. 2012. Data retrieved from the OECD's PISA database: http://www.oecd.org/pisa/

Ono, Hiroshi. 2007. 'Does the Examination Hell Pay Off? A Cost-Benefit Analysis of "Ronin" and College Education in Japan.' *Economics of Education Review* 26(3):271–284.

Östh, John, Eva Andersson, and Bo Malmberg. 2012. 'School Choice and Increasing Performance Difference: A Counterfactual Approach.' *Urban Studies* doi: 10.1177/0042098012452322.

Özek, Umut. 2009. 'The Effects of Open Enrollment on School Choice and Student Outcomes.' Working Paper 26, Urban Institute, Washington, DC.

Özek, Umut, Michael Hansen, and Thomas Gonzalez. 2012. 'A Leg Up or a Boot Out? Student Achievement and Mobility under School Restructuring.' CALDER Working Paper No. 78, National Center for Analysis of Longitudinal Data in Education Research, American Institutes for Research, Washington, DC.

Pal, Sarmistha. 2010. 'Public Infrastructure, Location of Private Schools and Primary School Attainment in an Emerging Economy.' *Economics of Education Review* 29(5):783–794.

Palomer, Cristian G. and Ricardo G. Paredes. 2010. 'Reducing the Educational Gap: Good Results in Vulnerable Groups.' *Journal of Development Studies* 46(3):535–555.

Park, Albert. Xinzheng Shi, Chang-tai Hsieh, and Xuehui An. 2010. 'Does School Quality Matter? Evidence from a Natural Experiment in Rural China.' Unpublished Manuscript, Department of Economics, University of Oxford.

Parry, Taryn R. 1997. 'Theory Meets Reality in the Education Voucher Debate: Some Evidence from Chile.' *Education Economics* 5(3):307–331.

Paton, Graeme. 2012. 'Ministers Scrap 24-Hour Notice on School Detentions.' *The Daily Telegraph*, 16 January, http://www.telegraph.co.uk/education/educationnews/ministers-scrap-24-hour-notice-on-school-detentions.html (accessed at 18.02.13).

Patrinos, Harry A. 2001. 'School Choice in Denmark.' Preliminary Report. World Bank, Washington, DC.

Patrinos, Harry A. 2002. 'Private Education Provision and Public Finance: The Netherlands as a Possible Model.' Occasional Paper No. 59, National Center for the Study of Privatization in Education, Columbia University, New York.

Patrinos, Harry A. 2011. 'Private Education Provision and Public Finance: The Netherlands.' *Education Economics* doi:10.1080/09645292.2011.568696.

Patrinos, Harry A. and Chris Sakellariou. 2011. 'Quality of Schooling, Returns to Schooling and the 1981 Vouchers Reform in Chile.' *World Development* 39(12):2245–2256.

Patton, Chris. 2012. 'Ofsted "Taking the Soul Out of School", Adviser Warns.' *The Daily Telegraph*. 29 October 2012, http://www.telegraph.co.uk/education/educationnews/9640875/ofsted-taking-the-soul-out-of-school-adviser-warns.html (accessed at 18.02.13).

Pekkarinen, Tuomas, Roope Uusitalo, and Sari Kerr. 2009. 'School Tracking and Development of Cognitive Skills.' Discussion Paper No. 4058, Institute for the Study of Labor, Bonn.

Perelman, Sergio and Daniel Santin. 2011. 'Measuring Educational Efficiency at the Student Level with Parametric Stochastic Distance Functions: An Application to Spanish PISA Results.' *Education Economics* 19(1):29–49.

Peterson, Paul. 2008. 'School Vouchers in the United States: Productivity in the Public and Private Sectors.' *Zeitschrift für Erziehungswissenschaft / Journal of Educational Science* 11(2):253–267.

Peterson, Paul E. and Matthew H. Chingos. 2009. 'Impact of For-Profit and Nonprofit Management on Student Achievement: The Philadelphia Intervention, 2002–2008.' Program on Education Policy and Governance Working Paper No. 09–02, Program on Education Policy and Governance, Taubman Center on State and Local Government, Harvard's Kennedy School of Government, Harvard University, Cambridge, MA.

Peterson, Paul E. and William E. Howell. 2004. 'Voucher Research Controversy: New Looks at the New York City Evaluation.' *Education Next*, Spring, 73–78.

Pierson, Paul. 1996. 'The New Politics of the Welfare State.' *World Politics* 48(2):143–179.

Pigou, Arthur C. 1935. *Economics in Practice: Six Lectures on Current Issues*. London: Macmillan.

Plucker, Jonathan, Patricia Muller, John Hansen, Russ Ravert, and Matthew Makel. 2006. 'Evaluation of the Cleveland Scholarship and Tutoring Program: Summary Report 1998–2004.' Report, Center for Evaluation & Education Policy, Indiana University, Bloomington, IN.

Ponzo, Michela. 2011. 'The Effects of School Competition on the Achievement of Italian Students.' *Managerial and Decision Economics* 32:53–61.

Pop-Eleches, Christian and Miguel Urquiola. 2011. 'Going to a Better School: Effects and Behavioral Responses.' NBER Working Paper No. 16886, National Bureau of Economic Research, Cambridge, MA.

Preston, Courtney, Ellen Goldring, Mark Berends, and Marisa Cannata. 2012. 'School Innovation in District Context: Comparing Traditional Public Schools and Charter Schools.' *Economics of Education Review* 31:318–330.

Propper, Carol and Jack Britton. 2012. 'Does Wage Regulation Harm Kids? Evidence from English Schools.' Working Paper No. 12/293, Centre for Market and Public Organisation, University of Bristol, Bristol.

Ragh, Mariella. 2012. 'Primary School Teaching Practices and Social Capital.' Master's Thesis, Sciences Po, Paris.

Rainey, Lydia. 2011. 'Making Sense of Charter School Studies – A Reporter's Guide.' Research Brief, National Charter School Research Project, Center on Reinventing Public Education, Washington DC.

Rangvid, Beatrice S. 2003. 'Do Schools Matter? The Influence of School Inputs on Student Performance and Outcomes.' PhD Dissertation, Department of Economics, Aarhus School of Business, Aarhus.

Rangvid, Beatrice S. 2008. 'Private School Diversity in Denmark's National Voucher System.' *Scandinavian Journal of Educational Research* 52(4):331–354.

Rangvid, Beatrice S. 2010. 'School Choice, Universal Vouchers and Native Flight from Local Schools.' *European Sociological Review* 26(3):319–335.

Rau, Thomás, Cristían Sánchez, and Sergio Urzúa. 2010. 'Unobserved Heterogeneity, School Choice and the Effect of Voucher Schools: Evidence from Chile.' Conference Paper, Network on Inequality and Poverty, Medellin, Colombia.

Reback, Randall. 2008. 'Demand (and Supply) in an Inter-District Public School Choice Program.' *Economics of Education Review* 27:402–416.

Ritzen, Jozef M., Jan van Dommelen, and Frans de Vijlder. 1997. 'School Finance and School Choice in the Netherlands.' *Economics of Education Review* 6(3):329–335.

Robert, Peter. 2010. 'Social Origin, School Choice, and Student Performance.' *Educational Research and Evaluation* 16(2):107–129.

Román, Marcela and Marcela Perticará. 2012. 'Student Mobility in Low Quality Schools: Segmentation among the Most Vulnerable Students.' *Estudios de Economía* 39(2):159–177.

Roth, Al. 2013. 'Market Design for Everyone (from Libertarians to Socialists).' Blog Post, Market Design Blog. Available at: http://marketdesigner.blogspot.co.uk/2013/01/market-design-for-everyone-from.html (accessed 18.02.13).

Rothstein, Jesse. 2006. 'Good Principals or Good Peers? Parental Valuation of School Characteristics, Tiebout Equilibrium, and the Effects of Inter-district Competition.' *American Economic Review* 96(4):1333–1350.

Rothstein, Jesse. 2007. 'Does Competition among Public Schools Benefit Students and Taxpayers? Comment.' *American Economic Review* 97(5):2026–2037.

Rouse, Cecilia E. 1998. 'Private School Vouchers and Student Achievement: An Evaluation of the Milwaukee Parental Choice Program.' *Quarterly Journal of Economics* 113(2):552–602.

Rouse, Cecilia E. and Lisa Barrow. 2009. 'School Vouchers and Student Achievement: Recent Evidence and Remaining Questions.' *Annual Review of Economics* 1(1):17–42.

Rutkowski, Leslie and David Rutkowski. 2010. 'Private and Public Education: A Cross-National Exploration with TIMSS 2003.' Occasional Paper No. 192, National Center for the Study of Privatization in Education, Columbia University, New York.

Ryu, Deockhyun and Changhui Kang. 2009. 'An International Comparison of the Effect of Private Education Spending on Student Academic Performance: Evidence from the Programme for International Student Assessment (PISA), 2006.' 노동경제논집 32(3):61–89.

Ryu, Deockhyun and Changhui Kang. Forthcoming. 'Do Private Tutoring Expenditures Raise Academic Performance? Evidence from Middle School Students in South Korea.' *Asian Economic Journal*.

Sacerdote, Bruce. 2011. 'Peer Effects in Education: How Might They Work, How Big Are They and How Much Do We Know Thus Far?' in Hanushek, Eric A., Stephen J. Machin, and Ludger Woessmann (eds), *Handbook of the Economics of Education*, pp. 249–277. Amsterdam: Elsevier/North-Holland.

Sacerdote, Bruce. 2012. 'When the Saints Go Marching Out: Long-Term Outcomes for Student Evacuees from Hurricanes Katrina and Rita.' *American Economic Journal: Applied Economics* 4(1):109–135.

Sahlgren, Gabriel H. 2011a. 'Schooling for Money: Swedish Education Reform and the Role of the Profit Motive.' *Economic Affairs* 32(3):28–35.

Sahlgren, Gabriel H. 2011b. 'Grade Inflation, Educational Achievement and the Profit Motive: A Comment on the SNS Report.' Blog Post, Personal Blog: http://gabrielsahlgren.blogspot.com/2011/09/grade-inflation-educational-achievement.html (accessed 18.02.13).

Sahlgren, Gabriel H. 2011c. 'Friskolereformen har förbättrat resultaten.' *Svenska Dagbladet*, 8 August. Available at: http://www.svd.se/opinion/brannpunkt/friskolereformen-har-forbattrat-resultaten_6374052.svd (accessed 18.02.13).

Sahlgren, Gabriel H. 2012. 'Viktiga kunskaper offras i det finländska skolmiraklet.' *Dagens Nyheter*, 15 June. Available at: http://www.dn.se/debatt/viktiga-kunskaper-offras-i-det-finlandska-skolmiraklet (accessed 18.02.13).

Sahlgren, Gabriel H. 2013. 'Skolval, segregation och likvärdighet: Vad säger forskningen?' Research Report, Friskolornas Riksförbund, Stockholm.

Sahlgren, Gabriel H. Forthcoming. 'Incentive to Invest? How Education Affects Economic Growth.' CMRE Research Paper, Centre for Market Reform of Education, London.

Salas-Velasco, Manuel. 2006. 'Do Private Schools Produce Better Outcomes than Public Schools? Evidence for Spain.' Conference Paper, Aarhus School of Business, Aarhus, Denmark.

Sandström, Mikael. 2002. *En riktig skolpeng*. Stockholm: Reforminstitutet.

Sandström, Mikael F. and Fredrik Bergström. 2005. 'School Vouchers in Practice: Competition Will Not Hurt You.' *Journal of Public Economics* 89:351–380.

Sapelli, Claudio. 2003. 'The Chilean Voucher System: Some New Results and Research Challenges.' *Cuadernos de economía* 40(121):530–538.

Sapelli, Claudio. 2010. 'Some Thoughts on the Evaluation of the Chilean Voucher System.' *Journal of School Choice* 4(2):222–231.

Sapelli, Claudio and Bernardita Vial. 2002. 'The Performance of Private and Public Schools in the Chilean Voucher System.' *Cuadernos de Economía* 39:423–454.

Sapelli, Claudio and Bernardita Vial. 2003. 'Peer Effects and Relative Performance of Voucher Schools in Chile.' Working Paper No. 256, Instituto de Economia, Pontificia Universidad Catolica de Chile, Santiago.

Sapelli, Claudio and Bernardita Vial. 2005. 'Private vs Public Voucher Schools in Chile: New Evidence on Efficiency and Peer Effects.' Working Paper No. 289, Instituto de Economia, Pontificia Universidad Catolica de Chile, Santiago.

Sass, Tim R. 2006. 'Charter Schools and Student Achievement in Florida.' *Education Finance and Policy* 1(1):50–90.

Schaeffer, Adam B. 2007. 'The Public Education Tax Credit.' Policy Analysis No. 605, Cato Institute, Washington, DC.

Schneeweis, Nicole and Rudolf Winter-Ebmer. 2007. 'Peer Effects in Austrian Schools.' *Empirical Economics* 32:387–409.

Schumpeter, Joseph A. 1994. *Capitalism, Socialism and Democracy.* New York: Routledge.

Schwerdt, Guido and Amelie C. Wuppermann. 2011. 'Is Traditional Teaching Really All That Bad? A Within-Student Between-Subject Approach.' *Economics of Education Review* 30(2):365–379.

Serritzlew, Søren. 2006. 'Linking Budgets to Activity: A Test of the Effect of Output-Purchase Budgeting.' *Public Budgeting and Finance* 26(2):101–120.

Shephard, Jessica. 2012. 'Most Free Schools Take Fewer Deprived Pupils than Local Average, Figures Show.' *The Guardian*, 23 April. Available at: http://www.guardian.co.uk/education/2012/apr/23/free-schools-deprived-pupils-average (accessed 18.02.13).

Shewbridge, Claire, Eunice Jang, Peter Matthews, and Paulo Santiago. 2011. 'OECD Reviews of Evaluation and Assessment in Education: Denmark.' OECD, Paris.

Sibieta, Luke, Haroon Chowdry, and Alastair Muriel. 2008. 'Level Playing Field? The Implications of School Funding.' Research Paper, CfBT Education Trust, London.

Sidak, J. Gregory. and David J. Teece. 2009. 'Dynamic Competition in Antitrust Law.' *Journal of Competition Law & Economics* 5(4):581–631.

Singh, Abhijeet. 2012. 'The Private School Premium: Size and Sources of the Private School Advantage in Test Scores in India.' Unpublished Manuscript, University of Oxford, Oxford.

Skolinspektionen. 2010. 'Orsaker till avslag för ansökningar om fristående skola – ansökningsomgång 2009.' Report Skolinspektionen, Stockholm.

Skolinspektionen. 2011a. 'Beslut om tillstånd för fristående skolor – ansökningsomgång 2010.' Dnr 30-2011:2346, Skolinspektionen, Stockholm.

Skolinspektionen. 2011b. 'Beslut om godkännande av fristående skolor – ansökningsomgång 2011.' Dnr 30-2011:5284, Skolinspektionen, Stockholm.

Skolinspektionen. 2011c. 'Skolbibliotek.' Information Leaflet, Skolinspektionen, Stockholm.

Skolinspektionen. 2012. 'Lika eller olika? Omrättning av nationella prov i grundskolan och gymnasieskolan under tre år.' Dnr: 01-2010:2643, Skolinspektionen, Stockholm.

Skolverket. 2005. 'Att mäta skolors relativa effektivitet – En modellanalys baserad på resurser och resultat.' Dnr 2004:1464. Stockholm: Skolverket.

Skolverket. 2009a. *Vad påverkar resultaten i svensk grundskola? Kunskapsöversikt om betydelsen av olika faktorer.* Stockholm: Skolverket.

Skolverket. 2009b. 'Likvärdig betygssättning i gymnasieskolan? En analys av sambandet mellan nationella prov och kursbetyg.' Report 338, Skolverket, Stockholm.

Skolverket. 2010a. 'Rustad att möta framtiden? PISA 2009 om 15-åringars läsförståelse och kunskaper i matematik och naturvetenskap.' Report 352. Stockholm: Skolverket.

Skolverket. 2010b. 'Redovisning av uppdrag om skillnaden mellan betygsresultat på nationella prov och ämnesbetyg i svenska, matematik och engelska i årskurs 9.' Dnr 01-2010:22, Skolverket, Stockholm.

Skolverket. 2012a. Data retrieved from the Swedish National Agency for Education's online database: http://www.skolverket.se.

Skolverket. 2012b. 'Mer om … Fristående skolor.' Leaflet, Skolverket, Stockholm.

Skolverket. 2012c. 'Redovisning av uppdrag om avvikelser mellan provresultat och betyg i grundskolans årskurs 9.' Dnr 75-2012:311, Skolverket, Stockholm.

Slater, Helen, Neil M. Davies, and Simon Burgess. 2011. 'Do Teachers Matter? Measuring the Variation in Teacher Effectiveness in England.' *Oxford Bulletin of Economics and Statistics* doi:10.1111/j.1468-0084.2011.00666.x.

Smithers, Alan. 2011. 'GCSE 2011.' Report, Centre for Education and Employment Research, University of Buckingham, Buckingham.

Smyth, Emer. 2008. 'The More, the Better? Intensity of Involvement in Private Tuition and Examination Performance.' *Educational Research and Evaluation: An International Journal on Theory and Practice* 14(5):465–476.

Smyth, Emer. 2009. 'Buying Your Way into College? Private Tuition and the Transition to Higher Education in Ireland.' *Oxford Review of Education* 35(1):1–22.

Sobel, Russell S. and Kerry A. King. 2008. 'Does School Choice Increase the Rate of Youth Entrepreneurship.' *Economics of Education Review* 27(4):429–438.

Söderström, Martin. 2006. 'School Choice and Student Achievement – New Evidence on Open-Enrolment.' Working Paper 2006:16, Institute for Labour Market Policy Evaluation, Stockholm.

Söderström, Martin and Roope Uusitalo. 2010. 'School Choice and Segregation: Evidence from an Admission Reform.' *Scandinavian Journal of Economics* 112(1):55–76.

Somers, Marie-Andrée, Patrick J. McEwan, and Douglas J. Willms. 2004. 'How Effective are Private Schools in Latin America?' *Comparative Education Review* 48(1):48–69.

Sprietsma, Maresa. 2008. 'Regional School Choice and School Selectivity: How Do They Relate to Student Performance? Evidence from PISA 2003.' *The European Journal of Comparative Economics* 5(2):155–178.

Springer, Matthew G., Dale Ballou, Laura Hamilton, Vi-Nhuan Le, J.R Lockwood, Daniel F. McCaffrey, Matthew Pepper, and Brian M. Stecher. 2010. 'Teacher Pay for Performance: Experimental Evidence from the Project on Incentives in Teaching.' Report, Vanderbilt Peabody College, National Center on Performance Incentives, Nashville, TN.

Springer, Matthew G., John F. Pane, Vi-Nhuan Le, Daniel F. McCaffrey, Susan Burns Freeman, Laura S. Hamilton, and Brian Stecher. 2012. 'Team Pay for Performance: Experimental Evidence from the Round Rock Pilot Project on Team Incentives.' *Educational Evaluation and Policy Analysis* doi:10.3102/0162373712439094.

Statens Offentliga Utredningar. 1999. 'Likvärdiga villkor?' SOU 1999:98, Ministry of Education, Stockholm.

Statens Offentliga Utredningar. 2008. 'En hållbar lärarutbildning.' SOU 2008:109, Ministry of Education, Stockholm.

Stewart, William. 2011. 'League Tables to Ignore Race and Poverty.' *TES*, 3 June. Available at: http://www.tes.co.uk/articl.aspx?storycode=6086535 (accessed 18.02.13).

Stoddard, Christina and Sean P. Corcoran. 2007. 'The Political Economy of School Choice: Support for Charter Schools across States and School Districts.' *Journal of Urban Economics* 62(1):27–54.

Stringer, Neil S. 2011. 'Setting and Maintaining GCSE and GCE Grading Standards: The Case for Contextualised Cohort-Referencing.' *Research Papers in Education* doi:10.108 0/02671522.2011.580364.

Stuit, David A. 2010. 'Are Bad Schools Immortal? The Scarcity of Turnarounds and Shutdowns in Both Charter and District Sectors.' Policy Report, Thomas B. Fordham Institute, Washington, DC.

Sullivan, Alice, Anthony Heath, and Catherine Rothon. 2011. 'Equalisation or Inflation? Social Class and Gender Differentials in England and Wales.' *Oxford Review of Education* 37(2):215–240.

Sund, Krister. 2009. 'Estimating Peer Effects in Swedish High School Using School, Teacher, and Student Fixed Effects.' *Economics of Education Review* 28:329–336.

Sund, Krister. 2011. 'Detracking Swedish Compulsory Schools: Any Losers, Any Winners?' *Empirical Economics* doi:10.1007/s00181-011-0532-6.

Sykes, Richard, Eric Anderson, Julia Buckingham, Robert Coe, Ron McLone, David Perks, Richard Pike, Amanda Spielman, Michael Wilshaw, and Alison Wolf. 2010. 'The Sir Richard Sykes Review.' London.

Tabarrok, Alexander. 2011. 'Private Education in India: A Novel Test of Cream Skimming.' *Contemporary Economic Policy* doi:10.1111/j.1465-7287.2011.00286.x.

Tegle, Stig. 2010. 'Påverkar förekomsten av friskolor betygen i grundskolan? En statistisk analys av samtliga elever i årskurs 9 år 2006.' Report, Svenskt Näringsliv, Stockholm.

Thapa, Amrit. 2011. 'Does Private School Competition Improve Public School Performance? The Case of Nepal.' PhD Dissertation, Graduate School of Arts and Sciences, Columbia University, New York.

Thieme, Claudio and Ernesto Treviño. 2011. 'School Choice and Market Imperfections: Evidence from Chile.' *Education and Urban Society* doi:10.1177/0013124511413387.

Tilak, Jandhyala, B.G. and Sudarshan M. Ratna. 2001. 'Private Schooling in Rural India.' Working Paper Series No. 76, National Council of Applied Economic Research, New Delhi.

Tokman, Andrea R. 2002. 'Is Private Education Better? Evidence from Chile.' Working Paper No. 147, Central Bank of Chile, Santiago.

Toma, Eugenia F. 1996. 'Public Funding and Private Schooling across Countries.' *Journal of Law and Economics* 39(1):121–148.

Tooley, James, Bao Yong, Pauline Dixon, and John Merrifield. 2011. 'School Choice and Academic Performance: Some Evidence from Developing Countries.' *Journal of School Choice* 5(1):1–39.

Törnroos, Jukka. 2006. 'Matematikkunskaper i Finland i internationell jämförelse.' Nämnaren, pp. 16–20. The figure regarding the percentage correct in algebra is available at: www.prim.su.se/seminarier/pdf/finnmatt.pdf.

Tuttle, Christina C., Philip Gleason, and Melissa Clark. 2012. 'Using Lotteries to Evaluate Schools of Choice: Evidence from a National Study of Charter School.' *Economics of Education Review* 31(2):237–253.

Tyrefors Hinnerich, Björn and Jonas Vlachos. 2012. 'Systematiska skillnader mellan interna och externa bedömningar av nationella prov.' Appendix 4 – Dnr. U2009/4877/G, Skolinspektionen, Stockholm.

Urquiola, Miguel. 2005. 'Does School Choice Lead to Sorting? Evidence from Tiebout Variation.' *American Economic Review* 95(4):1310–1326.

van Elk, Roel, Marc van der Steeg, and Dinand Webbink. 2011. 'Does the Timing of Tracking Affect Higher Education Completion?' *Economics of Education Review* 30(5):1009–1021.

Van Klaveren, Chris. 2011. 'Lecturing Style Teaching and Student Performance.' *Economics of Education Review* 30:729–739.

Vandenberghe, Vincent and Stéphane R. R. Robin. 2004. 'Evaluating the Effectiveness of Private Education across Countries: A Comparison of Methods.' *Labour Economics* 11(4):487–506.

Vasagar, Jeevan and Jessica Shephard. 2011. 'Free Schools Built in Mainly Middle-Class and Wealthy Areas.' *The Guardian*, 31 August. Available at: http://www.guardian.co.uk/education/2011/aug/31/free-schools-middle-class-areas (accessed 18.02.13).

Vegas, Emiliana. 2002. 'School Choice, Student Performance, and Teacher and School Characteristics.' Policy Research Working Paper No. 2833, Development Research Group, World Bank, Washington, DC.

Verschelde, Marijn, Jean Hindriks, and Glenn Rayp. 2011. 'School Autonomy and Educational Performance: Within-Country Evidence.' Workshop Paper. Faculty of Social Sciences and Technology Management, Faculty of Social Sciences and Technology Management, Norwegian University of Science and Technology, Trondheim.

Vlachos, Jonas 2011a. 'Friskolor i förändring' in Hartman, Laura (ed.), *Konkurrensens konsekvenser: Vad händer med svensk välfärd?*, pp. 66–110 Stockholm: SNS Förlag.

Vlachos, Jonas. 2011b. 'Betygets värde: En analys av hur konkurrens påverkar betygssättningen vid svenska skolor.' Report No. 2010:6, Konkurrensverket, Stockholm.

Vlachos, Jonas. 2012. 'Är vinst och konkurrens en bra modell för skolan?' *Ekonomisk debatt* 40(4):16–30.

Waldinger, Fabian. 2007. 'Does Ability Tracking Exacerbate the Role of Family Background for Students' Test Scores?' Unpublished Manuscript, Department of Economics, University of Warwick, Coventry.

Waldo, Staffan. 2007. 'Efficiency in Swedish Public Education: Competition and Voter Monitoring.' *Education Economics* 15(2):231–251.

Walford, Geoffrey. 1997. 'Sponsored Grant-Maintainted Schools: Extending the Franchise?' *Oxford Review of Education* 23(1):31–44.

West, Edwin G. 1997. 'Education Vouchers in Practice and Principle: A World Survey.' *World Bank Research Observer* 12(1):83–103.

West, Martin R. and Ludger Woessmann. 2010. '"Every Catholic Child in a Catholic School": Historical Resistance to State Schooling, Contemporary Private Competition, and Student Achievement across Countries.' *Economic Journal* 120:229–255.

Wikström, Christina and Magnus Wikström. 2005. 'Grade Inflation and School Competition: An Empirical Analysis Based on the Swedish Upper Secondary Schools.' *Economics of Education Review* 24(3):309–322.

Winnet, Robert, Holly Watt, and Claire Newell. 2011. 'Exam Boards Investigation: Michael Gove will Reform System to Prevent Boards Competing.' *The Daily Telegraph*, 9 December. Available at: http://www.telegraph.co.uk/education/educationnews/8947391/Exam-boards-investigation-Michael-Gove-will-reform-system-to-prevent-boards-competing.html.

Winters, Marcus A. 2011. 'Measuring the Effect of Charter Schools on Public School Student Achievement in an Urban Environment: Evidence from New York City.' *Economics of Education Review* doi:10.1016/j.econedurev.2011.08.014.

Winters, Marcus A. and Jay P. Greene. 2008. 'The Effect of Special Education Vouchers on Public School Achievement: Evidence From Florida's McKay Scholarship Program.' Civic Report No. 52, Centre for Civic Innovation, Manhattan Institute, New York.

Winters, Marcus A., Julie R. Trivitt, and Jay P. Green. 2010. 'The Impact of High-Stakes Testing on Student Proficiency in Low-Stakes Subjects: Evidence from Florida's Elementary Science Exam.' *Economics of Education Review* 29(1):138–146.

Witte, John F. 1997. 'Achievement Effects of the Milwaukee Voucher Program.' Unpublished Manuscript, University of Wisconson.

Witte, John F., Patrick J. Wolf, Alicia Dean, and Deven Carlson. 2011. 'Milwaukee Independent Charter Schools Study: Report on Two- and Three-Year Achievement Gains.' SCDP Milwaukee Evaluation Report No. 25, School Choice Demonstration Project, Department of Education Reform, University of Arkansas.

Wodon, Quentin and Yvonne Ying. 2009. 'Literacy and Numeracy in Faith-Based and Government Schools in Sierra Leone' in Barrera-Osorio, Felipe, Harry A. Patrinos, and Quentin Wodon (eds), *Emerging Evidence on Vouchers and Faith-Based Providers in Education: Case Studies from Africa, Latin America, and Asia*, pp. 99–118. Washington, DC: World Bank.

Woessmann, Ludger. 2003. 'Schooling Resources, Educational Institutions and Student Performance: The International Evidence.' *Oxford Bulletin of Economics and Statistics* 65(2):117–170.

Woessmann, Ludger. 2005. 'The Effect Heterogeneity of Central Examinations: Evidence from TIMSS, TIMSS-Repeat and PISA.' *Education Economics* 13(2):143–169.

Woessmann, Ludger. 2006. 'Public-Private Partnership and Schooling Outcomes across Countries.' CESifo Working Paper No. 1662, Centre for Economic Studies, Munich.

Woessmann, Ludger. 2010. 'Institutional Determinants of School Efficiency and Equity: German States as a Microcosm for OECD Countries.' *Jahrbücher für Nationalökonomie und Statistik* 230(2):234–270.

Woessmann, Ludger. 2011. 'Cross-Country Evidence on Teacher Performance Pay.' *Economics of Education Review* 39:404–418.

Woessmann, Ludger, Elke Lüdemann, Gabriela Schütz, and Martin R. West. 2007. 'School Accountability, Autonomy, Choice, and the Level of Student Achievement: International Evidence from PISA 2003.' Education Working Paper No. 13, OECD, Paris.

Wolf, Patrick J. 2007. 'Civics Exam: Schools of Choice Boost Civic Values.' PEPG/07–05, Program on Education Policy and Governance, Harvard University, Cambridge, MA.

Wolf, Patrick J. 2008. 'School Voucher Programs: What the Research Says.' *Brigham Young University Law Review*, 415–446.

Wolf, Patrick J. Brian Kisida, Babette Gutmann, Michael Puma, Nada Eissay and Lou Rizzo. 2013. 'School Vouchers and Student Outcomes: Experimental Evidence from Washington, DC.' *Journal of Policy Analysis and Management* doi:10.1002/pam.21691.

Zhang, Hongliang. 2012. 'The Mirage of Elite Schools: Evidence from Lottery-Based School Admissions in China.' Unpublished Manuscript, Department of Economics, Chinese University of Hong Kong.

Zhang, Yu. 2013. 'Does Private Tutoring Improve Students' National College Entrance Exam Performance? A Case Study from Jinan, China.' *Economics of Education Review* 32:1–28.

Zimmer, Karin, Miyako Ikeda, and Elke Lüdeman. 2011. 'School Competition, Institutional Differentiation, and the Quality and Equity of Education Systems' in Van den Branden, Kris, Piet Van Avermaet, and Mieke Van Houtte (eds), *Equity and Excellence in Education: Towards Maximal Learning Opportunities for All Students*, pp. 39–74. New York: Routledge.

Zimmer, Ron and Richard Buddin. 2006. 'Charter School Performance in Two Large Urban Districts.' *Journal of Urban Economics* 60:307–326.

Zimmer, Ron and Richard Buddin. 2009. 'Is Charter School Competition in California Improving the Performance of Traditional Public Schools?' *Public Administration Review* 69(5):831–845.

Zimmer, Ron and Richard Buddin. 2010. 'The Economics of Charter Schools' in Brewer, Dominic J. and Patrick J. McEwan (eds), *Economics of Education*, pp. 329–335. Oxford: Academic Press.

Zimmer, Ron, Brian Gill, Kevin Booker, Stéphane Lavertu, Tim R. Sass, and John Witte. 2009. 'Charter Schools in Eight States: Effects on Achievement, Attainment, Integration, and Competition.' Monograph, Rand Education, RAND Corporation, Santa Monica, CA.

Zimmer, Ron, Brian Gill, Kevin Booker, Stéphane Lavertu, and John Witte. 2011. 'Examining Charter Student Achievement Effects across Seven States.' *Economics of Education Review* doi:10.1016/j.econedurev.2011.05.005.

Zweimüller, Martina. 2012. 'The Long-Term Effects of School Entry Laws on Educational Attainment and Earnings in an Early Tracking System.' Unpublished Manuscript, Department of Economics, University of Linz, Linz.

INDEX

accessibility 117, 125

accountability: education markets 12–16, 124; importance 8, 95, 152; improvements 161–7; independent schools 68; lack of 42, 72; policy options 73; reforms 110; school choice 12–13, 167; schools 7–8, 13–17, 155; Sweden 45; teachers 164, 166

achievement: autonomy 103, 110; charter schools 83; competition 73–4, 92–3, 95, 99–100, 107; education 19; English academies 121; faith schools 102; grades 36–7; private schools 85–6; public schools 91; school choice 74, 75, 97, 125; school density 106; school switching 82; teachers 119; test scores 111–16; Tiebout choice 90; variations 38; vouchers 76, 80

admissions: decentralisation 45; proximity 148–9; qualifications 161; reforms 169; state schools 107–8, 127–8; test scores 44; universities 113–14, 159

African Americans 75–6

Australia 83–4

autonomy: achievement 110, 121; Belgium 84; competition 106, 110; cross-national studies 22–3; English academies 102–3; faith schools 102; foundation schools 102; funding 56; importance 75, 149; increased 149–52; lack of 58, 119, 121; Netherlands, The 60, 66; qualifications 159, 161, 163; schools 7–8, 13–17, 59, 78, 99, 168; test scores 89; voluntary-aided schools 108; vouchers 68, 133

Bangladesh 89

Belgium 84

Canada 83

career academies 80

Catholic schools 47, 80–1, 83

Catholicism 24–5, 60–1, 64, 69

charter schools: competition 91, 92–3; effects 95; funding 153; non-randomised studies 79–80; performance 81; quality 94; United States of America 74–5, 97; variations 82

Chile: education 46–59; franchise schools 59; funding 153; PISA 54; reforms 53; top-up fees 142–3; voucher system 9, 55

closure 137–9

cohort-referencing 159–60, 164–5, 169

Colombia 76, 87

competition: achievement 73–4, 99–100, 107; assumptions 4; autonomy 106, 149; changes in 30; Chile 46; Denmark 70, 71; e-learning 139, 157; education 163, 171; education provision 1, 2; educational achievement 52; effects 23–4, 29–33, 46, 92–4, 96, 103–10; evidence 59, 70, 121; exam boards 113–15, 116, 159; expenditure 25; failing schools 139; faith schools 109; for-profit schools 118; free schools 37, 40–1; impact 32–3, 41, 97; incentives 128; independent schools 25–6, 129; information 166; lack of 72, 78; long-term effects 28–9; measures 35, 48, 53; monopolies 157; municipal schools 50–1, 58; National Curriculum (Sweden) 39; Netherlands, The 62–3, 64; non-randomised studies 89–95; planning restrictions 156; profit motive 155; qualifications 161, 168, 169; quality 135; research 94–6; school choice 5; schools 16, 45; selection practices 56; state schools 136–7; success 125; Sweden 45; tax credits 127; test scores 44, 51, 110; voluntary-aided schools 108

expansion: e-learning 156; funding 136, 140; school choice 154; schools 5, 168; supply 158
expenditure 25, 103, 129
experimentation 7, 82, 144–8, 152

failing schools 137–9
faith schools 102, 109, 121
fee-paying schools: competition 90–1; evidence 131; Pakistan 87; performance 85, 103, 129; quality 152; vouchers 76, 136
Finland 26–7
for-profit schools 83, 118, 152–6, 168–9, 175
foundation schools 101–2, 106
franchise schools 49, 59
free schools: autonomy 149, 168; competition 40–1; costs 31–2; creation 156; educational achievement 69; efficiency 37; impact of increased enrolments 30–3; regulation 118; test scores 44
funding: autonomy 56; differentiated 139–42; e-learning 157; education 171; education markets 124; English schools 125; enrolments 99; equality 135–7; for-profit schools 152, 153; free schools 118; governments 175; grant-maintained schools 101; independent schools 68, 70, 132; means testing 141; municipal schools 50–1, 55, 70; parents 130; performance 136, 138; policy options 59, 68; quality 128; research 142; school choice 60; schools 9–10, 47, 96, 168; selection practices 145; state schools 108, 127–8, 137; top-up fees 142–4; voucher schools 57; vouchers 138

GCSE grades 110–11
governance 101–2
government: education 9–10, 133; funding 175; information provision 10–12, 164–7; policy options 8; private schools 88–9; role of 172, 173; schools 4
grade inflation 111–16, 158–9

grades 36–7
grant-maintained schools 100, 109
group work 40

Hungary 84

impact: competition 32, 41, 97, 107; grant-maintained schools 100; selection practices 145; test scores 40, 42–3; tracking 36–7, 147
implementation 124–3, 173
importance: accountability 8, 152; autonomy 75, 149; education 10; exams 161; programme design 171; school choice 77, 96; teaching 39, 119–20
independent schools: accountability 72; benefits 127; Catholicism 24–5; competition 25–6, 70; Denmark 68–9; Netherlands, The 60; number of schools 71; performance 84, 103; policy options 73; regulation 131–2; religion 60, 132; school density 107; selection practices 137; test scores 129; vouchers 136–7
India 77–8, 85–6, 129–30, 143
Indonesia 87
information: asymmetries 11, 130–1, 172; availability 58, 59; education markets 124; educational achievement 66–7; funding 136; improvements 161–7; lack of 15–16, 55, 66, 72, 120–1; policy options 68, 73; presentation 166; provision 110; qualifications 163; quality 96, 117; school choice 6–7, 43, 74, 161, 169; schools 165
innovation: charter schools 82; for-profit schools 155; information 166; lack of 64, 102, 121; schools 7
inspections 165–6, 167, 170
interventions 133, 173
Israel 84, 93

Japan 26, 84, 93

Kenya 87